MEDIATED MESSAGES AND AFRICAN-AMERICAN CULTURE

MEDIATED MESSAGES AND AFRICAN-AMERICAN CULTURE
Contemporary Issues

Venise T. Berry
Carmen L. Manning-Miller
editors

SAGE Publications
International Educational and Professional Publisher
Thousand Oaks   London   New Delhi

For information address:

 SAGE Publications, Inc.
2455 Teller Road
Thousand Oaks, California 91320
E-mail: order@sagepub.com

SAGE Publications Ltd.
6 Bonhill Street
London EC2A 4PU
United Kingdom

SAGE Publications India Pvt. Ltd.
M-32 Market
Greater Kailash I
New Delhi 110 048 India

Printed in the United States of America

Library of Congress Cataloging-in-Publication Data

Main entry under title:

Mediated messages and African-American culture: Contemporary issues /
editors, Venise T. Berry, Carmen L. Manning-Miller.
    p.   cm.
  Includes bibliographical references and index.
  ISBN 0-8039-7277-6 (cloth: acid-free paper).—ISBN
0-8039-7278-4 (pbk.: acid-free paper)
    1. Afro-Americans in motion pictures.   2. Afro-Americans in the
motion picture industry.   I. Berry, Venise T.   II. Manning-Miller,
Carmen L.
PN1995.9.N4M44   1996
791.43′08996073—dc20   95-32519

This book is printed on acid-free paper.

96 97 98 99 10 9 8 7 6 5 4 3 2 1

Sage Production Editor: Astrid Virding
Sage Typesetter: Andrea D. Swanson

Contents

Introduction

Racialism and the Media

VENISE T. BERRY

ultural studies scholar Stuart Hall (1981) argues that the mass media are the most important instruments of twentieth-century capitalism for maintaining ideological hegemony because the media provide the framework for perceiving reality. Bill Nichols (1981) goes on to explain how this reality evolves:

> Ideology is how the existing ensemble of social relations represents itself to individuals; it is the image a society gives of itself in order to perpetuate itself. These representations serve to constrain us (necessarily); they establish fixed places for us to occupy that work to guarantee coherent social actions over time. Ideology uses the fabrication of images and the processes of representation to persuade us that how things are is how they ought to be and that the place provided for us is the place we ought to have. (p. 1)

Sociologist Herman Gray (1989) moves this premise a step further with concern for African American culture. Gray argues that an ideological potency exists, specifically in representations of black people in the media. He suggests that this ideology occurs within a kind of gerrymandered framework producing and naturalizing racial representations.

Each of these scholars recognizes that mediated images and messages are an important part of how people see the world. And as Gray notes, this influence becomes even more crucial for African American culture because of its complex historical existence. Stereotypical ideals and attitudes have been formed and solidified over decades into accepted ideologies and norms about African Americans. Although I don't believe that the media have an all-encompassing power or control over their audience, I do recognize that they serve as a primary source of communication in this country, and, therefore, their images and ideals can affect specific people, at specific times, in specific ways, depending on the context of the situation.

The United States has always been a country where race is a crucial part of black identity. The black color on smooth, soft skin was used to force African people into slavery and it made them easier to catch when they escaped. The black color on smooth, soft skin created the need for a system of segregation and Jim Crow laws once slavery was abolished. The black color on smooth, soft skin made it easy to develop and maintain the stereotypical images and messages that developed concerning a community of people who were misplaced and misunderstood.

In contemporary American society, race remains a primary component of ideological consciousness. There are a variety of race theories that have been developed over the years to better explain how various cultures interact: cultural pluralism (Appleton, 1983; Washington, 1986); ethnicity (Aguirre, 1995; Grant, 1918; Hawkins, 1995); the melting pot (Moynihan & Glazer, 1970; Payton, 1986; Smith, 1971); multiculturalism (Kanpol & McLaren, 1995; Taylor, 1994); difference (Lorde, 1984; Rothenberg, 1990; West, 1990, 1995); marginalization (Whitaker, 1984; Willie, 1975); racism (Feagin & Vera, 1995; Katz & Taylor, 1988; Winant, 1994); modern or enlightened racism (Entman, 1990, 1992; Jhally & Lewis, 1992); cultural criticism (Dyson, 1993; hooks, 1990, 1994); critical race theory (Bell, 1992; Delgado, 1995); cultural identity (Collier & Thomas, 1988; Geertz, 1973); racial formation (Omi & Winant, 1986); genealogy (West, 1982); cultural politics (Angus & Jhally, 1989; Gilroy, 1987). The importance of race continually changes as American society evolves. While overt and malicious racism still exists, it has expanded to include various forms of modern racism or racialism.

Racialism serves as the umbrella for a wide range of racial ideology, theory, and practice. The notion encompases the ongoing doctrine of racism from past to present. It penetrates all aspects of our society, especially the media. Racialism molds itself into simpler and subtler forms of racial thought. It is born out of what Gray (1989) calls America's storehouse of racial memory, and it is perpetuated by the historical, sociological, and ideological distinction between races. It can be accepted, created, developed, and used by any individual from any culture. Examples include an insensitivity, bias, or complete disregard for different cultures; the inappropriate focus on race or race-based issues when an entity/situation involves different cultures; the use of stereotypical images or ideas concerning different racial histories, traditions, beliefs, and cultures; or the acceptance of anticultural attitudes based on a hostility or resentment for other races.

Racialism flows through the media in direct response to the presentation of America's racial experiences. Unfortunately, because of the normality of racialism today, problematic situations often go unnoticed or are ignored. Most individuals are not sensitive to the existence of racialism in the media. For example, an advertisement for Cover Girl that appeared in many of the fashion magazines featured five women: three white, one black, and one Asian. Despite the company's attempt at diversity (which should be applauded), there were two obvious racialism problems in the ad. First, the only difference between the five women was the slight difference in shades of skin color. The black and Asian women had what looked like the same hair texture, the same smiles, the same shape, even the same light-colored eyes. A second problem could be found in the caption, which read: "Redefining Beautiful." How beauty is defined and redefined is a major problem for African American women in this country, as the ad demonstrates.

In a second example, a few years ago, Epson computers took out a three-page advertisement in various magazines, and the first page read: "Our lasers are aimed at everyone." When you turned the page, there were several pictures of people standing next to Epson laser printers and "everyone" included two white men, two white women, and an Asian man. Another example was identified in the promotion for a brief-lived television show called *Class of '96* on Fox. One print promo showed several pictures of the main characters, who were college students. In the top right-hand corner were a white male and female laughing; next to that picture were three white women smiling; then beneath those two pictures was a lone black male sitting on a stairway

Photo: O. Toscani (Fall/Winter 1991-1992), "Angel and Devil," United Colors of Benetton; used by permission.

looking isolated and depressed. As if the image of a black male alone wasn't problematic enough, under his picture was a shot of the whole group sitting around a large table and you quickly noticed that the black male was missing; however, a closer look showed his arms and hands laying on the left side of the table—his body literally had been cut out of the shot.

Finally, examine the advertisements that are presented here. They each have similar subjects but present very different messages under the umbrella of racialism. The controversial ad for the United Colors of Benetton features a young white girl and a young black girl barely hugging. The white girl has curly golden locks. She is smiling and the light hits her hair almost as if to create a halo around her head. The black girl is not smiling and she has had her hair shaped into what looks like two horns. On the other hand, the Pizza Hut ad also shows us two young girls, black and white, hugging. But the message is very different. It presents a feeling of warmth and sincerity. Both girls are smiling. Their cheeks even touch and they seem happy to be together. Understanding racialism is not simply about recognizing the negative or

Pizza is a lot like life.

Pizza Hut; used by permission.

positive, it involves the complexity of such images and messages as they relate to the contextual ideology of contemporary American society.

Unfortunately, we all buy into elements of racialism. In the picture below two men are handcuffed together, one black and one white. When you look at this picture, which hand belongs to the criminal and

Source: United Colors of Benetton; used by permission.

which hand belongs to the officer? Too often the black hand is automatically associated with crime and the white hand means authority.

The examination of African American images and messages in the media has always been a complicated and controversial issue. Although the number of images and the variety of messages have increased, many critics and scholars have found that most remain problematic. For example, on television, African American characters seem abundant, yet they are found primarily in comedic roles reminiscent of the Zip Coon and Jim Crow stereotypes. Black artists are highly visible in the music industry, but rap music, particularly gangster rap, receives a disproportionate amount of negative media attention. Black film is said to be moving into another renaissance period, with more black filmmakers finding success than ever before, but many of these films continue to focus on images of violent black males and black females as sex objects. And in the news, it seems that black men have literally become the symbol of crime in society today.

So even though contemporary media can boast of slight increases in the number of images and small improvements have been made in the kinds of images, there is still much that needs to be done. In an effort to develop greater sensitivity and awareness among readers, this volume offers a better understanding of how racialism affects contemporary media.

Part I explores racialism in film. William Harris's chapter is an interesting construction of how Spike Lee's movies are tools of social change. In "Cultural Engineering and the Films of Spike Lee," Harris argues that Lee's films examine themes such as the oppression of African Americans, the exploitation of women, and black-on-black crime. Harris shows us that racialism can exist among black media practitioners as well as white.

In her chapter, "Intimations of Invisibility: Black Women and Contemporary Hollywood Cinema," Ruth Elizabeth Burks leads us to think about black women's plight in Hollywood. She explores how racialism is sometimes segmented through the critical orientations of Hollywood filmmakers. Her concern lies in the reliance on black independent films and filmmakers for corrective images despite the racist, sexist, and classist nature of many of these movies.

Jacquie Jones's republished article, "The New Ghetto Aesthetic," discusses today's black cinematic revolution. Jones notes that this surge of black filmmakers in Hollywood has raised important questions about the politics of representation in mainstream cinema. She explores the question: "Can 'black' and 'Hollywood' really exist in the same space, in the same time?"

Part II addresses various issues of racialism in print media. First, Oscar Gandy's chapter, "If It Weren't for Bad Luck: Framing Stories of Racially Comparative Risk," examines how the preferred mode of framing stories when African Americans are involved is usually in negative terms—such as the high probability of black loss in any given situation. His findings suggest that this approach is problematic because it consistently places the emphasis on failure rather than success.

"How Four Newspapers Covered the 1992 Los Angeles 'Riots' " is the title of Jyotika Ramaprasad's chapter. Ramaprasad argues that news coverage of African Americans during civil disorder situations has always been a concern, and reports on how the Los Angeles riots continued this practice. She discusses how assumptions and unbalanced coverage during situations like the L.A. riots create implications for individual blame rather than fostering a system, societal, or institutional examination.

Reginald Owens tackles the impact of oppression on the African American press today in "Entering the Twenty-First Century: Oppression and the African American Press." Building from a 91-year historical foundation, he demonstrates how publication and circulation increase for black newspapers and magazines when African American social conditions are oppressive. His conclusions deny that the African American press is dying, and reveal instead how this African American tradition continues to survive and grow.

The chapter "Carol Moseley-Braun: Black Women's Political Images in the Media" by Carmen Manning-Miller explores the 1992 Senate race in Illinois. Manning-Miller's examination notes the absence of a prominent set of political or cultural messages as well as values in the coverage of Braun's campaign. She found instead that a large amount of the coverage of Braun questioned her viability and personal attributes, and most of the media's quotes were solicited extensively from white external individuals, particularly white women.

Part III presents examples of racialism in the television and cable industries. In Herman Gray's republished article, "Television, Black Americans, and the American Dream," representations of black success and failure are examined. Gray's analysis explores the television industry's presentation of an idealized black middle class (*The Cosby Show*—fiction) in contrast to a menacing black underclass (*The Vanishing Family: Crisis in Black America*—nonfiction). His contention is that such conflictive images as part of the public discourse about American race relations and racial (in)equality create a powerful societal ideology.

Sharon Bramlett-Solomon and Tricia M. Farwell extend the study of sex and soap operas to include the issue of racialism in their chapter, "Sex on the Soaps: An Analysis of Black, White, and Interracial Couple Intimacy." In contrast to research that suggests things are changing in soap operas, their study finds that such changes, when race is involved, are slow and unstable. Although black and interracial couples exist in greater numbers today, intimacy between them is not a common or normal depiction.

The O. J. Simpson media circus is explored by Eddith Dashiell in "Broadcast TV Coverage of the O. J. Simpson Murder Case: Racist or Starstruck?" Many polls have suggested that the majority of white audiences tended to see the Simpson case as problematic because of his celebrity status, while most black viewers felt there were overt racial implications. Dashiell concludes that, despite the polls, broadcast television's evening news programs early in the coverage period usually shied away from the race issue unless it was specific to the case, and more often focused on Simpson's celebrity status.

I'll Fly Away was one of those really great television dramas that suffered from the boundaries of racialism. In "Advertising Discourse and the Marketing of *I'll Fly Away*," Karen Smith critically assesses the initial promotional campaign and how the stereotypical images may have affected the show's viewing audience and ultimate ratings. Smith explains how early advertising for the show featured Lily Harper, the main protagonist, as a mammy-type maid, when her true character was viable and progressive. She argues that network executives realized their mistake too late, and their efforts to save the exceptional show ultimately failed.

Black Entertainment Television (BET) has evolved as a dominant communication medium for African American culture. Alice Tait and John Barber's chapter, "Black Entertainment Television: Breaking New Ground and Accepting New Responsibilities?" describes the cable channel's efforts and assesses its impact. They argue that BET as an Afrocentric entity promotes cultural and racial images and messages, yet the primary influence of the cable network is its economic success as a black-owned company.

Part IV explores racialism as it manifests itself within specific areas of radio and music. African American community radio is the focus of Sharon Albert-Honore's chapter, "Empowering Voices: KUCB and Black Liberation Radio." Albert-Honore argues that First Amendment values of self-fulfillment and maintaining the search for truth are found in African American community radio. She documents the development of KUCB, an FCC-licensed community station in Des Moines, Iowa, and Black Liberation Radio, a pirate community station in Springfield, Illinois. Her analysis shows that such stations are necessary to provide a forum for minority voice.

In "'Pride and Profit' in Black Radio Promotions: Celebrating Family Days and Business Partnerships," Phylis Johnson and Thomas Birk develop the argument that many "black/urban" commercial radio stations are not simply profit-focused music meccas but are community- and education-oriented cultural systems as well. They describe two specific examples: WDAS's Unity Weekend 1992 in Philadelphia and WTLC's 1993 Black Expo in Indianapolis. Their evaluation explores how black/urban radio has established itself as a viable mode of economic and social change in America.

Portia Maultsby presents a crucial discussion on the relationship between music and culture in her chapter, "Music in African American Culture." She traces the role of music in the expression and context of black cultural identity, then demonstrates the need for more research on black popular music forms such as rhythm and blues, pop, and rap. Her chapter urges us to consider the social and cultural functions of music in African American communities, as an invaluable resource for documenting the complex and diverse nature of African American culture.

Finally, in my chapter with Harold Looney, "Rap Music, Black Men, and the Police," a contemporary black music form is examined in its cultural context. Research has found that black music has always been a prominent mode of communication in African American culture. We explore that cultural legacy in rap music within black identity and experience. Through rap music, black men have been able to find voice and to challenge what they see as an unfair authoritative system with that voice. We conclude that the problematic relationship between black men and police becomes an important lyrical topic of rap music based on the cultural experience of many urban black men.

Since 1968, when the Kerner Commission included media as an important component in the struggle between blacks and whites, various industries have strived to include more favorable images, ideas, and attitudes relating to African Americans. With racialism continually impacting the media, the problems have not gone away, they have only changed with the times. This book offers 16 examples of racialism in the media from movies and music to television and print. These chapters provide insight into the media's representation of African American culture and move readers toward a more complex understanding of the motivations, interactions, ideologies, and realities of such images and messages. It is an effort to help readers comprehend the kinds of racialism existing theory and to develop a sensitivity and awareness toward it. It is an important look at how the media intersects with African American culture in contemporary society.

REFERENCES

Aguirre, A. (1995). *American ethnicity: The dynamics and consequences of discrimination.* New York: McGraw-Hill.

Angus, I., & Jhally, S. (1989). *Cultural politics in contemporary America*. New York: Routledge.

Appleton, N. (1983). *Cultural pluralism in education: Theoretical foundations*. New York: Longman.

Bell, D. (1992). *Faces at the bottom of the well: The renaissance of racism*. New York: Basic Books.

Collier, M. J., & Thomas, M. (1988). Cultural identity: An interpretive perspective. In Y. Y. Kim & W. B. Gudykunst (Eds.), *Theories in intercultural communication* (pp. 99-120). Newbury Park, CA: Sage.

Delgado, R. (1995). *Critical race theory*. Philadelphia: Temple University Press.

Dyson, M. (1993). *Reflecting black: African-American cultural criticism*. Minneapolis: University of Minnesota Press.

Entman, R. (1990). Modern racism and the local television news. *Critical Studies in Mass Communication, 7*, 332-345.

Entman, R. (1992). Blacks in news: Television, modern racism and cultural change. *Journalism Quarterly, 29*(2), 341-361.

Feagin, J., & Vera, H. (1995). *White racism: The basics*. New York: Routledge.

Geertz, C. (1973). *The interpretation of cultures*. New York: Basic Books.

Gilroy, P. (1987). *There ain't no black in the Union Jack: The cultural politics of race and nation*. London: Hutchison.

Grant, M. (1918). *The passing of the great race*. New York: Scribner.

Gray, H. (1989). Television, black Americans, and the American dream. *Critical Studies in Mass Communication, 6*, 376-386.

Hall, S. (1981). Television as expression of ideology. *Communication Research Trends, 2*(3), pp. 5-6.

Hawkins, D. F. (Ed.). (1995). *Ethnicity, race and crime: Perspectives across time and place*. Albany: State University of New York Press.

hooks, b. (1990). *Yearning: Race, gender and cultural politics*. Boston: South End.

hooks, b. (1994). *Outlaw culture: Resisting representations*. New York: Routledge.

Jhally, S., & Lewis, J. (1992). *Enlightened racism: The Cosby Show, audiences and the myth of the American dream*. Boulder, CO: Westview.

Katz, P., & Taylor, D. (1988). *Eliminating racism: Profiles in controversy*. New York: Plenum.

Kanpol, B., & McLaren, P. (Eds.). (1995). *Critical multiculturalism: Uncommon voices in a common struggle*. Westport, CT: Bergin & Garvey.

Lorde, A. (1984). *Sister outsider*. Freedom, CA: Crossing Press.

Moynihan, D., & Glazer, N. (1970). *Beyond the melting pot: The Negroes, Puerto Ricans, Jews, Italians and Irish of New York City*. Cambridge: MIT Press.

Nichols, B. (1981). *Ideology and the image*. Bloomington: Indiana University Press.

Omi, M., & Winant, H. (1986). *Racial formation in the United States*. New York: Routledge & Kegan Paul.

Payton, R. (Ed.). (1986). *A melting pot or nation of minorities*. Austin: University of Texas Press.

Rothenberg, P. (1990). The construction, deconstruction and reconstruction of difference. *Hypatia, 5*(1), 42-58.

Smith, D. L. (1971). *The legacy of the melting pot*. North Quincy, MA: Christopher.

Taylor, C. (Ed.). (1994). *Multiculturalism: Examining the politics of recognition*. Princeton, NJ: Princeton University Press.

Washington, J. (1986). *Alain Locke and philosophy: A quest for cultural pluralism*. Westport, CT: Greenwood.

West, C. (1982). *Prophesy deliverance! An Afro-American revolutionary Christianity.* Philadelphia: Westminster.

West, C. (1990). The new cultural politics of difference. *October, 53,* 93-108.

West, C. (1995). Doing difference. *Gender & Society, 9*(1), 8-37.

Whitaker, B. (Ed.). (1984). *Minorities: A question of human rights.* New York: Pergamon.

Willie, C. (1975). *Oreo: A perspective on race and marginal men and women.* Wakefield, MA: Parameter.

Winant, H. (1994). *Racial conditions: Politics, theory, comparison.* Minneapolis: University of Minnesota Press.

PART I

Issues in Film

1

Cultural Engineering
and the Films of Spike Lee

WILLIAM A. HARRIS

The experience of African peoples during the past 500 years in the diaspora is continually being documented by researchers and addressed by political actors. The ravages of slavery, poverty, and discrimination have taken a toll in human lives and aspirations. Too often these deprivations are the main factors in the construction of the African American reality.

The attempts at bringing about positive change for the African American population have multiplied in the twentieth century. As the century draws to a close, we can clearly identify political forces both inside and outside the African American community that have targeted both internal and external conditions as the essential locus for change. Additionally, we can identify instances in which the media of information or entertainment have been used as vehicles for social change in the African American cause.

The civil rights movement, beginning with the efforts of Du Bois and continuing through the legalist strategies of the NAACP and

AUTHOR'S NOTE: This is a revised version of an article published in the *Journal of American and Canadian Studies, 11,* 129-154 (1994) (Sophia University, Japan). This research was supported, in part, by funds from the Minority Opportunity Research Experience grant awarded to the University of Iowa by the U.S. Department of Education.

beyond, used its protests and petitions to seek a more livable American society for African peoples. Through executive and legislative initiatives on employment, housing, and voting rights, the forces of government also centered their efforts at change on the greater society.

On the other hand, the government has implemented programs, such as Job Corps, MESBIC, and the War on Poverty, designed to improve the opportunity structure of the black community. And workers in many fields within the black community have created political, educational, and religious organizations providing guidance and training for thousands of African Americans.

Documentary and entertainment film and television products have served to persuade the general American public and inspire the African American public concerning our collective progress on the road to universal freedom. The past decade has seen a resurgence of African American filmmakers. Aside from their remunerative motives, our present-day black directors and film writers seem determined to use their medium as a force for positive change in African American society. This chapter analyzes the work of Spike Lee as a tool of social change.

In the decade since his first commercially distributed film was screened in America's theaters, Spike Lee has established a presence in the film industry and in the minds of his audience. His films are challenging and thought-provoking, with didactic messages for the several segments of his audience. Clearly, he is urging us to *wake up!* But over and above our somnolence, Spike is concerned about aspects of our interpersonal and collective behavior. In his first five films distributed to mass audiences,[1] certain themes appear continually. The analysis here focuses on the protagonists in these five films in terms of the representation and philosophy of four major themes contained therein. In the conclusion, the exhortatory function of Spike Lee's entertainment is placed within a conceptual framework known as cultural engineering.

THE OPPRESSION OF
AFRICAN AMERICAN WORKERS

African Americans face a cycle of deprivation regarding jobs, housing, and education. To develop socially and economically as an ethnic group, it is necessary to break into this cycle at some point. Spike Lee takes as a theme the oppression experienced by African American workers in the search for opportunity, and he depicts their struggle against that oppression. The inequities faced by the black worker are examined in *Jungle Fever, Mo' Better Blues,* and *Do the Right Thing.* In these three films, there are situations in which the hero is constrained in his efforts to actualize and progress in his career because of countervailing economic control by white entrepreneurs. The ethnicity of the white oppressor differs in each case, but the message is the same: There will be no increase in reward regardless of excellence in performance.

The inequities of the corporate world are shown to us in meetings between Flipper Purify and the bosses in *Jungle Fever.* When Flipper seeks the fulfillment of a promise that he would be made a partner in the firm, his quest is adamantly refused. The senselessness of the routine stifling of black ambition is made apparent to us. We are led to believe in the rightness of Flipper's position. But he is not to prevail in his quest for a partnership because of some reason that we cannot really understand: "We can't do it right now. Now is not the time." It is as though Jerry and Leslie, the partners, are treating him as a child or a pet who is told, "You can have the candy when I say and not before." It is an arbitrary and capricious refusal to recognize his ability and contribution. Flipper is being cozened by white liberals who are willing to suffer the black presence in the workplace as long as they can continue to exert white control (see Tucker, 1972). It is possible to trace Flipper's extramarital affair with Angela Tucci to a similar scene with the bosses, when they insist that his request for a black secretary is unreasonable. Flipper, in turn, sees as unreasonable his role as the token person of color in the company, but he acquiesces and gives Angie a trial. When asked about his workday, Flipper replies that he is "just a poor black man facing the struggle in corporate America." We take the statement as a bit of cant and with a grain of salt, but the intricacies of the struggle are apparent in the scenes with the bosses.

In *Mo' Better Blues*, Bleek Gilliam and his agent, Giant, face a similar scene of rejection by whites in power in the organization (Lee, 1990, pp. 239, 249-251). The petition in Bleek's case is for a more equitable share of the profits being generated by his celebrated jazz quintet. First, Bleek's boyhood buddy and manager, Giant, approaches the owners of "Beneath the Underdog." Giant tries to evoke the clearly apparent popularity of the band as grounds for an increase in salaries. His argument is refused because of the originally negotiated contract. Artistry is one thing but business is another.

> MOE: It's out of the question.
> GIANT: Everybody's making money except the artists.
> MOE: Don't hand me that artist doo-doo. They don't have any financial risks. Go listen to the music.
> (He dismisses Giant with a wave of the hand.)

In his round with the owners, Bleek initially bases his appeal on the fairness of the situation.

> BLEEK: . . . I came here to speak about the great sums of money you two are making off my music and the little I see in return.
> MOE: . . . Giant, your manager, was the one who negotiated this deal. One you agreed to.
> JOSH: And it's always been our business policy to never ever—
> MOE: —ever never—
> JOSH: —renegotiate the deal.

Failing this, Bleek attempts a humanitarian argument.

> BLEEK: I trust him. He's honest. I can't say that about you, Moe, or your first-class cousin.
> MOE: Nobody can be trusted. Everyone steals. Everyone is crooked. The trick is to walk out of the deal with as much of your shirt on as possible.
> BLEEK: Y'know what that sounds like? . . . like the long, long history of black artists being exploited.
> MOE: Everybody exploits everybody. Friendship is one thing but business is another.
> JOSH: We have a binding contract.

The club owners and the musician form a set piece in the entertainment world. The entertainer is always underpaid and the club owner is never making enough money. Yet, fortunes are made from the talents and careers of entertainers who die impoverished at an early age. Fairness is one thing but business is another. For all the good works of the John Hammonds and Norman Granzs in the music business, one wonders if our artistic geniuses would survive longer with less notoriety and a more equitable share of profits.

In *Do the Right Thing*, as Mookie attempts to discharge the duties of a young unwed father, it is clear that his job is a hindrance to his efforts. He is continually taunted and harassed by Pino, the boss's older son. And Sal, his boss, is unsympathetic to Mookie's needs, on the one hand, and crudely seductive toward Mookie's sister, Jade, on the other. In a brief scenario, Spike Lee reveals to us Sal's duplicity in his relations with Mookie. Following a break for a "quick shower" on the hottest day of the year, Mookie returns to face the music at Sal's Famous Pizzeria (Lee, 1989, pp. 204-205).

> SAL: Mookie, you are pushing it. You're really pushing it. I'm not paying you good money to fucking jerk me around.
> (Mookie has nothing to say.)
> SAL: You're gonna be in the street with the rest of your homeboys.
> PINO: 'Bout time, Pop.
> (ANGLE—DOOR)
> (Jade enters, and Sal looks up. He stops blasting Mookie and a very noticeable change comes over him.)
> SAL: Jade, we've been wondering when ya would pay us a visit.
> JADE: Hi, Sal, Pino, Vito.
> VITO: What's happening, Jade?
> JADE: Nuthin' really. How are you treating my brother?
> SAL: The Mook? Great. Mookie's a good kid.

It does not make for a good day at the office.

Mookie and Flipper, the protagonists who react against or in the face of economic oppression, suffer further loss. But even Bleek, who continues to pursue his art in the wake of inequity, suffers loss. What is the Leeian view of oppression? It is possible that he interprets oppression as an infection that emerges as a curse even if it is not directly hindering and disruptive.

Spike Lee's presentation of the continuing shortfalls of equity in the workplace of diversity forces white America to come to terms with the goals yet to be reached. One is moved to remove the blinders of denial and admit complicity in the daily grind of worker against worker. There is the need for a definition for "job" that differs from the definition of

"sentence," or a definition of "work" that differs from that of "war."
Spike Lee peeks behind the facade of the integrated workplace to
discover the micro-level events that belie the statistics seen in affirmative action reports.

THE EXPLOITATION OF WOMEN

A theme that emerges in each of Spike Lee's first five films concerns
the treatment of women by men. Spike's women are subject to the
whims and fantasies of men. The women are controlled by men. Men
are the actors, and women the acted upon. In *Jungle Fever*, the imbal-
ance of the relationships is seen most clearly. The ultimate justification
for Flipper's attraction to Angie and the disorganization of both their
lives is that he was "curious." He even attempts to extend his control
into her motivation for entering into the affair, by deeming her to have
been curious as well. Because of the racial dynamics of American society,
the concept of race leaps to mind as the motivating and salient element
in the interracial affair we see in *Jungle Fever.* We should consider the
matter further.

The seduction of Angie, although patently exploitative, is neither
crass nor compulsive as Spike Lee presents it. On the contrary, it is
extremely commonsensical and realistic. Flipper may be curious about
the white woman, but his curiosity remains dormant until the stranger
enters his space. Through a gradual process of overcoming prejudice,
comparing experiences, gaining confidential insights, and becoming
familiar, the two are drawn together. Their liaison is scripted and
predicted by Hannibal Lector's generalization: "We covet that which
we see every day" (Harris, 1989, p. 227).

Spike Lee has replicated the nuances of the archetypical extramarital
affair. The realistic and typical romance presented in *Jungle Fever*
originates in pedestrian rather than predatory urges and is enacted
between acquaintances who have become familiar. We do not bed the
hunk from the supermarket or the beauty from the laundromat. Instead,
we are attracted incrementally to those whose form and face we have
come to know. Our emotions are aroused by the familiar voice embod-
ied by the sexual mysteries that we can only wonder about. This is the
real love affair, the casting aside of discretion and frustration to act out

the irresistible fantasy. This is the love affair that occasions surprise on the part of friends and anguish on the part of spouses, the affair with the coworker or the spouse's close friend.

At the outset, Angie's complicity in the initiation of the affair is not completely manifest, if it exists at all. When Flipper tells her, "I've never cheated on my wife before," there seems to be no motivation for his confession. But before we can think twice, she has captured him completely. We learn later that we have probably witnessed the loss of her virginity, gone in the wink of an eye.

Angie's family life prior to Flipper is one of thankless drudgery. She is taken as a matter of fact to be the housekeeper and surrogate mother for her father and brothers, in addition to her frequent employment as a secretary. Her neighborhood boyfriend seems at first glance to be an equitable, though lackluster, partner. We must entertain the idea that Angie, at some point, sees Flipper as the exotic knight who will carry her away from a mean and predictable future. Her intention is not clear at the outset, but she eventually comes to broach the topic of bearing Flipper's child. She is not just having a fling.

In considering Flipper's motivation for beginning the affair, we should consider his work situation. Flipper has been rebuffed by the bosses in his request for an African American secretary. He grudgingly accepts Angie as an assistant; his grin often appears to be a gritting of teeth. He is also apprehensive about his chances for promotion at the firm. On the one hand, it is possible that Flipper, at some level, sees his seduction of Angie as a revenge against the bosses. On the other hand, Angie may represent a charm that Flipper must ingest in order to screw his courage in seeking the promotion. Note that it is only after the seduction that Flipper meets with the bosses about the partnership. And he emerges from the meeting enraged and empowered to go forth and found his own company. If the charm cannot work one magic, perhaps it can work another.

The concept of frustration and revenge arises again in connection with the behavior of Paulie Carbone, Angie's boyfriend in Bensonhurst. When we first see him, he is himself exploited in the same manner and for the same reasons as Angie. He is cast into the role of breadwinner and surrogate wife by his widowed father. In the end, however, he is seen to accost and approach a black woman, Orin Goode, for reasons that are not entirely clear. Is he exacting revenge against blacks, or perhaps against his father? It is of course entirely possible that he is, in fact, sincerely attracted to this lovely black woman. Whatever the case, in relationships constructed by Spike Lee, the male makes the moves, calls the shots, controls the pace of the affair.

Flipper's relations with his wife, Drew, are also self-absorbed. In their final scene, she is depicted crying while making love. Indications are that the errant husband has assumed and exercised a male prerogative in gaining access to her bed.

In his attack on the open secrets of American society, Spike Lee spares neither black nor white citizens. In the black community, his films often elicit the remark, "I'm not sure we should be talking about that." Surely those who make such remarks do not watch the 11 o'clock news. Spike invites us to abandon denial of negative patterns of behavior within the black community. He concentrates his commentary on the mutual mistreatment of black people in general and on the state of relations between males and females in particular.

One of the saddest exploitations of woman by man to be seen in films is suffered by Jane Toussaint in *School Daze* when she obeys the command to fornicate with Half-Pint. In the harsh initiation rite, Half-Pint was able to prevail in part because of the assistance of Jane and the other Gamma Rays. Julian, incensed, concocts a revenge to set his ego aright. Julian coerces Jane to lie with Half-Pint, offering her up as an inanimate "gift" (Lee, 1988, pp. 314-315).

> JULIAN: I told your cousin I would take care of you and that's what I'm goin' to do.
>
> HALF-PINT: Big Brother Almighty, what are you talking about?
>
> JULIAN: Tonight I'm giving you a gift, from me to you.
>
> (Julian takes Jane by the hand.)
>
> (CLOSE—JANE)
>
> HALF-PINT: I can't.
>
> (Jane looks as if somebody has just slit her throat. All the color is out of her face and the tears soon follow.)
>
> JULIAN: What do you mean? I know, we all know, you're still a virgin. Go.
>
> (ANGLE—GAMMAS)
>
> (They begin chanting.)
>
> GAMMAS: Go! Go! Go!

Jane complies and is devastated by the experience. But her degradation is not complete until Julian drives the final nail into the coffin of her self-esteem (Lee, 1988, pp. 319-320).

(Jane looks like a wreck, the tears have streaked her makeup. This is a woman who has lost all her self-worth.)

(. . . In rushes Julian. He grabs her by the hand and pulls her out from the Gammas.)

[In the hallway.]

JANE: I did what you said.

JULIAN: What is that?

JANE: I did it with Half-Pint.

JULIAN: What?

JANE: You told me.

JULIAN: The hell I did. You gave it up to Half-Pint? How could you? I thought you loved me. Now you're boning my own frat brother. My own frat brother. . . .

(At this point Jane is gone. She loses it. She's on the express to a breakdown.)

JANE: Why are you doing this to me?

She has become a used and discarded object. Our hearts go out to her and we fear for her sanity and survival. She has been a true believer in her man, right or wrong. But she is forced to accept betrayal.

Bleek Gilliam in *Mo' Better Blues* is the master of his horn and consort to two women. His world is under his control. His behavior is brazen and self-centered. A woman is, in fact, an object for Bleek, albeit a beautiful object such as a rare musical instrument. She exists to be mastered and performed upon, a medium in which to express the virtuosity of his sexual prowess. There are scenes between a commanding Bleek and each of the women, Indigo and Clarke, in which he boldly expresses his cocksman's philosophy (Lee, 1990, pp. 228, 231).

INDIGO: Bleek, you're a good brother, but you still don't know what you want.

BLEEK: Now I guess it's time for Confessions of a Modern Day Dog.

INDIGO: Like it or not, Bleek, you're a dog. A nice dog, but a dog, nonetheless.

BLEEK: I won't argue the point. You know how I am. It's no secret. With men—It's a dick thing.

CLARKE: . . . Let's be real. What you and I do is not make love.

BLEEK: What would you call it?

CLARKE: It's definitely not making love!

BLEEK: Boning!

CLARKE: You've been a lot more imaginative.

BLEEK: I got a million of them. The Mo' Better.

CLARKE: Mo' what?

BLEEK: The Mo' Better makes it Mo' Better.

CLARKE: Anyway, . . . we don't make love, you don't love me. But in the meantime I'll settle for some of that Mo' Better.

BLEEK: I also got some of that In Case of Emergency Break Glass Dick. . . .

The women do not go gladly to their debasement. There are scenes between a contrite Bleek and each of the women in which they confront him about his lack of focus and commitment in the relationship. The motivation for the ending of these affairs is represented in a montage of misnaming and complaining in which each of the women rails against Bleek's infidelity. Bleek brushes off their challenges with a smirk and a shrug. After their departures, he makes a halfhearted attempt to fill his bed. It is clear throughout, however, that his principal muse is the muse of music, Terpsichore, and not the muse of romance, Erato. Only when his world is brutally crushed and his talent destroyed does Bleek come to earth and settle for the mundane existence of wife and home.

In *Do the Right Thing*, Tina gives us the impression that she is the harridan, the nagger, the constant complainer. Tina, in fact, represents a community of women who are courted at an early age with promises that are never kept. They are compromised at first in terms of their reputations, and soon in terms of the time they must spend performing motherly duties. The rancor of their rhetoric matches the quality of male trustworthiness.

Mookie is a hustler. He is constrained from a serene and orderly lifestyle by the conditions of his existence. In Mookie's world, opportunities for remunerative work are few and opportunities for hedonistic play are many. Jobs are hard to find and paychecks are skimpy. Mookie gives us the impression of a person constantly on the move to ferret out the next slim opportunity. Mookie has obligations in the form of a woman and her son, whom he fathered. He has obligations to his reference group in the neighborhood. He has obligations to perform on the job. Rushing from one obligation to another, he fully discharges none. In a scene in which Tina has ordered a pizza, we see the frantic attempt by Mookie to cover all the bases. Neither Speedy Gonzales nor Superman could cover all the ground that Mookie attempts (Lee, 1989, pp. 225-228).

> MOOKIE: Shit! I forgot [the ice cream].
> TINA: Your memory is really getting bad. . . .
> MOOKIE: I can run out and get it.
> TINA: No! No! You won't come back either.
> MOOKIE: I can't be staying long anyway.
> TINA: How long then?
> MOOKIE: Long enough for us to do the nasty.
> TINA: That's out. No! It's too hot! You think I'm gonna let you get some, put on your clothes, then run outta here and never see you again in who knows when?
> MOOKIE: A quickie is good every once in a blue moon.
> TINA: You a blue-moon fool.
> MOOKIE: Then we'll do something else.
> TINA: What else?
> MOOKIE: Trust me.
> TINA: Trust you? Because of trusting you we have a son. Remember your son?

The lone exception to Spike Lee's gallery of exploited women is Nola Darling in *She's Gotta Have It*. Nola is so completely liberated, so predatory, so accultured to the masculine approach to romance that she perplexes her lovers (Lee, 1987, pp. 340-341, 293).

> MARS: Dependable? What? Are you on drugs? [Nola is] 'bout dependable as a ripped diaphragm.
> JAMIE: That's cold.
> MARS: I'm not lying. Make a date with her, it's fifty-fifty she shows at all, let alone late. Last year I got two playoff tickets, y'know, da Knicks against the Celtics. . . .I asked Nola if she wanted to go and she said, "Yes, I've always wanted to go to a Knick [sic] game." . . .

(CLOSE—MARS)

MARS: Do you know, she never showed. I missed the goddam first two quarters and guess what? Bernard King scored thirty-five points, just in the first half. . . . I wouldn't say Nola was dependable.

JAMIE: It was bad enough, Nola and all her male friends, but on top of that she had this one particular woman after her. That was a bit much for me. I had my suspicions about the both of them. I asked Nola point blank, was she involved with this female or what? She said no.

Nola is presented as happy and in control of her world. She sips the nectar from the flowers of manhood, but she does not entirely relinquish her space or her persona. She is centered. Although we are never quite sure of Nola's grand plan, she gives the impression of one who is surefooted in rocky terrain and trekking toward an ultimate Nirvana. The men cannot fathom her motive nor can they abide her equanimity (Lee, 1987, p. 336).

JAMIE: . . . You can see anybody but I can't. This shit has gone on long enough. I've tried to be open-minded but instead I'm being played for a sucker.

They do not recognize that she is recycling their own behavior, and without a doubt she populates their worst nightmares. Through Nola's eyes, we gain a view of male society as it appears to women in the boudoir. It is quite different than the view presented to men in the locker room. Spike Lee uses the character of Nola to hold up a mirror to male society (Lee, 1987, pp. 285-288).

[The COME-ON scene: Quick cuts of BOGUS MEN talking as if they were trying to rap to Nola.]

DOG #1: Slim, you so fine I'd drink a tub of your bath water.

DOG #2: I wanna rock ya world.

DOG #3: If I was you, I'm the kinda guy you'd want to take home to meet your mother. Don't you agree?

DOG #4: Baby, it's got to be you and me.

DOG #5: You may not realize this but you are sending out strong vibes tonight. May I continue? You're lonely, you're alone, you're sad, you're confused, you're horny. You need a man like me to understand you, to hold you, to caress, to looove you. You need me. What's your phone number?

DOG #6: I know I only saw you for the first time in my life one minute ago but I love you.

DOG #7: I know I only saw you for the first time in my life one minute ago but I love you.

DOG #8: I love you.

DOG #9: I love you.

DOG #10: I—

DOG #11: —love—

DOG #12: —you.

DOG #13: I got my B.A. from Morehouse, my M.B.A. from Harvard. I own a new BMW 318i, I make fifty-three thou a year after taxes and I want you to want me.

DOG #14: Did you know I'm related to Michael Jackson on my mother's side of the family and Prince on my father's? No lie. We can call 'em up right now.

DOG #15: Baby, I got plenty of what you need. Ten throbbing inches of USDA government-inspected prime-cut grade-A TUBESTEAK!!!

(He sticks out his tongue.)

Spike Lee forces us to consider black male repertoires and the possibility of role reversal. Through Nola's point of view, Spike Lee reveals males who act on the belief that "you're fine and you're mine." But, has he built the character of Nola on a real character type in the black community? Probably not. A black woman with multiple partners is a woman besieged, controlled, put upon, and demanded of on all sides. She has not the comfort and serenity of a Nola no matter what her age, income, or physical attributes are. Patently, Spike Lee is justly criticized by Simmonds (1988), who reminds us that liberation has economic and political dimensions that outweigh sexual freedom. Nola is, in fact, a man in a woman suit, a persona constructed from the male standpoint.

BLACK-ON-BLACK CRIME

When we think of the violence that people wreak on one another, we must consider little murders of the soul as well as street violence in our communities. In large part, Spike's concerns about the ill treatment of black people by black people are reflected in his portrayal of relations between males and females. In addition to this, however, there are several other instances that bear analysis. In *School Daze,* for example, the brief confrontation between the college students and the townies represents the deteriorating connections between the socioeconomic classes of the black American population (see Wilson, 1980). At first glance, the townies' animosity appears to be related to folkways of territoriality. Obviously, the restaurant is a local hangout and not intimately identified with the campus. On closer examination, however, there is revealed a difference in worldview concerning intellectual manhood, political rhetoric, and black identity (Lee, 1988, pp. 274-278).

> LEEDS: . . . We may not have your ed-u-ca-tion, but we ain't dirt either. . . . Are you black?
>
> (Those three words stop Slice in his tracks.) . . .
>
> (Slice walks up to Leeds, he's right in his face. The Fellas follow.)
>
> SLICE: You got a legitimate beef, but it's not with us.
>
> LEEDS: Who then?
>
> SLICE: Don't ever question whether I'm black. In fact, I was gonna ask your country, BAMA ass, why do you put those Jerri-curl, drip-drip chemicals in your black nappy hair?
>
> EDGE: That's right, goddammit.
>
> SLICE: And on top of that, come out in public with those plastic shower caps on your heads.
>
> JORDAN: Just like a bitch.
>
> MOSES: Who you calling a bitch?
>
> BOOKER T.: If the shoe fits.
>
> (Leeds steps back, trying to take back the upper hand that the local yokels have obviously lost.)
>
> LEEDS: I betcha you niggers think y'all are white. College don't mean shit, you'll always be niggers, always, just like us.
>
> SLICE: You're not niggers.
>
> (The Fellas leave, walking backwards, though; you never turn your back.) . . .

The rage of the townies is spontaneous and diffuse. The bewilderment of the college students is nearly complete; they grope for understanding. The scene is a border dispute between populations alien to one another. They are two groups with much in common who, because of the accidents of birth and background, are bound for different destinies. Yet, on each side, the possibility of acquiring the other's destiny is clearly so near and still so far.

Although the rage expressed in the standoff in *School Daze* is fairly gratuitous, a more brutal confrontation, for cause, is enacted in *Mo' Better Blues* when Bleek and Giant are severely beaten in the alley behind the club. Bleek loses more than a battle in that dark back alley; he loses the value of his artistic gift. He is never again to work as a performing artist. Bleek's fate is determined by the depth of his loyalty to his friend Giant, an addicted gambler. Giant himself has earlier fallen prey to the violence that accompanies his gambling habit. In a sickening scene, "Madlock methodically breaks all of Giant's five fingers on his left hand" (Lee, 1990, pp. 257-258). The message is that our weaknesses lead us to destruction and to the destruction of our loved ones.

The weakness of drug addiction creates the symbiosis between the predatory drug dealer and the hapless junkie. The dealer has a serpentine reputation in the African American community: menacing, fascinating, treacherous, slick, and above all deadly. Gator's weakness in *Jungle Fever* leads to his death, made more tragic because his father is the executioner. Sam Jackson's portrayal and Spike Lee's direction reveal the descending way stations in the degrading spiral of the junkie's career. We are amused, we are horrified, we are immersed in the den of iniquity.

Aside from veiled or outright violence, Spike comments broadly and boldly on the divisive issue of skin color as it affects the minds and lives of African Americans. In *School Daze,* the issue assumes tribalistic proportions (Lee, 1988, pp. 220-221).

(Jane gives Rachel a long, hard look. She then flips her hair at Rachel and the Gamma Rays follow suit.)

DORIS: It's not real.

DINA: Say what?

LIZZIE: You heard.

(The Jigs stand up and the battle lines are drawn.)

RACHEL: It ain't even real.

JANE: You wish you had hair like this.

DORIS: Girl, y'know you weren't born with green eyes.

LIZZIE: Green contact lenses.

DINA: They're just jealous.

RACHEL: Jealous?

JANE: Rachel, I've been watching you look at Julian. You're not slick.

RACHEL: If that was true he's not much to look at.

JANE: Pickaninny.

DORIS: Barbie doll.
RACHEL: High-yellow heifer.
DINA: Tar Baby!
VIVIAN: Wanna Be White!
KIM: Jigaboo!
RACHEL: Don't start.
JANE: We're gonna finish it.
[Musical production number]

The Jigaboos and Wannabees are mobilized against one another while they ignore a common heritage. As African Americans, they suffer because their misguided focus allows the perpetuation of social inequities. As women, they suffer because they lack a unified and shared understanding of their subdominant status vis-à-vis males.

In *Jungle Fever*, both Flipper and Drew are haunted by childhood memories of taunts received because of a skin color that was said to be too light or too dark. The women's "war council" dwells on and revolves around the topic of complexion.

The issue of skin color as a divisive irritant within the African American population is an issue that will not be wished away or denied. In fact, possibly the best prospect for a solution is technological. A report from Arizona tells of research on Melanotan, a compound that can increase the production of melanin and permanently darken skin (Freundlich, 1989). And there is the imminent possibility of genetic alteration, which can affect the physical characteristics of progeny far into the future (Kolata, 1994). The research is at the stage of animal trials. Help is on the way—for those who truly want it. The rest of Spike's representations of intragroup conflict are the teasings, cussings, and scuffling that are too often seen as merely cultural. Spike Lee is bent on cultural change; his motive is as much to teach as to entertain.

TRANQUILITY IS A SOMETIMES THING

In reflecting on these themes in Spike Lee's films, one cannot help but be struck by the fact that they constitute a catalogue of misery, treachery, and deceit. Are we choosing to take the narrow, pessimistic view? Have we ignored the scenes of happiness and contentment, and chosen to dwell instead on the deviance and violence? Admittedly there is joy in Spike's magic lantern. Nola's birthday fete is a creative tribute concocted by Jamie, the devoted lover. Spike frames it as a special moment by rendering the scene in color.

School Daze has moments of festivity and tenderness amidst scenes of intergroup rivalry and sexual exploitation. The Splash Jam is an unqualified gala, enjoyed with wild abandon by all factions of the college student bodies. The film has other celebrations, however, such as the Greek Show and the Homecoming parade, that are marred by the intergroup conflicts that infest the small campus.

The marriage between Bleek and Indigo marks a happy ending to *Mo' Better Blues,* as does the final scene between Da Mayor and Mother Sister in *Do the Right Thing* (Lee, 1989, pp. 258-259).

(MOTHER SISTER'S BEDROOM—DAY)
(Da Mayor wakes up in Mother Sister's big brass bed (she was born in it). At first he has no idea where he's at, then he sees Mother Sister sitting down across the room smiling at him.)
MOTHER SISTER: Good morning.
DA MAYOR: Is it a good morning?
MOTHER SISTER: Yes indeed. You almost got yourself killed last night.
DA MAYOR: I've done that before.
(Da Mayor gets up out of her big brass bed.)
DA MAYOR: Where did you sleep?
MOTHER SISTER: I didn't.
DA MAYOR: I hope the block is still standing.
MOTHER SISTER: We're still standing.

The opening scene of family life in the Purify household contains most of the tranquility to be found in *Jungle Fever.* Tranquility there is in Spike Lee's films, but mostly it is a sometimes thing.

Spike Lee seems to be a man mobilized by the clear and present danger to the African American social environment. He insists that we wake up and face the danger. And he will not cease in warning us of the enemy within and without.

In addition, there is a subtext in Spike Lee's work concerning the fleeting nature of life and its events. His treatment of the pleasures we derive from our existence, the products we create during our lives, and the relationships we form often emphasizes the transitoriness of the things we most enjoy and esteem. In *Jungle Fever*, the carnal pleasures of romance lead directly to trouble. By contrast, Nola in *She's Gotta Have It* is depicted exuberantly reveling in her sexual liberation. But as the tale ends, she makes a decision for self-imposed celibacy, however briefly it is enacted. Her contemplation of change from a life of worldly pleasure to the life of a nun is almost Buddhistic in its presentation. The soporific pleasure of narcotics leads to depravity and death in *Jungle Fever* and the hedonistic addiction to gambling leads to pain and destruction in *Mo' Better Blues*. Even the comforting pleasures of spiritual life enjoyed by the Good Reverend Doctor are wrenched and buffeted by an ugly reality in *Jungle Fever.*

Flipper's work is devalued by his bosses in *Jungle Fever.* Adding destruction to insult, his wife, in a fit of righteous rage, defenestrates all of his architectural drawings and equipment. Sal's pizza parlor in *Do the Right Thing* is reduced to a burnt-out hulk in the space of a few minutes of violence, the violence triggered by Sal's fit of pique. In *Mo' Better Blues,* Bleek is stripped of his musical artistry in a back alley brawl. Finally, the gala productions of the students in *School Daze* consist solely of ephemera—floats, costumes, dance routines; none of these will outlive even the mayfly.

Relationships in Spike Lee's films can spontaneously destruct. The elusive Nola is plainly not the woman who wants your engagement ring. In *School Daze*, even the seemingly durable relationship between Dap and Rachel, fired in the crucible of activism, cannot withstand the misunderstanding and slights that tarnish its luster. There is a contrary observation to be seen in *Do the Right Thing;* the Mayor and Mother Sister find common ground amidst the turmoil of the neighborhood. The multiple romances of Bleek in *Mo' Better Blues* are clearly destined for disaster; we see this plainly from the outset. Finally, *Jungle Fever* presents us with a panorama of tenuous relationships. We can imagine further turmoil that is likely to occur in the collective lives of these characters after the curtain falls.

ON THE UPSIDE:
SCENES OF CHANGE AND RESISTANCE

Along with scenes of joy, Spike Lee offers us the vision of reconstructed social roles among African Americans. Flipper in *Jungle Fever* addresses the psychic battering of the corporate world with an entrepreneurial strategy of his own. His decision is emblematic of Walter Rodney's (1990) admonition against stagnation in the struggle:

> If a person gets trapped in a previous moment of history, you find it hard to carry on a conversation with him or her because they are still out to defend something that you're not against, but you're not with because it is no longer the relevant thing. Why should we caught get up in making tremendous tirades against . . . the Europeans . . ., look how these fellows exploited us? Why should we continually speak in this grand singular—the African is this and the European is the other? That was a formulation that was necessary at a particular point in time, when we were still within the whole identity crisis, when we were trying to evolve a peoplehood. But the moment we move beyond that . . .we must look at real life. (p. 69)

There is the ongoing necessity to "keep on steppin'." Now that African American society has committed slavery and oppression to its collective cultural memory, the task becomes less one of protesting the past and more one of planning for the future. We are treated to a reaffirmation of family roles as they are ultimately assumed by Bleek and Indigo in *Mo' Better Blues,* by the old couple in *Do the Right Thing,* as well as by Flipper and his family.

Spike Lee, in the sheer making of his films and in the themes therein, reflects the essence of Rodney's statement. We can also see how Lee's work resonates with the ultimate level of Afrocentric awareness, described by Asante (1988, p. 49). It is a case study in going beyond lament and ascending the learning curve of consciousness and contribution.

In a discussion of the East African context, Ali Mazrui (1972) provides some general principles for the conceptualization of media's role in social change strategies. Cultural engineering, according to Mazrui, involves using cultural products "for purposes of deflecting human habit in the direction of new and perhaps constructive endeavors" (p. xv). As the magic lantern of the cinema projects the magic mirror of our societal role models, our collective identity is reinforced through the wide dissemination of cultural images and political statements.

Without a great stretch of imagination, it is possible to transfer Mazrui's (1972, pp. 23-37) conceptualization of the relationship between societal development and the creative arts to the African American context. Cultural products, such as those generated by Spike Lee, serve three separate but essential purposes in the development process. Clearly, the content of the film conveys a powerful visual and verbal statement to the audience. Of equal importance, also, is the African American identity of the cultural worker. The cultural pride attached to productions by African American cultural workers enhances and magnifies the message of the films and their impact on the black audience. The third important role of these works is that of a bridge to the greater society. The American public gains access to authentic portrayals of black hopes and aspirations as well as black tribulations and motives. Further, the films eminently meet the exacting technical standards of the film industry. They bring new talent and ideas, on and off camera, to the development of society and the arts.

Spike Lee's art is an art of advocacy. He is speaking in favor of the need for African American social solidarity even in his later films *Crooklyn* and *Drop Squad*. In his titles and credits, he is seen to juxtapose the images and ideas of Malcolm X and Martin Luther King Jr. By doing so, he demonstrates to us that factions purported to be antagonistic in African American society have much in common. The best outcome of the widespread donning of "X" regalia in connection with the screening of *Malcolm X* (Lee, 1992) would be an affirmation that " 'X' marks the spot where plans for African American progress begin." Through unity, there is a viable society to be gained; through conflict, there is a people to be lost.

NOTE

1. Spike Lee's first films are as follows: *She's Gotta Have It* (1986, distributed by Island Pictures, Los Angeles); *School Daze* (1988, distributed by Columbia Pictures, Culver City, CA); *Do the Right Thing* (1989, distributed by Universal Pictures, Universal City, CA); *Mo' Better Blues* (1990, distributed by Universal Pictures, Universal City, CA); *Jungle Fever* (1991, distributed by Universal Pictures, Universal City, CA); *Malcolm X* (1992, distributed by Warner Brothers, Burbank, CA) (all films produced by 40 Acres and a Mule Filmworks, Brooklyn, NY). All quotations from these films are used by permission of Spike Lee.

REFERENCES

Asante, M. K. (1988). *Afrocentricity*. Trenton, NJ: Africa World Press.

Freundlich, N. (1989, March 27). This hormone may give you what the sun can't: A safe tan. *Business Week*, p. 64.

Harris, T. (1989). *The silence of the lambs*. New York: St. Martin's.

Kolata, G. (1994, November 22). Gene technique can shape future generations. *New York Times*, pp. A-1 ff.

Lee, S. (1987). *Spike Lee's gotta have it*. New York: Simon & Schuster.

Lee, S. (1988). *Uplift the race*. New York: Simon & Schuster.

Lee, S. (1989). *Do the right thing*. New York: Simon & Schuster.

Lee, S. (1990). *Mo' better blues*. New York: Simon & Schuster.

Lee, S. (1991). *Five for five*. New York: Stewart, Tabori & Chang.

Mazrui, A. A. (1972). *Cultural engineering and nation-building in East Africa*. Evanston, IL: Northwestern University Press.

Rodney, W. (1990). *Walter Rodney speaks: The making of an African intellectual*. Trenton, NJ: Africa World Press.

Simmonds, F. N. (1988). She's gotta have it: The representation of black female sexuality on film. *Feminist Review, 29*, 10-22.

Tucker, R. (1972). Some observations on neo-paternalism in black-white managerial relations. *African-American Studies, 3*, 7-11.

Wilson, W. J. (1980). *The declining significance of race*. Chicago: University of Chicago Press.

2

Intimations of Invisibility

Black Women and Contemporary Hollywood Cinema

RUTH ELIZABETH BURKS

> *The most desirable option for people of color who promote the new cultural politics of difference is to be a critical organic catalyst. By this I mean a person who stays attuned to the best of what the mainstream has to offer—its paradigms, viewpoints and methods—yet maintains a grounding in affirming and enabling subcultures of criticism. Prophetic critics and artists of color should be exemplars of what it means to be intellectual freedom fighters, that is, cultural workers who simultaneously position themselves within (or alongside) the mainstream while clearly aligned with groups who vow to keep alive potent traditions of critique and resistance.*
>
> West, 1992, p. 33

In 1985, Whoopi Goldberg, as Celie in Steven Spielberg's film adaptation of Alice Walker's *The Color Purple*, drew nationwide attention to the doubly negative predicament of the black woman in the United States. The media, however, chose to focus on the black man, whom Spielberg's production had visually portrayed as the miscreant responsible for the black woman's plight, rather than on the underlying culprits—pervasive racism, sexism, and classism in the United States.

The controversy surrounding Spielberg's depiction of the black male in *The Color Purple* was the reason given by producer Diane Silver for omitting most of Bessie Mear's scenes from her 1986 cinematic version of Richard Wright's *Native Son*—a peculiar choice given the fact that in his own 1951 film adaptation of his classic novel, Wright had augmented Bessie's already significant role. But Silver's pretense for Bessie's conspicuous absence from much of her film was motivated more by a desire for fame and financial gain than by any compulsion to maintain the artistic integrity of the original source. As Silver rationalized it, if Bigger Thomas's killing of Bessie could militate against audience empathy for him, and thereby curb favorable reviews and box office revenue, then Bessie would just have to go.

Silver's decision to sacrifice Bessie to render Bigger's dilemma more sympathetically is indicative of the fate that black female representation in commercial cinema in the late 1980s and early 1990s would take. Her/story would be passed over for his/story, and the roles allotted to African American women in feature-length Hollywood films would become primarily supportive ones. Equally insidious, those supporting roles would recall the bitches, mammies, tragic mulattos, and whores already overdetermined in films of the not too distant past. And most perfidiously, for it would completely stifle the voice that Celie, as a black woman, had attained in Walker's novel, the African American woman would begin to be erased and replaced by an "other": a female with no clearly designated race—just an obvious black countenance—who possesses many of the negative and stereotypical traits previously reserved for Hollywood's distorted image of the black woman.

Before, however, even beginning to categorize and describe the new stereotypes of black females that have begun to appear in films such as *The Bodyguard* (1992), *Do the Right Thing* (1989), *Malcolm X* (1992), *Passion Fish* (1992), and *Sister Act* (1992), stereotypes that obstruct a realistic, multifarious representation of black women in contemporary Hollywood films, a more immediate problem needs to be addressed. The current critical practice of bypassing analyses of black female representations in commercial Hollywood cinema to call attention to representations of the black community in independent productions has created a new problematic: a critical orientation that (a) valorizes black independent films, even when they are racist, sexist, and classist; (b) fails to address the fact that a plethora of both male and female African Americans—not to mention most Americans—still shape their perceptions of themselves as well as others by what they see on Hollywood's silver screen; and (c) leaves mainstream Hollywood producers free to do what they want with the construction of our black female image. In essence, contemporary black film criticism creates an endangered female species by neglecting to insist on authentic and multiplicitous depictions of African American women in Hollywood as well as in independently produced cinema.

Needless to say, black independent filmmaking has a significant place in black culture. Films created, marketed, and distributed by filmmakers whose works are not bound by either the commercial constraints or the narrative modes that Hollywood imposes on its products are our best means for visualizing the nuances of black life in all of its complexity. Nevertheless, even though black independent filmmaking—by presenting other ways of seeing, other images of blacks—can and does serve as a corrective to Hollywood cinema, black independent films cannot be viewed as the only tools capable of remedying the constant visual distortion of black reality. Not only is the impact of black independent cinema too often muted by low budgets and the absence of readily available distribution outlets—which means, of course, that few independent black films reach a large audience, so few exert influence on those who write, direct, and produce African American films for the mainstream moviegoing American public—but, also, black independent cinema is not necessarily free of the dominant white, male, heterosexual hegemony that has succeeded, at one point or another, in colonizing us all. In other words, I want to suggest that the following definition of black independent filmmaking is far more utopian than real, particularly when it comes to the portrayal of black women:

> Black independent cinema, like most independent film practices, approaches film as a research tool. The filmmakers investigate the possibilities of representing alternative Black images on the screen; bringing to the foreground issues central to Black communities in America; criticizing sexism and homophobia in the Black community; and deploying Afrafemcentric discourses that empower Black women. The narratives of such films are not always linear; the characters represent a tapestry of voices from W. E. B. Du Bois, Frantz Fanon, Toni Morrison, Malcolm X, Martin Luther King, Jr., Karl Marx, Angela Davis, Alice Walker, and Zora Neale Hurston. (Diawara, 1993, p. 5)

I see two significant problems with the above generalizations about black independent filmmaking offered by Manthia Diawara in *Black*

American Cinema. First, the characters created by independent black filmmakers do not always represent "a tapestry of voices," for one can effectively argue that Spike Lee's independently produced *She's Gotta Have It* (1986) exploits the voice of Zora Neale Hurston's *Their Eyes Were Watching God* just as his commercially produced *Do the Right Thing* (1989) and *Malcolm X* (1992) diminish the vision of Martin Luther King Jr. and Malcolm X, respectively. Second, the dearth of black feminist films by black males as well as the absence of films by black male heterosexuals that explore black male homosexuality speak to the extent to which black independent film is reflexive of both the individuals who produce it and the culture from which it springs. Consequently, critical support of black independent cinema should neither excuse those elements of independent films that would be decried if they had appeared in Hollywood productions nor require that one forgo attention to commercial film products. In fact, if black independent cinema is analogous to other independent cinema, as Diawara contends, it should thrive on being critiqued and received in similar ways. Independent films not only coexist with those produced in Hollywood but also provide the source material for commercial films when Hollywood recognizes the need to revitalize itself, which brings us to a disturbing conundrum when it comes to black women and independently produced cinema.

Most film scholars divide nondocumentary shorts or feature-length films into two stylistic categories—narrative or nonnarrative—even though both can exist in the same work. Whereas most narrative films are linear and often follow a pattern not unlike that of classical Hollywood films in which there is a hero or antihero whose actions or inaction constitute the major focus of the story and plot, nonnarrative cinema tends to be abstract, complex, circuitous, and nonlinear. An example of a recent and well-known black independent feature film that employs a nonnarrative mode of presentation is Julie Dash's *Daughters of the Dust* (1991). *Daughters of the Dust*, like other black feminist films, exhibits a counterhegemonic, dialogic style—one that in many ways is analogous to the works of contemporary African American women writers such as Toni Morrison and Gloria Naylor, works that deliberately resist dominant discursive patterns. Nevertheless, the nonlinear formal pattern that frames *Daughters*, and that seems ideally suited to black feminist discourse, is often too problematic for a mainstream cinematic audience, either black or white, who have been acclimatized to films that fit within the Hollywood formal system. Concurrently, black independent cinema that adopts a linear mode of presentation— and, subsequently, conforms stylistically to the classic Hollywood para- digm—has a much better chance of crossing over and reaching a large, mainstream audience.

A recent example of a well-known black independent feature film that uses the linear or narrative mode of presentation is John Singleton's *Boyz N the Hood* (1991). *Boyz*'s cinematic lineage can be traced back to Melvin Van Peebles's *Sweet Sweetback's Baadasss Song* (1971), and Singleton's creative vision can be likened to Wright's in *Native Son*; it is a vision that attempts to reverse prior images of black American culture by placing the black male at the center of his own story; nevertheless, it retards that culture by relegating the equally oppressed black female to the periphery.

John Singleton is not alone; indeed, his efforts to redress the misogynistic depiction of black women in *Boyz N the Hood* by centering his second film, *Poetic Justice* (1993), around an African American woman is noteworthy, even if the film is not. Nevertheless, too many of the new, black, heterocentric filmmakers—Spike Lee, Bill Duke, Mario Van Peebles, and Robert Townsend, to name just a few—con- tinue to marginalize black female representation in a unilateral and ultimately genocidal desire to convey what they envision as the fatal, singular predicament of the black male. The high level of redundancy that shapes a number of these films (in this case, prior viewer familiarity with the linear, narrative mode of presentation as well as with generic expectations) facilitates their acceptance by a mainstream audience. A film such as *Daughters of the Dust,* on the other hand, with its high degree of entropy (in this case, viewer unfamiliarity with both the nonnarrative mode as well as the subject matter), inauspiciously fosters audience rejection and results in a relatively small following at best. Consequently, black feminist films, which often succeed in opening up new discursive terrains for the cinematic revisioning of black women, remain the purview of a few while racist and sexist depictions of black women are reinforced in the heralding of a plethora of popular, male- centered films that purport to present a black worldview.

As a case in point, I quote from an essay by Houston A. Baker Jr. (1993) titled "Spike Lee and the Commerce of Culture" in which he responds to Lee's own acknowledgment of the need to "beef up" the portrayal of black female characters in *Do the Right Thing*:

> "Beefing up" is an unfortunate term for what, in any case, Lee forgot to do. . . . *Do The Right Thing* fails to provide either visualizations or intelligent hearings of creative, culturally resistant black women. . . . At the moment of uprising against Sal's, women do not provide revolutionary counsel or energy; they only scream. (p. 175)

Although Baker (1993) notes that "in our age of an advanced black feminist critique . . . it seems a pity that Lee's revolution and resistance are confined almost exclusively to a black male cast of characters" (p. 175), it is apparent in his concluding paragraphs that Baker considers the lack of black female character development a minor flaw—one of a few, in fact, that minimally detracts from Lee's overall achievement:

> There are still manifold territories for Spike Lee to master (including a black woman's critique), but it does seem to me that few black artists, past or present—few, that is, who carry what the religion of conjuring calls "power"—would hesitate to welcome him into their energetic company. And in the manner of a true postmodern, Lee understands that his job is to get "paid in full" so that he can continue producing films of black cultural resistance. (p. 175)

Like a number of critics and scholars, it seems to me that Baker is far too willing to overlook major gaps in Lee's cinematic depiction of black women in his zest to applaud black male artistic accomplishment.

I, too, saw *Do the Right Thing*, five times, in fact, in an honest attempt to locate black cultural resistance. Unlike Baker, however, each of *my* screenings of Lee's film merely reinforced the absence of any revolutionary fervor. Not only are Lee's female representations problematic, but also his male characters are equally so. Buggin' Out's desire to boycott Sal's Pizzeria is provoked as much from not getting enough cheese on his pizza as it is from a politically inspired desire to see photographs of black women and men hung on Sal's walls. Radio Raheem's death at the hands of the police—a murder promulgated, in part, by his decision to join Buggin' Out's boycott when Sal wouldn't let him blast his boombox in the pizzeria—not only plays into white fantasies that blacks protest and riot over trivial slights but also high-

lights the impotency of an entire black community who watch flaccidly
as the police slay one of their own. Nor was I surprised that the ending
of *Do the Right Thing* reassures whites that they have little to fear from
a mass black attack, for the film's characterization of black females
merely reaffirms the fact that black cultural resistance cannot exist
concomitantly with a hatred of black women. bell hooks (1990)
theorizes the conflict in an essay titled "Reflections on Race and Sex":

> Black liberation struggle must be re-visioned so that it is no longer
> equated with maleness. We need a revolutionary vision of black libera-
> tion, one that emerges from a feminist standpoint and addresses the
> collective plight of black people. (p. 64)

Until the new wave of young, black, male, independent filmmakers
acknowledge the collusion between racism and sexism and refuse to
visualize one without playing off of the other, black women have little
choice but to deplore sexist depictions of themselves wherever they
occur and to look to other sources for cinematic empowerment:
independent films produced by black feminist filmmakers *and* commercial, Hollywood films produced by those who try to convey more
multifaceted, multiplicitous depictions of black women.

Theoretically, black independent feminist filmmakers posit the most
immediate and long-term promise for the transmutation of existing
stereotypes of black women as well as for the radical transformation of
Hollywood's antiquated and redundant cinematic conventions. Black
feminist filmmakers such as Camille Billops, Kathleen Collins, Ayoka
Chenzira, Julie Dash, and Alile Sharon Larkin have already begun to
produce counterhegemonic texts that open up new, positive spaces for
the revisioning of black culture.

Realistically, however, as important as the works of these and other,
independent, black, feminist filmmakers are to feminist struggle, we
cannot simply leave the reconstruction of our image exclusively to them
while we ignore what occurs in commercially produced cinema. The
fact that few, if any, black independent feminist films ever reach a
mainstream audience compared with the fact that most commercially
produced Hollywood films do command a large, popular market,
militates against adopting a passive response to the latter.

Whether we like it or not, commercial Hollywood cinema remains
particularly instrumental in determining the current social, intellectual,

political, and cultural values that all Americans embrace: The very fabric of life—the clothes we wear, the values we hold, the consequences we fear—are determined in large measure by the images we see on the screen. Not only do black audiences make up almost one-third of Hollywood's consumers (Guerrero, 1993, p. 6), but also, film, more than any other media, "determines how blackness and black people are seen and how other groups will respond to us based on their relation to these constructed and consumed images" (hooks, 1992, p. 5). Yet, despite the effects that commercial Hollywood cinema has on its audience, a number of black film critics refuse to interrogate it because of its negative track record in rendering black culture:

> With *The Birth of a Nation* came the ban on Blacks participating in bourgeois humanism on Hollywood screens. In other words, there are no simple stories about Black people loving each other, hating each other, or enjoying their private possessions without reference to the White world, because the spaces of those stories are occupied by newer forms of race relation stories which have been overdetermined by Griffith's master text. (Diawara, 1993, pp. 3-4)

I do not disagree with the above assessment of established conventions omnipresent in Hollywood's representations of blacks. Nonetheless, I believe that a sweeping dismissal of ideological tools—as potent as Hollywood films reveal themselves to be—finally does more harm than good, particularly when, as the following quotation shows, it disparages those who are interested in examining these influential and widely disseminated cultural products.

> Some of the prominent Black film historians and critics, such as Albert Johnson, Donald Bogle, and Thomas Cripps, emphasize mainly mainstream cinema when discussing Black films. With the exception of a few breakthrough films, such as those by Micheaux, Van Peebles, and Lee, these historians are primarily concerned with the issues of integration and race relations in mainstream films, Black actors and actresses on the big screen, and the construction of stereotypes in Hollywood films. They rarely pay attention to independent cinema, which includes far more Black directors than Hollywood, and in which aesthetics, political concerns such as authorship and spectatorship, and the politics of representation with respect to Black cinema are more prevalent. (Diawara, 1993, p. 4)

The above excerpt is both prescriptive and proscriptive; in belittling other critical approaches to black American cinema and presenting its position alone as authentic, it inhibits debate and appears blind to its obvious bias. For example, in an essay titled "Fire and Desire: Race, Melodrama, and Oscar Micheaux," Jane Gaines (1993) suggests that "the jury is still out on Oscar Micheaux" (p. 63). In refuting the claim that Micheaux was innovative, Gaines not only asserts that Micheaux should be situated firmly within the classical Hollywood system that he tried so hard to imitate but also contends that the new Micheaux criticism devises "inventive ways to move beyond his reputation for creating unflattering characterizations of blacks, as well as his reputation for technical amateurism and aesthetic poverty" (p. 63). Similar criticism can and has been applied to the films of Van Peebles and Lee, a fact that leads one to surmise that attention to classical Hollywood paradigms does not necessarily result in a completely flawed product.

But an even more serious problem is created by a totalizing repudiation of commercial Hollywood cinema: It denies the black woman representation within mainstream films. Lest we forget how devastating invisibility can be, in an essay titled "Modernism, Postmodernism, and the Problem of the Visual in Afro-American Culture," Michelle Wallace (1992) recalls Ralph Ellison's *Invisible Man* and reminds us that the absence of black images in mass media is as devastating as the presence of "negative" black stereotypes. Wallace's point is pivotal, for I can remember when images of black women in Hollywood films, or for that matter on my parents' television set, were virtually nonexistent. As much as I, too, lament the one-dimensional, stereotypical, contemporary media images of black women, a return to the days when few black females or males appeared on screen would not be welcomed. Could it be that critics who propose distancing themselves from white-controlled mass media no longer remember? If so, we risk falling prey to the adage that a people who forget their past are doomed to repeat it.

One way for black film critics and scholars to avoid retracing ground that has already been trod is to draw upon existing parallels between black American cinema and black American literature. In *The Signifying Monkey,* Henry Louis Gates Jr. (1988) delineates a gendered difference in the strategies pioneering black men and women took in their attempts to write themselves into humanity. Gates notes that where male writers were preoccupied with white racism, black women writers were more concerned with general feelings. As a result, even as late as the mid-twentieth century, black female and male authors often found themselves fighting between themselves, even though their underlying goals were similar. Indeed, the literary antagonism between Zora Neale Hurston and Richard Wright is a matter of public record.

When Wright reviewed *Their Eyes Were Watching God* for *New Masses,* he declared that "the sensory sweep of her novel carries no theme, no message, no thought" (Wright, 1937, p. 26). Although, according to his biographer (Fabre, 1973), Wright assessed that Hurston "wrote with facility," but nevertheless insisted that her corrupted vision perpetuated the "minstrel show tradition and the clichés about black life so dear to the writing public" (p. 143). When Hurston critiqued *Uncle Tom's Children* for the *Saturday Review of Literature,* she responded in kind with a response that, as Fabre notes, "hardly came as a surprise, however, since Wright's criticisms of her novel had shown how divergent their viewpoints were" (p. 162).

Yet, today, I teach a Zora Neale Hurston/Richard Wright seminar because of the number of likenesses I see between the two. In addition to drawing upon analogous materials and experimenting with similar genres, both Hurston and Wright stand at the forefront of an impressive African American literary tradition that each helped to define. Unpropitiously, Hurston and Wright's points of convergence, as well as the similitude between other black female and male authors, are too often overlooked, for, as black feminist literary critic Mary Helen Washington (1990) points out, black women writers were viewed as apolitical because of their concern for the personal (p. 36). Needless to say, in such a male-dominated culture, the consequence of this insistence upon a homogeneous rather than a heterogeneous approach to social justice was that the black woman's voice was silenced. Unfortunately, the earlier demand for homogeneity in African American literature seems to circumscribe black American film currently and to generate an unwarranted schism between those who wish to examine Hollywood's representations of blacks and those who prefer to confine themselves to independent black cinema. Moreover, as one might expect, this unnecessary bifurcation exerts the greatest toll on black women.

Given the prior history of African American female cinematic representation, the black woman's desire to see herself contemporaneously on the silver screen in a less negative light is an understandably human one. During a large group discussion, which I led at a small, liberal arts college in California, I discovered that young, intelligent, and politically aware black women found *Boomerang* as empowering as *Daughters of the Dust*. The mere fact of being represented as accomplished, desirable, independent black women—rather than as self-effacing mammies or expendable, sexual victims of rapacious black and white males—heightened their image of self-in-the-world.

Ironically, Ed Guerrero (1993) in *Framing Blackness: The African-American Image in Film*, one of the most recent books on the subject of black cinematic representation, omits any mention of black female leading roles in his predominantly negative reading of *Boomerang*:

> By way of guilty compensation to the political consciousness of the film's mostly lower-class, inner-city black audience, *Boomerang* vaguely acknowledges, in a formulaic way reminiscent of the screwball comedy resolution, that corporate culture and the high fashion executive life may not be the answer to its protagonist's problems. In this case, boy (Murphy) gets the right girl (Berry) and discovers that he is unhappy with corporate values, be they black or white, and the film ends on a dominant cinema cliche with the once-selfish Marcus deciding to quit the corporation to serve humanity in the form of teaching black children. (p. 197)

As the above excerpt also demonstrates, the black female spectator never enters into Guerrero's consideration of the film. In fact, his primary objection to *Boomerang* is that it follows the classic Hollywood formula. That it uses that formula in an attempt to transform it, by placing black females as well as males at its center and by rejecting the commerce culture that Baker so heartily praises Spike Lee for co-opting, is less important to Guerrero than the fact that it epitomizes the "low art" (quotation marks mine) of commercial Hollywood cinema.

"Low art," now that's the clincher.

The notion of *high art* and *low art* is not unique to film. Critics and scholars in the arts and the humanities have wrestled with these interrelated concepts for centuries. Although no connotation of either of the two concepts has as yet been definitively agreed upon, contemporary cultural critics would tend to agree that one term is used in an oppositional relation to the other. Of tantamount importance, however, is the fact that the terms *high art* and *low art* tend to divide rather than unite and, at least since Matthew Arnold, are too frequently used to create an elite rather than to democratize. Consequently, Guerrero's use of the term *low art* in his unfavorable review of *Boomerang* should be viewed as much as an attempt to negate the opinions of those who might disagree with him as well as to ground his argument theoretically. In fact, as the following extract shows, critics who object to the amount of attention paid to Hollywood films frequently justify their disdain aesthetically:

> The relations between Black independent cinema and . . . Hollywood cinema . . . parallel those between Blackness and Americanness; the dichotomy between the so-called marked cultures and unmarked cultures; but also the relations between "high art" and "low art." (Diawara, 1993, p. 4)

The syntax in the preceding sentence leaves no doubt that black independent cinema and blackness are analogous here with "high art" while Hollywood cinema and Americanness, in this instance at least, are associated with "low art."

Black feminist literary critic Barbara Christian (1990), however, warns us against this binary opposition. In an essay titled "The Highs and Lows of Black Feminist Criticism," Christian shows how such a linear way of thinking contributed to the silencing of black women writers and to the development of internecine strife among women. As Christian traces the markers distinguishing the high and the low, she demonstrates how black feminist critics were compelled to reevaluate the signs before they could progress meaningfully:

> Yet even as we moved, the high, the low persisted, in fact moved further and further apart. For we now confronted the revelation we always knew, that there is both a She and there are many she's. And that sometimes, in our work we seemed to reduce the *both-and* to *either-or.* That revelation made itself strongly felt in the exclusion that women of color protested when Woman was defined, in the rejection that many working-class women experienced when Woman was described. The awareness that we too seek to homogenize the world of our Sisters, to fix ourselves in boxes and categories through jargon, theory, abstraction, is upon us. (p. 49)

Christian's remarks can be appreciated by all women—the women in the kitchen as well as the women in academe—even though they are addressed to other black feminist critic/scholars, who, as Christian reminds us, are far more likely to stress theory rather than praxis in a university setting where language is privileged over action. Equally important, Christian's admonitions are as pertinent to black film criticism as to black literary criticism, particularly in light of the current misogynistic representation of black women in independent as well as commercially produced cinema.

Black feminist film criticism is only beginning to emerge in a field that has been dominated by whites and an occasional black male; nevertheless, it behooves us to consider what Christian has to say. Clearly, theory is important in sustaining our inquiries, but it is also possible to theorize to abstraction and, in the process, succumb to what Cornell West (1992) calls the "Talented Tenth Seduction" and defines as a "move toward arrogant group insularity," a move away from the black community (p. 33). Without being too critical, because I admire much of bell hooks's work immensely, I believe that, in certain respects, in the area of black American cinema, hooks's demand for a radical feminist agenda is as delimiting as some of the other critics whom I mentioned earlier in this chapter.

Although I do not find hooks's (1992) call for a "critical practice that enables production of feminist film theory that theorizes black female spectatorship" problematic (p. 131), I am disturbed by remarks such as the following:

> The extent to which black women feel devalued, objectified, dehumanized in this society determines the scope and texture of their looking relations. Those black women whose identities were constructed in resistance, by practices that oppose the dominant order, were most inclined to develop an oppositional gaze. (p. 127)

> Critical black female spectatorship emerges as a site of resistance only when individual black women active[ly] resist the imposition of dominant ways of knowing and looking. While every black woman I talked to was aware of racism, that awareness did not automatically correspond with politicization, the development of an oppositional gaze. (p. 128)

Both passages are troubling: the first because it's too prescriptive, and the second because it's too proscriptive. Taken together, both excerpts signify the beginning of a new hierarchy built upon one's degree of politicization. By privileging an oppositional gaze that can develop only out of active resistance, both statements overlook the women in the kitchen whose circumstances may not permit them to resist actively. Furthermore, hooks's conviction that an oppositional gaze is the only valid one presages a homogeneous rather than a heterogeneous approach to mass media.

In place of the division that hooks inauspiciously formulates in making theoretical distinctions between black women who actively resist colonization and black women who do not, Jacqueline Bobo's (1993) examination of black women's reactions to the film adaptation of *The Color Purple* illustrates that an oppositional gaze is not dependent on one's degree of politicization. In an attempt to understand how black women were able to read through a white-controlled mainstream Hollywood product and to extract meanings they considered satisfactory, Bobo studied black women's responses and arrived at the following conclusion:

> The preoccupations and concerns of black women activists and writers resonate with the lives of many black women. As such, the issues they addressed can be seen as constituting a reservoir of background knowledge that black women used as a discursive strategy for meaning[ful] construction of the film *The Color Purple*. This does not mean that the women who engaged positively with the film were aware of this heritage of black women's activism. It means that the issues that these women considered to be important were pervasive ones in black women's lives; thus, the women could be interpellated, or hailed, by a creative work in which these elements were present. (p. 285)

Bobo's findings are significant: They open rather than close the realm of black female spectatorship and suggest that an individual act of resistance often reflects a communal response to oppression. Bobo's findings also reaffirm Christian's (1990) reflections and practical suggestions for the future of black feminist literary criticism, recommendations that enable all black women:

> But as we look high, we might also look low, lest we devalue women in the world even as we define Woman. In ignoring their voices, we may not only truncate our movement but we may also limit our own process until our voices no longer sound like women's voices anymore. (p. 51)

In an ideal culture, in a culture not already riddled with racism, sexism, and classism, a culture not already anesthetized to all but linear, classic Hollywood film, black independent filmmaking, if it, itself, were free of colonizing influence, might posit the ideal way to represent blackness in all of its complexity. But in a culture such as ours, a culture in which mass media greatly determine the quality of our lives, to depend solely on black feminist independent filmmakers to revision our image is suicidal. Black feminist independent filmmakers, who already struggle to bring their individual creative vision to public view, do not need the onus of supplying the only authentic images of black women. Also, many might profit from having their products distributed or financed by Hollywood's film industry—even if, at times, that vision is somewhat muted by being filtered through the Hollywood classical system.

Commercial Hollywood films as well as black independent feminist cinema both have a place in black female representation. Our task, as black feminist critics, is to hold Hollywood accountable for the images of African American women it frequently mass produces as well as to create a critically receptive space for the revisioning of black women's images within the type of films that Hollywood propagates; moreover, it is crucial that we refrain from privileging the "high art" of independent filmmaking and refusing to interrogate the "low art" Hollywood-generated cinema, a "low art" that actually exerts tremendous influence over our daily lives.

Finally, to return to a point brought up in the opening of this essay, the producer of the 1986 film adaptation of Richard Wright's *Native Son* revised her initial conception of that film in direct response to the negative criticism *The Color Purple* elicited from African Americans regarding its depiction of black men. Although in this particular instance, Silver's deviations ricocheted against black female representation in her film, for Bessie's role was diminished; still it signifies that criticism directed at Hollywood film portrayals of African Americans does not always go unheard. As black women, who need to see ourselves and be seen by others as the complex, vibrant people we are, we need to ensure our continued visibility by supporting independent black feminist filmmaking; by insisting that Hollywood include realistic, multifarious, and, consequently, empowering representations of us in what they too produce; and by opening up a space for an inclusive black feminist critique of both.

REFERENCES

Baker, H. A., Jr. (1993). Spike Lee and the commerce of culture. In M. Diawara (Ed.), *Black American cinema* (pp. 154-176). New York: Routledge.

Bobo, J. (1993). Reading through the text: The black woman as audience. In M. Diawara (Ed.), *Black American cinema* (pp. 272-287). New York: Routledge.

Christian, B. (1990). The highs and lows of black feminist criticism. In H. L. Gates Jr. (Ed.), *Reading black, reading feminist: A critical anthology* (pp. 44-51). New York: Meridian.

Diawara, M. (1993). Black American cinema: The new realism. In M. Diawara (Ed.), *Black American cinema* (pp. 3-25). New York: Routledge.

Fabre, M. (1973). *The unfinished quest of Richard Wright* (2nd ed.). New York: Morrow.

Gaines, J. (1993). Fire and desire: Race, melodrama, and Oscar Micheaux. In M. Diawara (Ed.), *Black American cinema* (pp. 49-70). New York: Routledge.

Gates, H. L., Jr. (1988). *The signifying monkey: A theory of African-American literary criticism.* New York: Oxford University Press.

Guerrero, E. (1993). *Framing blackness: The African-American image in film.* Philadelphia: Temple University Press.

hooks, b. (1990). *Yearning: Race, gender, and cultural politics.* Boston: South End.

hooks, b. (1992). *Black looks: Race and representation.* Boston: South End.

Wallace, M. (1992). Modernism, postmodernism, and the problem of the visual in Afro-American culture. In R. Ferguson, M. Gever, T. T. Minh-ha, & C. West (Eds.), *Out there: Marginalization and contemporary cultures* (pp. 39-50). Cambridge: MIT Press.

Washington, M. H. (1990). "The darkened eye restored": Notes toward a literary history of black women. In H. L. Gates Jr. (Ed.), *Reading black, reading feminist: A critical anthology* (pp. 30-43). New York: Meridian.

West, C. (1992). The new cultural politics of difference. In R. Ferguson, M. Gever, T. T. Minh-ha, & C. West (Eds.), *Out there: Marginalization and contemporary cultures* (pp. 19-36). Cambridge: MIT Press.

3

The New Ghetto Aesthetic

JACQUIE JONES

B y the end of 1991, at least twelve feature films directed by African Americans will be released to mainstream audiences by Hollywood studios and major independents. Seven more are scheduled to be released by smaller independents or are still seeking distributors. And while this phenomenon means, for audiences, an unprecedented exposure to images generated by anyone other than whites, it does not, on the surface, offer much in the way of imaging the experience of the African American community at large. In fact, of the films scheduled for wide release, only three—*A Rage in Harlem, The Five Heartbeats*, and *True Identity*—did not concentrate on the contemporary urban ghetto. Only one—*A Rage in Harlem*—contains a valuable leading role for a black female actor. And none are directed by black women.

Nonetheless, this veritable explosion of black films raises old and important questions about the politics of representation in mainstream cinema as well as new ones about the cinematic intentions and realities of black filmmakers in Hollywood today. Is the goal of black filmmakers, ultimately, to be included, integrated into the existing protocol of mainstream cinema? Or is it to transform the language of mainstream

SOURCE: This chapter originally appeared in *Wide Angle, 13*(3-4), 32-43 (1991, July-October); used and slightly modified by permission.

cinema, to force it to acknowledge the plurality of American culture? And, if the primary charge of popular cinema is to impart hegemonic social values, can "black" and "Hollywood" really exist in the same space, in the same time?

Like most trends in popular culture, the precedents for this new black male cinema have been clearly set out, its marketability all but assured. Hollywood hopes to capitalize on the success of recent low-budget black-made films (most notably those written and directed by Spike Lee) as well as on the phenomenal success of rap music, not to mention paranoid fantasies inspired by headlines announcing a "black-on-black" war raging in major metropolitan areas. So American audiences will be treated to a battery of films that "illuminate" the life of the young black male, the nation's most recent sociological curiosity.

Unlike rap music, which can be seen as a reformulation of popular music—a synthesis and, in some instances, elevation of form and content—this new homeboy cinema does not threaten existing conventions. Instead, it exists as a modification of sensationalist Hollywood formulae. Some will argue that, like rap, these films present warped perceptions shaped in the space between disenfranchisement and escalating consumerism—that both are, at their core, violent, bitterly misogynist, and nonredemptive. But there is a profound dissimilarity between contemporary black Hollywood cinema and rap music: As a phenomenon, black Hollywood is necessarily not of its own creation. And the reason, as *Los Angeles Times* staff writer Nina Easton notes, is economics:

> At a time when movie production costs are soaring, profitable films are the exception, rather than the rule. Over the past four years, these young filmmakers proved to Hollywood that making cheap movies aimed at a core black audience can mean lucrative business. (p. A-1)

Sadly, the monolith of imagery spawned by the current interest in black film may threaten the viability of other types of mainstream black cinematic expression. And it promises to codify a range of behaviors as uncharacteristic of the black experience as those represented in films made by whites (though they may be executed with a greater degree of truth and sensibility). Films that attempt to delve more deeply into any cultural actuality not directly associated with teenagers and crime have no better chance of being widely distributed today than they did five years ago. Indeed, their chances may be worsening.

Award-winning filmmaker Wendell Harris provides a case in point. His *Chameleon Street*, a psychologically probing and deeply clever film, won the Grand Jury Prize at the Sundance Film Festival in 1990, an award that should have immediately guaranteed him a distributor. The film was repeatedly passed over by major distributors, although one was eventually successful in securing remake rights. The distributors intend to remake *Chameleon Street* with white principals, as do the procurers of the remake rights to Charles Lane's critically acclaimed first feature, *Sidewalk Stories*.

Although black film critic Clyde Taylor has argued that Spike Lee's rise to popular and critical success forced black filmmaking to a crossroads of mission, Lee's films now stand as an example of what many hoped was the best that could possibly be gleaned from Hollywood: money to finance an independent vision—one that, for all its contrivances and faults, was determined to reconstruct the image and scope of African Americans within contemporary popular film culture. First Island, then Columbia, Universal, and finally Warner Brothers bought into "Spike Lee." His budgets were relatively stingy; in exchange he was offered free reign. But now, years after the release of *She's Gotta Have It*, Hollywood is choosing not only the black film artists who will reach mass audiences but their vehicles as well. The question has become, as Taylor (1990) poignantly poses it, "How has the goal of building a black film culture beyond Hollywood control been affected?"

THE NEW JACK AESTHETIC

Mario Van Peebles makes his feature directorial debut with the slick shoot-'em-up *New Jack City*, the first black film released in 1991 and the first real black gangster film in two decades. Yet *New Jack City's* sensibilities are perhaps more deeply rooted in American cinematic convention than any such film preceding it. This action-adventure film depicts frenzied, vulgar Americanism run amok in Hollywood's new fantasy land: the crime-infested black ghetto. (That this particular ghetto happens to be Harlem, the legendary mecca of black creative spunk, is as irrelevant to the film's text as the black women who race across the screen stripping, sniveling, and killing.) Less than four months after its release, *New Jack City* had grossed over $40 million, making it the most lucrative black film since the blaxploitation films of the 1970s.

Mario Van Peebles, of course, is the son of legendary guerilla filmmaker Melvin Van Peebles, who achieved a similar feat with *Sweet Sweetback's Badasssss Song* 20 years ago. Sweetback was a pimp/stud, a classic antihero, who achieved cult hero status by murdering two abusive white policemen and eluding the law long enough to cross the border into Mexico. The film grossed over $20 million in its first few months of release in 1971. Yet while the elder Van Peebles envisioned the law as a necessary enemy of black people, the younger position it as a savior to black people in communities fraught with self-imposed lawlessness (i.e., "black-on-black" crime). That the renegade law enforcement officers of *New Jack City* are an interracial lot in no way compromises their adherence to the customary hyperaggressive, vigilante-style personalization of "justice" that African Americans have come to expect and fear from police. (In one scene, a white officer calls a black gangster "Buck-wheat" before shooting him dead.)

New Jack City is the kind of propaganda film that allows for the easy dismissal of problems ravaging the black community. It suggests that the problem with communities plagued by drugs and crime is that the residents are either dealers, users, or complicit bystanders—all unwilling or unable to help themselves. The opening credits roll over an inventory of Reagan-era fallout: images of poverty, homelessness, and unemployment. What might have followed is an examination of how these realities breathe life into a sophisticated, entrepreneurial drug culture. Instead, we get the standard romp through tastefully furnished kingpin quarters, numerous acts of savagery on the part of both gangsters and police, and no indication whatsoever of the humanity that necessarily survives any epidemic. Coscreenwriter Barry Cooper (who is credited with coining the phrase *New Jack*), himself an ex-crack addict and native of the mean streets, could hardly have survived such a scenario.

Also glaringly prominent is the standard rap treatment of women as "bitches" and "ho's." That one "bitch" is elevated to the status of psychopathic murderer hardly seems an achievement. *New Jack City* fails to establish even one nuanced female character with singular relevance or value to the film's text. But perhaps such territory lies beyond the concerns of those whom Karen Brailsford (1991) refers to as "black filmmakers that record the evolution of black boys into invisible men (should they live so long)."

New Jack City is also the first film to attempt to cinematize a "New Jack" or rap aesthetic. It draws its text directly from the lyrics of hip-hoppers such as rap artist and costar Ice T. In his rap repertoire, Ice T covers a range of topics, from his own experience as a gang member in Los Angeles to a memorable account of a dehumanizing sexual act involving a flashlight. *New Jack City* positions this figure as a hero, a champion of the people. Yet, while it adeptly cinematizes the themes and nuances inherent in many rap lyrics—the unidimensional and problematic approach to solving the problems of drugs and violence and the fanatic hystericization of racism—*New Jack City* fails to convey the authenticity rap artists themselves bring to the topics with which they grapple. Instead, it emerges as a smooth new age gangster tale with little cultural reference. Ultimately, it looms as little more than a blackface *Scarface*.

GHETTOCENTRICITY

23-year-old John Singleton is perhaps one of the most high-profile mean streets' natives to lend his voice to Hollywood. *Boyz N the Hood*, the first of three pictures to be produced under his contract with Columbia Pictures, went to Cannes less than a year after his graduation from USC film school. With *Boyz N the Hood*, Singleton manages to synthesize every element in the current trend in black imaging in mainstream cinema.

Drawn directly from newspaper headlines and Singleton's own South Central L.A. biography, *Boyz N the Hood* depicts with cinematic fluency the senseless self-destruction of young black men—it also promotes the casual dismissal and denigration of black women and perpetuates the assumption that black women are ineffectual in communal black problem solving. The film unapologetically asserts that the problems facing the black community might easily and best be solved by the reintroduction of the term *father* as that term is understood in

American mythology: that no-nonsense figure who teaches his son how to fish (even in an environment as urbane as Los Angeles), to practice safe sex (to "keep your dick from falling off"), and to use a gun (to protect your property and not, under any circumstances, for the purpose of exacting revenge).

Boyz N the Hood engages in the constant, hostile objectification of women through the standard bitch/ho device. But Singleton goes one step further by removing the black mother from the life of his protagonist, Tre, the only central character in *Boyz N the Hood* to survive. Doughboy and Ricky, the other two principals, are brought up by their ineffectual mother, and as Singleton's logic would have it, both perish in the brutality of L.A. gang warfare.

In the foreground of this macho epic are two straight-laced, ambitious, and responsible young men. One, Ricky, is struggling to escape a family legacy of marginality. His unmarried mother—whose two sons have different and absent fathers—is every bus rider's worst nightmare, the kind who slaps and curses her kids for not "being still." And his brother, Doughboy, is a loud-mouthed loafer. Ricky's life is defined by limitations. Instead of striving for anything as clichéd as academic excellence, Ricky aspires to the more *realistic* road out of the ghetto: football. Tre, on the other hand, has a self-employed black nationalist father, Furious, who willingly accepts responsibility for raising his young son when the child proves too much for Tre's mother, Vera, to handle. (In an early scene, Vera admits to Furious, "I can't teach him how to be a man.") Unlike Vera, who holds a master's degree, Furious has resisted the tide pulling the black middle class out of the ghetto. He has only his own sensibly stern fatherliness to guide Tre down the very straight and very narrow.

But, as essayist Lett Proctor argues in *Black Film Review*, although *Boyz N the Hood* attempts to

> establish a 'Just say No' subtext, it underscores an age-old, fundamental paradox of the ghetto film: Is [its] purpose to inspire reflection on the erupting fury in inner cities or merely to magnify the grim realities of life for far too many black youths?

Boyz does not succeed beyond the latter, while *Straight out of Brooklyn* achieves the former. Made for less than $100,000, *Straight out of*

Brooklyn would be remarkable if only because its writer, director, and producer was 19-year-old Matty Rich. As a former resident of the Red Hook Housing Project, where the action of the film takes place (most of the scenes were shot in his grandmother's apartment there), Rich articulates many of the factors that lead to the development of people like *New Jack City*'s Nino Brown or *Boyz N the Hood*'s Doughboy. Lawrence Gillard, who plays *Straight out of Brooklyn*'s protagonist, Dennis, is painfully successful at rendering the hopelessness and confinement of inner-city youth, victims not only of rampant crime but also of the abandoned dreams of their parents and community. Escape— its conditionless eventuality—is the fever of Rich's Brooklyn. One comes to understand the confidence with which many of his peers accept the chance of death. Death, at least, provides deliverance.

The script and canvas of *Straight out of Brooklyn* are expectedly raw, unlike those of *Boyz N the Hood*. Yet the truth found in *Straight out of Brooklyn* is so personal and unglamorous that it ultimately convinces. No doubt, some will argue that here I am equating cinematic poverty with virtue. The fact that Rich's vision is executed in raw neorealist time, without benefit of seamless editing or buttery smooth cinematography, might detract from the viewing experience for some. But his treatment of violence as pedestrian and exceptional rather than exciting and obligatory sets the film apart from others of its kind. Unlike directors of studio-financed films, Rich had no need to invent easy solutions. *Straight out of Brooklyn,* along with Norman Loftis's *Small Time* (which has also been unsuccessful in acquiring theatrical distribution), are perhaps the only believable visions in the exploitative business of contemporary ghetto cinema.

Small Time, an independent feature not mentioned in any of the recently released lists of new black films, adopts the same gritty approach as *Straight out of Brooklyn*. Without pretense or apology, *Small Time* flings the viewer straight into the sordid, trivial life of Vance, played by Richard Barboza. Like *Straight out of Brooklyn,* the film successfully eludes false notions of enfranchisement or settlement and instead forces the viewer into an uncomfortable association with the realities of contemporary urban life. Like Rich, Loftis proves his protagonist's humanity by simply insisting on its existence.

BITCHES AND HO'S

As the heroine of Spike Lee's first feature film, *She's Gotta Have It,* Nola Darling ushered in contemporary commercial black cinema. Nola ostensibly represented a postmodern black woman, grappling not only with the political management of her own body but also with more metaphysical issues such as the nature of sexuality and monogamy. Lee was hailed as a visionary healer, a savior of the black cinematic image, for his creation of this character, played by Tracy Camila Johns.

Yet even five years later, it is difficult to view the opening segments of *She's Gotta Have It*—which feature a litany of sexual slander and macho posturing—as revolutionary, cinematically or otherwise. Finally, Nola Darling is a fantasy who can only be understood in the context of thwarted male desire and sexual repression, a context in which rejection is rationalized by assigning immoral aspirations to an ultimately powerless pawn. Nola is entirely defined by her suitor's desire to control not only her body but her will. Indeed, her character can only be understood in relation to the three male characters who, as the film would have it, give her existence and meaning.

It is ironic that Nola Darling should be the mother of black female characters in contemporary mainstream black film—and it is eerie to watch Tracy Camila Johns stripping down to red satin lingerie in Mario Van Peebles's *New Jack City.* The significance of John's two major roles to date is profound because, unfortunately, they express the entire range of female representation in commercial films made by black men. Black women are allowed to occupy two narrow categories in this cinema: that of the bitch and that of the ho.

In *She's Gotta Have It,* John's character does double duty as both bitch (read: willful, ripe for bringing down) and ho (read: sexually demanding, not easily satisfied). In *New Jack City,* she loses even the perfunctory endowments of job and friends, functioning solely as a self-serving temptress and the catalyst for an unmendable rift between friends, brothers. While Johns plays the ho in *New Jack City,* Vanessa Williams plays Keisha, the bitch. Keisha explodes as a maniacal, cold-blooded henchwoman, equal in enmity to any on the Cash Money Brothers's lethal crew. Yet she is the most significantly marginal of any on Nino Brown's squad. While other gang members participate and are held responsible by Nino, Keisha waits silently for the chance to kill again. Because of the boundaries placed on her participation, it is difficult to even analyze her role, yet the feminization of her character is clearly intentional. The filmmakers may have been attempting even-handedness: to show that a woman can be as brutal and nihilistic as a man. But the audience gets to know the male characters through personal histories, dialogues, and their residence within the text, while Keisha emerges as little more than a well-placed bitch, sufficiently mean and contextually impotent.

John Singleton is far more parochial in his designations. The three principal female characters in his *Boyz N the Hood* are Vera, Tre's mother, Brandi, his girlfriend, and Mrs. Baker, the mother of Ricky and Doughboy. (Here again, no female character can be defined apart from her relationships to male characters.) Both Vera and Brandi function as sanitized bitches. Vera is the stronger of the two, as her character actively engages the assumption that she is perceived as such. But the protagonist Tre thrives in spite of—if not because of—her absence in his formative adolescent years.

Brandi achieves real presence in only three scenes in the film. In the first, she becomes angered when she is not properly acknowledged as Tre's girlfriend by the other teenage girls attending a barbecue (after which she scolds Tre for not calling her). In the second, she withholds sex from Tre while wearing a Catholic school uniform, and in the third, she succumbs to Tre's desire for sex after witnessing a moving instance of his vulnerability. In the last two instances, her manipulation of sex strengthens the popular postulate that women possess sexuality purely for the purpose of giving it to (or withholding it from) men, and have no sexual desire of their own (unless, of course, they are ho's).

Mrs. Baker is perhaps the most problematic of the three. She is the vision of the aged ho. Early on, her unwanted interest in Furious is depicted as improper and loose. And the mere existence of her two illegitimate children with different absent fathers alludes to her promiscuous character. Presented as the typical, Mrs. Baker is a lazy, permissive parent with no ostensible source of earned income. She functions as a foil to Furious, the industrious, committed nationalist and dutiful father. Mrs. Baker's boys run amok, ravaging the neighborhood stores of South Central, while Tre mows the lawn and fishes with Furious. Ultimately, Tre gets a job while Doughboy goes to jail and Ricky fathers an illegitimate child.

Singleton has said that, "A young boy needs a man to show him how to be a man." Unfortunately, he translates this revelation into a scenario in which women are incapable of raising male children, while men can singularly achieve the feat. Given the fact that virtually no black men actually raise young boys single-handedly while a large percentage of black women do, and given the fact that Tre survives while Ricky and Doughboy do not—especially because Ricky is an upright youth with solid values and the promise of a future—Singleton comes dangerously close to blaming black women for the tragedies currently ransacking black communities.

The other female characters in the film are explicitly referred to as bitches and ho's. In the barbecue scene, for example, Doughboy publicly announces that "bitches gotta eat, too," a comment for which he is duly reprimanded. He corrects himself by substituting "ho's" for "bitches." As a throng of teenage girls amble up to the grill, half-heartedly rebuffing Doughboy, the other boys join him in laughter. If the scene were isolated, perhaps, it might indicate something like boyish ambivalence toward ensuing maturity. But *Boyz N the Hood* has such a preponderance of similarly unchallenged verbal assaults on women that they exist as a separate theme of hostility.

BEYOND GHETTO

Bill Duke attempts to reconfigure this dynamic in *A Rage in Harlem.* (Duke, familiar to audiences as a menacing antagonist in mainstream films such as *American Gigolo,* has also been quietly honing his skills behind the camera on prime time television. He has more than 100 directing credits, including programs such as *Dallas, Hill Street Blues,* and *Miami Vice.*) At the center of his 1950s Harlem underworld, Duke places Immabelle, a conniving but good-hearted vixen. And although Immabelle is excessively dependent on her overstated sexuality, she is empowered in a manner that no other black female character has been in recent commercial black films.

Thinking that her lover and his parents have been killed in a shootout, Immabelle flees Natchez, Mississippi, with a trunk full of ill-gotten gold. Finding her way to Harlem, she establishes contacts in the underworld with shrewd professionalism, honing in on a hapless pawn and exploiting him. It is unfortunate that the film ultimately reduces her to a victim in the classic damsel in distress scenario. Had she been allowed to follow the path initially laid for her, she might have taken the first steps toward realizing participation in this new black film culture. (*A Rage in Harlem* is also significant in its characterization and normalization of a range of nontraditional sexual orientations: characters include a cross-dressing lesbian, a man exhibiting traces of bestiality and a transvestite madam.)

On the periphery of this gangster flick also reside hardworking, noncriminal, nonvictims who greatly enhance the depiction of the community in which the tale unfolds (unlike in *New Jack City* or *Boyz N the Hood*). Duke opts for colorful, fantastic characters whose often murderous actions are softened by their well-developed personalities and the specificity of their involvement. Like Duke, veteran director Michael Schultz chooses fantasy over realism and makes a bold step away from crime as a central motif, although his film *Livin' Large* brings the treatment of inner-city male youth back into focus.

The film depicts the exploits of a would-be newscaster, presser at a family dry cleaning establishment, Dexter Jackson. The steps that lead Dexter to realize his dream reflect the conflict between career and consciousness for black people involved in media with humor and insight. Largely, though, *Livin' Large* is too cartooned to be successful on any level below the surface.

CONCLUSION:
RAP, YOUTH AND URBAN CATHARSIS

The glaring absence of African Americans in commercial cinema has spawned a generation of moviegoers unaccustomed to big screen treatment of black youth in the form of television and music video, most specifically rap music video. Provocative and uncompromising, rap music has best utilized video technology by politicizing and reconstructing American iconography while speaking directly to and from the experience of inner-city youth, most often male youth.

The introduction of rap to the feature-length film has been a gradual and easy one. First, Spike Lee introduced the premiere political rap group Public Enemy to film culture with "Fight the Power," the anthem of *Do the Right Thing*. Then Reginald Hudlin's *House Party* starred rap duo Kid N Play. Later, Mario Van Peebles incorporated not only the music and artists but also the themes dominating hip-hop culture in his *New Jack City*. (These three films also had the distinction of being the biggest box office earners of contemporary black films.) The torch has been passed to younger filmmakers, such as John Singleton and Matty Rich, who speak not only from the perspective of black youth but also from the experience of coming of age in inner cities plagued by the sensational stuff of drugs and violence. And Hollywood has promised that more films illuminating these elements—"rap, youth, and urban catharsis," as Nelson George (1991, p. 24) puts it—will come.

Unfortunately, even a cursory examination of the recent wave of black films financed with studio capital reveals that the age-old ghettoization of black products remains unchanged. The industry's wholesale investment in films that explore only ghettoes and male youth ignores the existence of a black community beyond these narrow confines—inclusive of women as valuable participants—as well as films that refuse to cater to these prescriptions.

REFERENCES

Brailsford, K. (1991, June). A rage comes of age. *Elle*.
Easton, N. (1991, May 3). New black films, new insights. *Los Angeles Times*, pp. A-1, 1.
George, N. (1991, May 28). Native son: Ghetto centricity. *Village Voice, 36*(22), 24.
Proctor, L. (1991). A rage in Hollywood. *Black Film Review, 6*(4), 8-9.
Taylor, C. (1990). The future of black film: The debate continues. *Black Film Review, 5*(4), 7-11.

PART II

Issues in Print

4

If It Weren't for Bad Luck

Framing Stories of Racially Comparative Risk

OSCAR H. GANDY JR.

R obert Stallings (1990) suggests that "the reality of risks for most of us exists mainly in images created by others" (p. 81). Although our friends, and our social and professional contacts, may be important sources of risk perceptions, for the bulk of risks that operate outside the boundaries of common everyday experience, we depend upon information provided by the press.

Because the press plays such a critical role in determining how we understand the risks we face, and because this understanding is a fundamental part of other decisions we make about education, work, recreation, investment, and other aspects of life involving risk, it is important for us to study how well, or how poorly, the press informs us about those risks.

RACISM AND THE RISK OF DISCRIMINATION

The literature on the communication of risk has traditionally been concerned with technological risk. The environmental movement has

AUTHOR'S NOTE: The research for this chapter was performed while the author was a Fellow at the Freedom Forum Media Studies Center at Columbia University, and reflects the valuable contributions of his research assistant, Jennifer Imperio.

helped to increase the level of public discussion about the risks to the quality of life that flow from ill-considered use of the earth's resources. The antinuclear movement has performed a similar function with regard to the risks associated with nuclear energy. Disasters such as the chemical spill at Bhopal help to focus our concerns upon the risks associated with the unregulated manufacturing and shipping of dangerous chemicals. In the context of policy debates about financing the health care system, discussion of the particular risks associated with HIV and sexual activity has taken on a particularly urgent tone within the press. Even though the risks that befall individuals as a result of their membership in a racial or ethnic group are seen by some as being of critical importance, these risks are not granted a similar status within the risk agendas of the nation's press (Singer & Endreny, 1993). The risk of racial discrimination is rarely examined in those terms, despite the fact that it is real and ripe with consequence.

We should be clear that communication about the risk of discrimination is important for blacks and other victims of discrimination. Because discrimination generally refers to an activity that is experienced in an institutional context, and is thereby a valid target for a public policy response, other citizens who either are concerned about the consequences that flow from continued discrimination or are attuned to fundamental debates regarding justice and equality have a need to be well informed about the distribution of this risk.

THE PRESS AND RACE

The ways in which the press helps us understand the risk of discrimination are complicated because of the ways in which the press has traditionally covered race from outside the frame of risk. Racism, and the ways it has been covered by the press, has been studied by a small community of devoted scholars who have attempted to note changes both in racism and in its representation over time. Teun van Dijk has written extensively on the role of the press in the reproduction of racism (van Dijk, 1991). His microanalysis of press coverage provides numerous examples of the ways in which editorial decisions are likely to produce different impressions of the nature, cause, and consequences of institutional practices. The ways that stories about African Americans are framed are primarily seen to influence how nonblacks feel about the demands that blacks make for equality, fair play, or, on occasion, special affirmative advantage.

We see in Robert Entman's writing on the construct of modern racism (1990) that news reporting, especially crime reporting on television, might contribute to whites' opposition to granting the political demands of African Americans because blacks are presented in these stories as being particularly threatening. Nadeau, Niemi, and Levine (1993) found a strong correlation between perceived threat and estimates of the size of the minority group populations that were seen as especially threatening. These misperceptions of size and scope are likely to be reflected in a distorted awareness of the nature and extent of crime, unemployment, and other socioeconomic conditions that are linked to public policy debates involving African Americans.

FRAMING AND ITS CONSEQUENCES

Within the expanding literature on press performance, there is an increased emphasis on the ways in which stories are framed, or positioned. The literature suggests that framing plays a critical role in determining how social reality is understood, including who might be to blame or should be held responsible for correcting any problems. Shanto Iyengar (1991) suggests that differences as subtle as the use of episodic rather than thematic frames can influence how people understand public issues. In studies of television, Iyengar notes that television news tends to favor episodic framing because "episodic reports make 'good pictures,' while thematic reports feature 'talking heads' " (p. 14). He notes, however, that there is a slight tendency for television coverage of racial inequality to use thematic more than episodic framing, although in stories that focused on poverty or economic inequality, episodic frames were relatively more prominent. Yet, an experimental study that showed respondents episodic or thematic presentations produced the expected result. That is, thematic frames generated more comments of institutional responsibility than did episodic frames. Unfortunately, in terms of the consequences for social policy, the anger that respondents apparently felt was directed toward the government for its pursuit of policies showing favoritism toward blacks.

Whether episodic or thematic, there is a common tendency within investigative reports to identify someone to blame. David Protess and his colleagues (Protess et al., 1991) refer to investigative reporting in general as a "journalism of outrage." They suggest that "investigative journalists intend to provoke outrage in their reports of malfeasance. The work is validated when citizens respond by demanding change from their leaders" (p. 5). A preliminary examination of documents for 30 investigative stories that had been entered into competitions for professional awards (Investigative Reporters and Editors) supports this claim in that nearly all the submissions proudly reported changes in policy and practice as outcomes flowing from their investigations. In general, then, investigative stories follow an underlying script reflecting a shared vision of the world (Ettema & Glasser, 1987, 1988; Glasser & Ettema, 1989). This script requires that there must be a victim or, more likely, hundreds of victims who have been harmed by the targets of the investigation—the villains who have to be brought to justice because they "have deviated from societal standards of conduct" (Protess et al., 1991, p. 9).

Not all observers share the assumptions underling the modern social responsibility theory of the press (McQuail, 1992). Some suggest that the effort to mobilize public opinion in support of public policy goals introduces an interpretive form of reporting that paradoxically threatens the democratic process by placing the press between the citizen and the public official or political candidate (Entman, 1989; Patterson, 1993).

Students of the press tend to think of the audience as a homogeneous group (Protess & McCombs, 1991), although the literature on media effects provides numerous studies with evidence of differences in reception, including differences associated with race, class, and gender (Atkin, Greenberg, & McDermott, 1983; Gandy & Matabane, 1989). Indeed, Entman (1993) suggests that the notion of framing itself "implies that the frame has a common effect on large portions of the receiving audience, though it is not likely to have a universal effect on all" (p. 54).

Some of the differences in responsiveness to framing may be due in part to differences in the extent to which the public *identifies* with the victims in investigative reports. If either the victims or the villains are representative of some subpopulation, as may be identified by race, class, or sexual orientation, we should expect to find differences within the general audience in their attention, understanding, and emotional response to any reported malfeasance.

It is not my intention to overemphasize the importance of press reports in shaping public understanding of the risk of discrimination. Clearly, personal experience is the most powerful teacher and the most reliable source of information. It is also clear that cold statistics are not by themselves nearly as compelling as a recent personal experience. Indeed, Cose (1993) suggests that

> in the real world, such statistics are almost irrelevant, for rage does not flow from dry numerical analyses of discrimination or from professional prospects projected on a statistician's screen. It flows from the felt experiences of everyday life, from lessons learned in run-of-the-mill human encounters, from the struggles and disappointments of family members and peers. (p. 40)

Yet, the role of the mass media in the social construction of risk ought not be ignored, for the evidence that the press plays a critical role, especially for those whose personal experience is limited, is substantial and quite well known (Gerbner, Gross, Morgan, & Signorielli, 1994).

If we grant that the mass media have, and will continue to play, an important role in determining how people understand and think about risk and its distribution in society, and, further, if we believe that this influence reflects differences in the ways that this information is framed, then we need not hesitate any further in exploring how this role is played.

THE ACTUARIAL ASSUMPTION
AND THE COMMUNICATION OF RISK

There is a tendency to report facts of the past in terms of probability. This tendency is well ingrained in everyday speech, and therefore this tendency is generally unquestioned in day-to-day decisions about how to report the findings of statistical research. Often we make an *actuarial assumption* that relationships that have been noted in the past, and are reflected in comparisons of relative frequency, or rates, are actually *predictions* about outcomes in the future. That relationship is expressed in some detail and with some precision, as if the relation between the past and the future were fully determined, especially when the linkage is presented in probabilistic terms: "Among those aged thirty-five to fifty-four, who have five or more years of college, it turns out that black men are twice as likely to be separated or divorced" (Hacker, 1992, p. 75). Even though this quote is expressly limited to historical data, the use of the language of probability in this manner contributes to the spread of the actuarial assumption regarding life chances. When we observe, for example, that a higher proportion of black men than white men have died before the age of 25, then it is common for us to go on to say, "Black men are more likely to die young."

Statements about the probability of negative outcomes are commonly understood as statements about risk. When those statements are about the disparity in the hardships that whites and blacks are likely to experience, we are making assessments of racially comparative risk. As we have suggested, understanding statistical representations in the context of communication about risk is important because of the role that risk assessment plays in a variety of decisions an individual makes each day. Cognitive scientists examining decision making under uncertainty develop elaborate models that purport to identify the rational choices that individuals would make once they have produced the appropriate subjective estimates of outcomes and values. The fact that these subjective estimates are based upon rather unreliable sources of information is being recognized with increasing frequency (Kahneman & Tversky, 1986).

Even entertainment media have been identified as important sources of information that individuals use in estimating the nature of risks in their environment. The visibility of the Cultural Indicators Project (Gerbner, 1973) and the importance of its contribution to the study of media and cultivation (Signorielli & Morgan, 1990) were due in no small part to its early association with public concerns about the risk of violence. Initial conceptions of a "mean world," and the association of heavy television viewing with expressions of fear and mistrust, served to underscore the relationship between media representations of risk in the environment and people's understanding of their options. Functionalist theories of the press continue to emphasize the importance of the mass media's surveillance of the environment, presumably for the purpose of giving advance warning about risks (McQuail, 1992; Wright, 1960).

The literature on the communication of risk is quite extensive, although, as we have noted, this literature is deficient in two ways that are important for this study: (a) Racial comparisons are rare, and (b) the risks that matter are primarily technological rather than social (Liss, 1989). The narrowness of this vision is similar to that which characterizes the literature of crime and victimization (Elias, 1986).

IDENTIFICATION AND REFLECTION
OF DIFFERENTIAL RISK

Decision theorists conceptualize rational choices among alternatives in the context of a payoff matrix. Knowledge about the likelihood of outcomes and consequences must be combined with awareness of the economic, and perhaps even the social, costs associated with realizing an outcome or avoiding its alternative. Comparisons within the matrix are influenced by variations in estimates of probability and value. The efforts of social psychologists have demonstrated that these estimates consistently fail to behave according to formal logical rules, and as a result, people are seen to act irrationally. More recently, these researchers have argued that this tendency is linked in part to the ways in which we frame the problems or, of more interest, how the problems are framed for us.

Frequently when an example is needed to help an audience understand how framing operates to influence the way individuals understand outcomes that are risky or uncertain, theorists turn to the classic experiment by Kahneman and Tversky (1986). Subjects are informed about a "disease" that is certain to kill 600 people unless some action is taken. Two options having identical expected outcomes are seen to be differentially preferred, depending upon whether the outcomes are framed in terms of lives saved or lives lost. People become risk-avoiding in the context of lives being saved, and risk-seeking in the context of almost certain loss of life.

If the victims were identified by race, class, gender, or nationality, I believe we would find quite substantial differences in the extent of the shifts in risk orientation. Indeed, I believe we would find still other significant differences if the respondents' *answers* were compared by race, gender, or social class. Although we might hope that the personal characteristics of victims or perpetrators don't influence our feelings about providing emergency assistance, there is considerable evidence to the contrary. Racism is a significant constraint on the impulse toward good works.

As Tversky and Kahneman remind us in other reported studies (1990), subtle framing differences generate substantial variance in expressed preference for, or willingness to accept, the actions of others. Whether a monetary charge is identified as a tax or a discount, a credit or a fee, greatly influences the way we feel about its payment or its loss, even though the amount is precisely the same. Indeed, even the value of the raise we last received is seen to shrink upon hearing about the more substantial raises our colleagues have received.

Stories about race and risk are, therefore, likely to produce quite different levels of awareness and concern depending upon the ways in which they are framed. Consider the simple facts that might have been uncovered in an analysis of unemployment statistics. Average unemployment for the last month may have been 8% of the population. We might note, however, that unemployment for whites was 6.4% and unemployment for blacks was 18.1%, with unemployment for young black males reaching 43%. We don't feel the same way about all of these victims of a stagnant economy! Let us see how these differences might be exacerbated by subtle framing of the facts.

One story that was reported fairly widely in 1993 was a report that African Americans were more likely to be laid off in the most recent recession. The facts might have been something to the effect that among the major firms reporting, blacks had a 1 in 10 chance of being laid off, while whites had a 1 in 25 chance of being laid off. This fact might have been presented in one of four ways that emphasized this outcome in probabilistic terms: (a) Blacks were more likely (than whites) to be laid off (high probability of black loss); (b) blacks were less likely (than whites) to keep their jobs (low probability of black gain); (c) whites were less likely (than blacks) to be laid off (low probability of white loss); or (d) whites were more likely (than blacks) to keep their jobs (high probability of white gain).

In the same way that differences in outcome preferences were produced by emphasizing lives saved over lives lost, by taking advantage of the tendency to seek risk so as to avoid a more certain loss, we can imagine how estimates of the severity of the last recession might be influenced as a function of which representation those four frames presented. And, as I have suggested, it is also likely that the differences in these estimates of severity will vary with the race (and extent of racial identification) of the readers of stories framed in one of these four ways.

NUMBERS AND NUANCES

Ulrich Beck (1992) suggests that inequality has lost much of its significance as an issue over the past two decades. In its place, we have seen a "process of individualization." Social problems are no longer considered to be experienced by classes or groups but increasingly are "perceived in terms of psychological dispositions: as personal inadequacies, guilt feelings, anxieties, conflicts, and neuroses" (p. 100). Yet, we still understand risk in terms of groups. The claim I am making is that what we feel about groups at risk may be influenced greatly by what has been said by the press about these groups and this class of risks.

Because most of us live in cities where there is only a single daily newspaper, we are likely to be presented with only one framing of this issue at a time. It may also be the case that because of the operation of professional standards or other structural influences, we are exposed to similar framings of risk over time. Because of the structural constraints that influence newspapers and other information media, we might find that differences in political awareness and concern generally reflect the influence of economic geography. Tichenor, Olien, and Donohue (1987) suggest that what you know depends largely upon where you live. In their development of a research program geared toward understanding the gaps in public affairs knowledge that were consistently linked with educational attainment, Tichenor and his colleagues identified factors that might influence the quality of information that was available in different newspaper markets. In their view: "Differences in media structure, as an aspect of total community structure, appear to have considerable impact on levels of knowledge about public affairs" (Olien, Donohue, & Tichenor, 1983, p. 459). Cecilie Gaziano (1984) found these gaps in public affairs knowledge to vary with readership of the neighborhood newspapers that she suggests "often address the concerns of the disadvantaged in their reporting of local public affairs issues" (p. 556), while the mainstream papers tend to ignore those concerns.

Structural influences thought to determine media content include the nature of ownership, competition within the marketplace, and, increasingly, the perceived importance of segments of the readership to particular advertisers (Baker, 1994; Olien, Tichenor, & Donohue, 1988; Picard, McCombs, Winter, & Lacy, 1988).

Depending upon the audience that is the primary target of the article, differences in emphasis may characterize the reporting of statistics about risk (Cohn, 1989; Mauro, 1992). This is just as likely to be true with regard to stories about the risk of discrimination as it is with regard to the risk of criminal assault.

DESIGN/RESEARCH QUESTIONS

The following research questions guided the design of this early study of the framing of racially comparative risk: (a) What patterns characterize the representation of social risks that are experienced by African Americans? (b) Do these risks have a special character when they are presented in comparative terms? (c) What structural influences are involved in the determination of different frames or stories about the social risks faced by African Americans?

Using the "major papers" database within the DIALOG system, a search was made to identify all the stories published in those papers between January 1992 and September 1993 that included the word *black* within 10 words of the words *more likely* or *less likely*. Preliminary investigations had determined that using *more likely* alone would identify the overwhelming majority of the items that would be identified by using *less likely*, but there were a still a significant number of stories that would be missed using *more likely* alone. Using *white* generated a few additional unduplicated stories, but produced far more items that were not related to racial comparisons.

Upon reviewing the headlines and leads, it was determined that many of the stories involved activities in which there was no victimization; that is, individuals either put themselves at risk by engaging in risky behavior (unprotected sex, smoking, and so on) or faced a higher risk because of factors beyond individual control (genetic predisposition, poverty, and so on). These risks were not of primary interest because they differed from risks that had been generated or assigned by the discriminatory actions of individuals in institutions.

Murray Edelman (1983) suggests that we ought to focus on the role of institutions and the administrative decisions that are repeated daily and combine to produce and reproduce the inequalities that we see reflected in statistical comparisons. He suggests that "thousands of such actions occur every day at every level of government, most of them unnoticed by the press, few of them [are] discussed, debated, or known outside the enclaves of professionals, corporate managers, technicians, and interest-group representatives" (p. 134). Thus, with this policy focus in mind, the criterion used for including stories within the primary analysis was that they involve decisions by an institutionalized authority that could be seen as placing African Americans at risk.

Six general subject categories were developed, as follows: (a) The *financial* category contains stories about difficulties African Americans faced in gaining residential mortgages. (b) The category of *health* contains stories about the differential treatment African Americans received from health care professionals; the quality of health care is seen to vary with the race of the patient. (c) The category *education* contains stories about the differential assignment of African American youngsters to lower level/less challenging classes and sections in schools; these are frequently stories about integrated schools with segregated classes. (d) The *government services* category contains stories about the differential success African Americans achieved in gaining government benefits and services, such as disability payments from the Social Security Administration. (e) The category *criminal justice* contains stories about the differential probabilities that African Americans faced as victims of crime seeking justice or as persons charged with crimes facing sentence. (f) The category of *employment* contains stories about the differential probability that African Americans would be hired, promoted, or fired.

This initial sampling was used in two ways to address the primary research questions. The stories in the "major papers" file were used to describe the distribution of items by subject as they were reported in 1992. This description emphasized the framing of the stories in the headlines and in the lead, or first three paragraphs. Because most of the stories involving the use of statistics for the presentation of comparative risk estimates were based upon wire service accounts, the stories could be expected to be quite similar from paper to paper. By selecting those stories that had been reproduced in at least half of the major papers, it was possible to classify the story as a *major event* and to use that fact in pursuing similarities and differences in coverage in other papers in American cities.

Four stories were identified as major stories: (a) a 1992 story that indicated that blacks with similar medical conditions were less likely than whites to receive aggressive cardiac care, as with angioplasty or bypass surgery; (b) a similar story in 1993 that indicated that the racial differences in cardiac care were not explained by differences in insurance; (c) a story in 1992 that indicated that blacks with similar physical conditions were less likely than whites to be granted disability benefits; and (d) several stories related to the difficulties that blacks, relative to whites, Hispanics, and Asians, faced in getting mortgages for the purchase of homes. The most important story was a report by the Federal Reserve Bank of Boston that concluded that racial discrimination could not be ruled out as a factor.

The "papers" database in DIALOG, as well as the *New York Times* file in the Nexis/Lexis database, were used to identify all the published stories that were in some identifiable way related to these four major stories (potentially published in 54 newspapers). In addition to the stories that were either photocopied or reproduced with full text from the database, information about the percentage of African Americans represented in the population of the metropolitan area in which the newspaper was published was gathered for each newspaper in the database. Identifying information included the paper; the length of the article; whether or not it included pictures, graphs, and tables; and who, including wire services, was given credit for the story.

Because the primary focus of the analysis is on the ways in which the stories are framed, the headlines and the first three paragraphs, or what the database identified as the "lead," were used in the analysis. Several variables were developed to characterize the framing of stories. Nearly all were coded as dichotomous dummy variables, where presence = 1 and absence = 0. All coding was accomplished by a single coder. Acceptable levels of reliability were achieved after initial training. Continued improvement in reliability was assumed to follow ongoing discussions of items identified as problematic. The discussions that follow have been limited to those enjoying the highest levels of reliability.

TABLE 4.1 Patterns of Risk (the probable winners and losers in phrases using *more likely* or *less likely*; $N = 411$)

	BGAIN	BLOSE	WGAIN	WLOSE
Proportion coded = 1	.088	.749	.160	.021

FINDINGS

Table 4.1 presents an assessment of the orientation toward African American risk in the major newspapers in the United States. On the basis of the initial search of the databases, we identified 411 qualifying phrases that made use of the actuarial assumption, that is, used probabilistic language to comment on risk, such as "blacks were more likely to be denied mortgages than whites, Asians, or Hispanics." Four outcomes were considered, and for the purposes of this analysis, they were coded as mutually exclusive. BGAIN was the low probability of black gain; BLOSE was the high probability of black loss; WGAIN was the high probability of white gain; and WLOSE was the low probability of white loss. The resultant proportions indicate that the overwhelming tendency in these stories was to use phrases emphasizing the high probability of black loss (nearly 75% of all phrases).

Table 4.2 presents the results of an examination of a narrower sample. The 79 stories used in this analysis involve only those stories where differences in outcome, or comparative risk, can be seen as reflecting institutional decision making. We note that 40% of the headlines present the story in terms of black loss, while another 30% frame the story as one of disparity. These codings are not mutually exclusive; indeed, the correlation between these two attributes is positive. Some 26% of the headlines frame the story as being about race, and this frame is considerably more likely to involve disparity ($r = .29$). Episodic leads are relatively rare (7%), and headlines do not usually frame stories in probabilistic terms (9%).

Table 4.2 also includes assessments of the explanatory power of five nominal variables (as measured by eta-squared). Knowing the subject of the story (health, finance, government services, and so on) is useful in predicting the framing of the story as being about bias or discrimination (.21) or the high probability of blacks losing (.18). Knowing

TABLE 4.2 Determinants of Risk Framing in Stories of Organizational Decision Making (eta-squared; $n = 79$)

Variables	% (N = 1)	Subject	Study	Credit	Wire	Paper
Actuary	.089	.147	.033	.099	.129	.126
Bias	.278	.209	.172	.094	.048	.067
Blacknot	.405	.113	.189	.133	.091	.107
Disparit	.317	.084	.083	.074	.034	.088
Episodic	.076	.061	.120	.084	.040	.167
Graphics	.177	.092	.128	.221	.106	.264
Past	.114	.717	.247	.131	.459	.063
Precise	.291	.331	.188	.076	.221	.091
Question	.101	.044	.134	.031	.161	.128
Race	.266	.091	.064	.118	.161	.113
Whites	.051	.076	.075	.095	.079	.135
BNOT		.179	.200	.047	.067	.091
BWIN		.045	.571	.081	.018	.153
WWIN		.164	.125	.128	.348	.168

the source of the data used in the story is considerably more useful in predicting whether or not the story would be framed in terms of the low probability of black success (BWIN = .57). Along those lines, knowing which newspaper or wire service was the source of the story is also helpful in predicting whether the leads would frame the story in terms of the high probability of white success (WWIN = .35).

Table 4.3 presents the results of the analysis of the four major stories that were identified on the basis of their being repeated in the "major papers" database. We note that even though the Heart92 and Heart93 stories are fundamentally about the same sort of disparity, they are framed quite differently. In 1992, there was a greater tendency to frame the story in terms of black loss than in 1993 (62% versus 35%). There was also a greater tendency of the stories to raise doubts about the conclusions from data in 1993 than in 1992 (22% versus 4%). We note that the use of the bias or discrimination frame was used more often in stories about mortgages (51%) and was almost never invoked in the stories about disparity in medical care published in 1992 (4%).

Because it is clear that different stories tend to be framed differently, Table 4.4 presents the relationship between one possible influence, black presence in the market, measured in terms of the proportion of African Americans in the metropolitan area, and the use of particular

TABLE 4.3 Risk Framing in Major Stories ($n = 197$; % coded = 1)

Variables	Disability	Heart92	Heart93	Mortgage
Actuary	25.7	27.1	22.5	1.4
Blacknot	65.7	62.5	37.5	39.2
Bias	28.6	4.2	17.5	51.4
Disparit	17.1	54.2	47.5	31.1
Episodic	2.9	0.0	0.0	37.8
Graphics	0.0	10.4	5.0	24.3
Past	62.9	4.2	17.5	4.1
Precise	60.0	43.8	37.5	16.2
Question	22.9	4.2	22.5	14.9
Race	14.3	33.3	45.0	20.3
Whites	8.6	14.6	37.5	1.4
$N =$	35	48	40	74

frames in these individual stories. Here we note that in both the Heart92 and the Disability story, there was a tendency in markets with a greater black presence to frame those stories in terms of the past ($r = 34$, $r = 33$). The Mortgage story was the most important of all stories in terms of the number of papers in markets that carried one or more stories about disparity in mortgage lending. It thus appears that the tendency to frame stories in terms of bias or discrimination in markets with a stronger black presence was more consistent with regard to this story than with any other ($r = .26$). It is also worth noting that the presence of blacks in the market was important in determining if the paper would include indications of uncertainty about the facts or conclusions about disparities in health care delivery. The fewer blacks in the market, the more likely the story would be framed in terms of uncertainty ($r = -.32$).

Table 4.5 presents the results of efforts to explore other structural influences on the framing of racially comparative risk. The individual, or organization, given credit for the story is not a very reliable source of knowledge about story framing. It is most useful in suggesting whether the story will have graphics or not (.26) or whether the story will have an episodic lead (.19). There is considerably more to be gained from knowing which wire service was the source. This knowledge is useful in predicting whether the stories will be framed in terms of the

TABLE 4.4 The Relationship Between Black Presence in the Market and Risk Frames Used (Pearson's *r*)

	Story			
Frames	*Heart92*	*Disability*	*Heart93*	*Mortgage*
Actuary	.024	.190	.011	−.124
Bias	.108	.101	−.065	.261
Blacknot	−.199	.210	−.153	.012
BNOT	.215	.272	.099	.130
BWIN	.443	−.207	.114	*
Disparit	−.112	.011	−.040	−.073
Episodic	*	.128	*	−.006
Graphics	.192	*	−.008	.011
Length	.099	.110	.071	.095
Local	−.004	−.189	.039	.064
Past	.342	.332	.076	.191
Precise	−.228	.320	.004	.179
Question	.085	−.181	−.320	.047
Race	.074	−.031	.120	−.202
Whites	.164	.001	−.177	−.079
WWIN	−.158	−.034	−.084	*

*Computation not possible.

past (.39), make use of an episodic lead (.21), or use a higher level of precision (.21), perhaps when framing the story in terms of the high probability of black loss (.24). Knowledge of the paper's identity is similarly important as a predictor of characteristic frames, which includes, of course, whether it will carry the story at all. The proportion of African Americans in the newspaper's market is not a very powerful predictor of framing overall, but there are several relationships worth noting.

There is a tendency, at least regarding these stories, to frame the concern as being about bias or discrimination in markets where there are relatively more African Americans in the population ($r = .21$). Of interest, there is a similar tendency to frame those stories in terms of things that were likely to occur in the past ($r = .15$). Despite the fact that leads emphasizing the high probability that whites would experience positive outcomes (WWIN) were really quite rare, we still find a clear indication that such leads tended not to be used in markets where blacks were a more visible presence ($r = −.21$).

When we examine the correlations between frames and the proportion of minorities among professionals at least in newspapers (as

TABLE 4.5 Determinants of Risk Factors for Major Stories Combined (eta-squared; $N = 197$)

Variables	Credit	Wire	Paper	% Black (r)	% Minority (r)
Actuary	.130	.099	.194	−.022	.047
Bias	.110	.135	.354	.211	−.097
Blacknot	.057	.109	.283	−.050	.070
BNOT	.083	.240	.316	.189	.209
BWIN	.053	.181	.226	−.011	−.064
Disparit	.060	.081	.205	−.098	−.008
Episodic	.189	.214	.211	.100	−.049
Graphics	.262	.145	.258	.067	.046
Past	.089	.394	.187	.155	.057
Precise	.051	.204	.269	.013	.128
Question	.025	.052	.242	−.071	.011
Race	.048	.054	.252	−.069	.138
WWIN	.102	.180	.235	−.209	−.073
Whites	.030	.042	.199	−.078	.032

reported to the American Society of Newspaper Editors [ASNE]; see Foote, 1993), we find some interesting departures. First, we should note that the proportion of minorities on staff is directly correlated with the proportion of African Americans in the market ($r = .425$). The correlation is not perfect, however, for a great many reasons, including the fact that African Americans represent only 58% of the minorities being counted in the ASNE study.

We can see that minority presence in the organization does not operate in the same way that blacks in the marketplace seem to operate. Where the newspapers are more likely to frame stories in terms of bias when there is more of a black presence in the market ($r = .21$), they are less likely to do so if they have a substantial minority presence on their professional staff ($r = −.097$). Although both presence on staff and presence in the market are associated with a tendency to emphasize the high probability of black loss (BNOT $= .19, .21$), such is not the case with regard to the framing of the story as being about race. There is a tendency to *avoid* such framing where there is a black presence in the market, but a tendency to emphasize it when there is a minority presence on the staff (Race, $−.07, .14$). Although the coefficients suggest that the pressures go in the same direction, the size of the

TABLE 4.6 Contributions to Variance in the Framing of Risk in Major Stories Combined (N = 187), Multiple Regression (betas)

	Bias	BNOT	WWIN
Wealth	.079	.034	−.068
% Minority	−.132	.182	−.042
% Black	.231	.190	−.198
R-squared	.065	.080	.046

coefficients (−.20 versus −.07) point to a difference in terms of a preference for talking about the high probability of white success (WWIN).

The final table (Table 4.6) is an effort to examine several influences simultaneously. The beta coefficients in multiple regression can be interpreted as an estimate of the relationship between an influence and a selected outcome when the influence of other measured variables is held constant statistically. These models include two market variables: the wealth of households, and the proportion of African Americans in the metropolitan area (negatively correlated with each other), as well as an estimate of the proportion of minorities on staff. R-squared is interpreted much like eta-squared to mean the proportion of the variance in the dependent variable that is explained by the measured variance in the independent variables.

The explained variance is not high, and the coefficients are not reliable indicators because this analysis uses a small number of similar stories. The coefficients do, however, tell a story. When wealth and minority staff are controlled, the most important predictor of the use of the bias or discrimination frame is the proportion of blacks in the market. Indeed, in every case, that variable is the most important predictor.

DISCUSSION

Because the scope of this study has been limited to a relatively brief period, and has focused primarily on newspaper coverage in 1992, and further because the number of stories that are published about the risks that African Americans face is relatively small, it would be unwise to treat these patterns as describing some fundamental tendency. Yet, these data are highly suggestive of underlying journalistic tendencies in the framing of stories about blacks at risk. It is clear that the preferred mode for discussing comparative risks for blacks is in terms of *the high probability of black loss*, even when logic dictates that at least three other options might be used to present the very same statistical reality. Journalists may be trained in school and on the job to emphasize failure rather than success, but there may be unfortunate negative consequences that flow from reproducing this professional bias.

These data give support to the conclusions reached by Tichenor, Donohue, and Olien that what you know is a function of where you live. Newspapers differ in terms of what they choose to publish with regard to black risk, and they also differ in terms of how they frame those stories. Because framing influences how those risks are understood, both in terms of magnitude or likelihood as well as in terms of social justice or fairness, an understanding of what governs these differences is important for us to attain.

These preliminary data suggest that a variety of factors are involved in determining which frames are used for particular stories in particular newspaper markets. Although it is clear that different sources including different news and wire services have identifiable tendencies when it comes to framing stories about racial disparity, the final decision is made at the level of the newspaper that chooses, sizes, places, and frames the story. The fact that the proportion of African Americans in the metropolitan area served by these papers emerges as an important predictor of coverage and framing raises critical questions about how well the press is serving its privileged functions.

It would be premature to conclude that economic self-interest guides the framing of stories to reflect the importance of black readers to the bottom line of the paper. In the 54 markets studied, the presence of African American households was associated with the level of household income. The presence of blacks in the market was greatest in the poorest newspaper markets. This pattern points to a problem for editors who seek to attract black circulation in ways that do not risk white readership or advertising support. Arthur Chandler of the *Los Angeles Times* is quoted as suggesting that "giving more attention to minority issues 'would not make sense financially . . . [because] that audience does not have the purchasing power and is not responsive to the kind of advertising we carry' " (Baker, 1994, p. 68). Of course the determination of editorial content is bound to be more complicated than that. Concerns about community, the level of racial conflict, and even the level of activism among African American professionals on the newspaper's staff may all intervene to influence how particular stories are framed. These are questions that ought to be pursued, and this has been just a tentative initial step.

Future studies should expand the number of years that are examined, thereby increasing the number of stories about particular issues, from particular news services, and at different moments in a newspaper's publishing history. Structural information should be expanded to include information about racial conflict within a paper's community, more detail about the racial composition of a newspaper's professional staff, as well as information about circulation in urban and suburban areas that might indicate the economic basis for racial sensitivity.

REFERENCES

Atkin, C., Greenberg, B., & McDermott, S. (1983). Television and race role socialization. *Journalism Quarterly, 60*(3), 407-414.
Baker, E. (1994). *Advertising and a democratic press*. Princeton, NJ: Princeton University Press.
Beck, U. (1992). *Risk society: Towards a new modernity*. London: Sage.
Cohn, V. (1989). *News and numbers*. Ames: Iowa State University Press.
Cose, E. (1993). *The rage of a privileged class*. New York: HarperCollins.
Edelman, M. (1983). Systematic confusions in the evaluation of implementing decisions. In S. Spiro & E. Yuchtman-Yaar (Eds.), *Evaluating the welfare state* (pp. 131-147). New York: Academic Press.
Elias, R. (1986). *The politics of victimization*. New York: Oxford University Press.
Entman, R. (1989). *Democracy without citizens*. New York: Oxford University Press.
Entman, R. (1990). Racism and local TV news. *Critical Studies in Mass Communication, 7*(4), 332-345.
Entman, R. (1993). Framing: Toward clarification of a fractured paradigm. *Journal of Communication, 43*(4), 51-58.
Ettema, J., & Glasser, T. (1987). On the epistemology of investigative journalism. In M. Gurevitch & M. Levy (Eds.), *Mass communication review yearbook* (Vol. 6, pp. 338-361). Newbury Park, CA: Sage.
Ettema, J., & Glasser, T. (1988). Narrative form and moral force: The realization of innocence and guilt through investigative journalism. *Journal of Communication, 38*(3), 8-26.
Foote, C. (1993, May-June). More than half of U.S. dailies employ newsroom minorities. *ASNE Bulletin*, pp. 20-25.
Gandy, O., & Matabane, P. (1989). Television and social perceptions among African-Americans and Hispanics. In M. Asante & W. Gudykunst (Eds.), *Handbook of*

intercultural and development communication (pp. 318-348). Newbury Park, CA: Sage.

Gaziano, C. (1984). Neighborhood newspapers, citizen groups and public affairs knowledge gaps. *Journalism Quarterly, 61*(3), 556-566.

Gerbner, G. (1973). Cultural indicators: The third voice. In G. Gerbner, L. Gross, & W. Melody (Eds.), *Communications technology and social policy* (pp. 555-573). New York: Wiley.

Gerbner, G., Gross, L., Morgan, M., & Signorielli, N. (1994). Growing up with television: The cultivation perspective. In J. Bryant & D. Zillmann (Eds.), *Media effects: Advances in theory and research* (pp. 17-41). Hillsdale, NJ: Lawrence Erlbaum.

Glasser, T., & Ettema, T. (1989). Investigative journalism and the moral order. *Critical Studies in Mass Communication, 6*(1), 1-20.

Hacker, A. (1992). *Two nations: Black and white, separate, hostile, unequal.* New York: Scribner.

Iyengar, S. (1991). *Is anybody responsible? How television frames political issues.* Chicago: University of Chicago Press.

Kahneman, D., & Tversky, A. (1986). Choices, values and frames. In N. Smelser & D. Gerstein (Eds.), *Behavioral and social science* (pp. 153-172). Washington, DC: National Academy Press.

Liss, W. (Ed.). (1989). *Prospects and problems in risk communication.* Waterloo, Ontario: University of Calgary Press.

Mauro, J. (1992). *Statistical deception at work.* Hillsdale, NJ: Lawrence Erlbaum.

McQuail, D. (1992). *Media performance.* London: Sage.

Nadeau, R., Niemi, R., & Levine, R. (1993). Innumeracy about minority populations. *Public Opinion Quarterly, 57*(3), 332-347.

Olien, C., Donohue, G., & Tichenor, P. (1983). Structure, communication and social power: The evolution of the knowledge gap hypothesis. In E. Wartella, D. Whitney, & S. Windahl (Eds.), *Mass communication review yearbook* (Vol. 4, pp. 455-461). Beverly Hills, CA: Sage.

Olien, C., Tichenor, P., & Donohue, G. (1988). Relation between corporate ownership and editor attitudes about business. *Journalism Quarterly, 65*(2), 259-266.

Patterson, T. (1993). *Out of order.* New York: Knopf.

Picard, R., McCombs, M., Winter, J., & Lacy, S. (Eds.). (1988). *Press concentration and monopoly: New perspectives on newspaper ownership and operation.* Norwood, NJ: Ablex.

Protess, D., Cook, F., Doppelt, J., Ettema, J., Gordon, T., Leff, D., & Miller, P. (1991). *The journalism of outrage.* New York: Guilford.

Protess, D., & McCombs, M. (Eds.). (1991). *Agenda setting.* Hillsdale, NJ: Lawrence Erlbaum.

Signorielli, N., & Morgan, M. (Eds.). (1990). *Cultivation analysis.* Newbury Park, CA: Sage.

Singer, E., & Endreny, P. (1993). *Reporting on risk: How the mass media portray accidents, diseases, disasters and other hazards.* New York: Russell Sage.

Stallings, R. (1990). Media discourse and the social construction of risk. *Social Problems, 37*(1), 80-93.

Tichenor, P., Olien, C., & Donohue, G. (1987). Effects of use of metro dailies on knowledge gap in small towns. *Journalism Quarterly, 64*(2-3), 329-336.

Tversky, A., & Kahneman, D. (1990). Rational choice and the framing of decisions. In K. Cook & M. Levi (Eds.), *The limits of rationality* (pp. 60-89). Chicago: University of Chicago Press.

van Dijk, T. A. (1991). *Racism and the press.* London: Routledge.

Wright, C. (1960). Functional analysis of mass communication. *Public Opinion Quarterly, 24,* 606-620.

5

How Four Newspapers Covered the 1992 Los Angeles "Riots"

JYOTIKA RAMAPRASAD

Complaints about the quantity and quality of media coverage, both in news and in entertainment content, of groups of people—defined by nationality, gender, race, and so on—are not uncommon. For example, scant coverage apart, the Third World is angry about its "coups and earthquakes" coverage, women complain about sexist coverage, and people of color dislike their stereotypical coverage.

This chapter singles out coverage of racial groups, specifically African Americans, for examination. In particular, it examines how newspapers from different parts of the United States covered the "riots" spurred by the acquittal of the police officers in the Rodney King beating case. The basic premise of the chapter is that a better understanding of newspaper coverage of certain events can lead to a better understanding of mediated messages concerning certain groups. Specifically, because the events in Los Angeles were spurred by the acquittal of the white police officers tried in the beating case of an African American, the assumption is that most of the coverage of the event referred to African Americans.

AUTHOR'S NOTE: This chapter is based on a paper presented to the Minorities and Communication Division, AEJMC, at the national convention (Kansas City, Kansas, August 1993).

GENERAL MEDIA COVERAGE
OF AFRICAN AMERICANS

Concern about media coverage of African Americans outside of and, particularly, within civil disorder situations, although recent in intensity is long-standing in expression. As early as 1922, the report of the Chicago Committee on Race Relations condemned the practices and policies of the Chicago press with respect to routine news about African Americans and laid part of the blame for the 1919 racial conflict on their reportage (Chicago Commission on Race Relations, 1922). Somewhat similar sentiments were echoed in 1968 in the *Report of the National Advisory Commission on Civil Disorders* (also see Midura, 1971).

Also long-standing is concern over coverage of the actual riots themselves, which typically tends to portray the African American participants as demanding and aggressive (Klein, 1968; Lyle, 1968; Rosenberg, 1992). It is argued that routine stereotypical and negative coverage of African Americans in the media does not provide an understanding of black reality. This results in racial disharmony, which in turn leads to conflict. Media coverage of the conflict often confirms racial stereotypes and keeps the vicious cycle going.

The discussion of African American coverage in both routine and extreme situations has moved from concern to specific examinations. This scholarship, although initially sparse, has over time documented the scant, stereotypical, and slanted nature of the coverage. Specifically, studies outside the framework of civil disorder news have examined black visibility and found it to be limited and skewed.

For example, Gist (1932) found that the press not only minimized news about African Americans but also subordinated general news about them to antisocial news. Carter (1957) found that southern newspapers gave little attention to the story of desegregation and made no attempt to "delve into the issue or 'background' it" (p. 18). Sentman (1983) reported that coverage of African Americans formed only a very small portion of *Life*'s content in sample years from 1937 to 1972, and coverage of everyday black life was more or less absent. Roberts (1975) found that the type of story in which African Americans appeared most often had to do with civil rights, and the positions blacks were shown occupying were blue-collar. Tracing longitudinal (from 1892 to 1968) coverage of African Americans in two Los Angeles newspapers, Johnson,

Sears, and McConahay (1971) concluded: "It is just as well that press coverage of blacks was so rare for so many years, because the content of it was mostly degrading" (p. 710).

More recent studies have found increased coverage of blacks but not necessarily a change in skew. For example, Chaudhary (1980) found that although articles about black officials were longer, they were placed in less desirable positions and were more negative than articles about white officials. Roberts (1975) found that although blacks were in about one-fourth of the sample newscasts, they were "seen but not heard," suggesting that "in the context of world and national affairs, the viewpoint of blacks is seldom expressed" (p. 55).

Longitudinal studies have, however, found changes in coverage with time. For example, Stempel (1971) found that pictorial coverage of blacks, although limited in 1960, had increased in 1970 in both news and advertising content. Colle (1968) traced positive changes in black images in film and television. Lambert (1965) found that 1964 articles about African Americans in *Look* magazine were more favorable than 1959 articles; the 1964 articles also covered African Americans as members of society. In a study of newspaper pictures, Lester and Smith (1990) found that the early years (1937 to 1952) reflected stereotyping, the middle years (1957 to 1972) reflected an increased reporting of causes of riots and urban disturbances, and the later years (1978 to 1988) covered the attempts of black leaders to effect change by working within the system.

Reasons suggested for the improvement in coverage over time have included the hiring of more black reporters,[1] the greater participation of blacks in visible civic activities (Martindale, 1985; Stempel, 1971), and the increased sensitivity of reporters (Lester & Smith, 1990). Martindale (1985) provided yet another reason for her study's finding of reduced stereotypical coverage in the 1970s over the 1950s in four leading U.S. dailies: the absence of protest activity in the 1970s.

MEDIA COVERAGE OF
AFRICAN AMERICANS IN RIOT SITUATIONS

Historically, when protest activity is present, coverage of African Americans has tended to be negative. For example, in one of the few studies of the 1917 riots, Rudwick (1964) pointed out the detrimental nature of the coverage wherein the press "encouraged as well as reflected racial tensions" (p. 70) by presenting African Americans as vindictive "criminals, rapists, and dupes of corrupt politicians" (p. 71).

Although study of the next major outbreak in 1943 is almost nonexistent, criticisms of the "riot exacerbation" (p. 330) role of the media (before and) once riots broke out resurfaced in studies of the 1960s riots (see Paletz & Dunn, 1969, for a review). Breen's (1968) study of the 1967 Detroit riots found that "each of the eight [sample] papers presented accounts of riots that dealt, mainly, with reports of fires and looting" (p. 545). Martindale (1985) found that protest coverage in the 1960s tended to focus on incidents, number of people involved, attendant violence, and perhaps a brief quote about the cause of the riot from a black spokesperson.

More recently, based on a study of 10 publications in July and August 1992, Bridge (1992) concluded the following about the coverage of the 1992 riots:

> The media fanned the flames of racial and ethnic unrest between blacks and whites, blacks and Latinos, and other groups by reducing complex events to short phrases which were then repeated again and again in news stories. These phrases or key descriptors were often misleading. (n.p.)

Even when riot coverage is not directly provocative and in fact is deliberately restrained and exemplary, it may still fail "to provide a truthful, comprehensive, and intelligent account of the day's events" because it does not contribute "to an understanding of the nature of Afro-American grievances or of conditions in that community" (Paletz & Dunn, 1969, p. 345). Articles published in the *Detroit Free Press* reporting on a survey conducted soon after the July 1967 riots in Detroit indicated that rioters were more bitterly resentful and alienated than nonrioters. Rioters rated overcrowded living conditions, police brutality, poor housing, lack of jobs, poverty, and anger with business as their major grievances contributing to the riot. Survey findings also suggested that those blacks who least expected a change in white attitudes were the most likely to riot (cited in Rosenthal, 1978).

Martindale (1989), in particular, but others too (Hartmann & Husband, 1974) have pointed out this lack of media attention to the root causes of riots and other protest activity. Martindale (1989) found that during the 1960s, when newspapers gave the most extensive coverage to black protest, they gave the least coverage to causes of the protests. Coverage of such events as sit-ins, marches, and so on, when no description of cause is given, gives the impression of blacks being unreasonable and demanding; it also makes it appear that blacks are reacting to some "mild inconvenience" (Fisher & Lowenstein, cited in Martindale, 1989). Rosenthal (1978) found a correlation between community self-interest and newspaper orientation in the coverage of the Detroit riots of 1967 in the one year following the riots. The greater the black population in the community and the further from Detroit its location, the more the papers had the problems-and-solutions (prevention) approach, which included articles on understanding causes of riots so as to ameliorate problems. The smaller the black population in the community and the closer to Detroit its location, the more the papers had the preparedness theme.

THE CONSEQUENCES AND
CAUSES OF MEDIA COVERAGE

Concern about, and study of, media coverage of groups is rooted in a recognition of the consequences of such coverage. According to Sentman (1983), coverage influences understanding and "the impression of that group's place in society" (p. 501). The Kerner Commission (*Report of the National Advisory Commission on Civil Disorders*, 1968) suggested that inadequate and negative coverage of blacks was at least partially responsible for the "black-white schism." Such coverage, according to Johnson et al. (1971), has confused whites' understanding of racism, has facilitated the exploitation of black people by whites, and has created white fear of blacks. Gist (1932) suggests that it is highly plausible that such coverage "might be a factor in engendering racial antipathies and prejudices" (p. 409). More recently, Gandy (1994) wrote:

> Because of the media's role in the cultivation of social perceptions, there is reason to be concerned about the tendency for African-Americans and Hispanics to be presented in media roles that define them as violent criminals. Not only do such representations operate to reproduce racism,

but the cumulative impact of such coverage may be a reduction in the general audience's willingness to support public policies designed to help blacks escape poverty and criminal victimization. (p. 41)

Consequences apart, researchers have also attempted to address reasons for such coverage. Lack of black staff members (Paletz & Dunn, 1969) and hypersensitivity to white readers (Gist, 1932) are offered as reasons. The way "the press is organized and manned to obtain and publish news" (Paletz & Dunn, 1969, p. 345), however, is an additional factor. For example, Gist's (1932) survey of editors indicated that " 'news value' was the deciding factor" in determining coverage (p. 410). Lyle (1968) offered the "objectivity fetish" (p. xii) as another reason; reporters are expected to cover the who, what, when, where, and how, but the why comes at the end because the reporter is not supposed to indulge in interpretation. Coupled with these professional and organizational influences is the status quo orientation of the press.

According to Paletz and Dunn (1969), their sample newspaper "presented the [1967 Winston-Salem] riot almost exclusively from the perspective of law enforcement and city officials" (p. 339). Paletz and Dunn concluded that "media act to maintain socio-cultural consensus. . . . All may not be well in the society, but this is no way to change the situation" (pp. 344-345). Similarly, Johnson et al. (1971) considered "formula reporting" (i.e., reporting from the perspective of the status quo, for example, blacks as disrupting the peace of civilized society) to be responsible for such coverage. Hartmann and Husband (1974) studied racism and the mass media in Britain and found that the media use a news frame to cover colored people that indicates they are a problem. Martindale (1989) concluded similarly: Protests are often portrayed by the media as the work of deviants and the protestors as being "irrational, dangerous, or not to be taken seriously" (p. 921). Blanchard (1968) also pointed to the "law-and-order" line of coverage (of the Poor People's Campaign demonstration), which reflects not only "the grab-and-run habits of fact- and quote-gathering but institutional bias" (p. 63). The Kerner report (*Report of the National Advisory Commission on Civil Disorders,* 1968) said that reliance on official sources and coverage of law enforcement activities result in an "exaggeration of mood and event" (p. 363) and lead blacks to consider the media as part of the "white power structure" (p. 374).

Much of this type of literature has now been organized into a theory of news content that includes personal biases and values, workplace values, routines of news production, organizational imperatives, and ideology as factors that influence news content (Shoemaker & Reese, 1991). Generally, as a result of a combination of these factors, less powerful people, groups, and causes receive little attention in the media. Often, increased attention is focused on them only when they become "extremists," and then this attention is filtered through estab- lishment eyes. One of the consequences of such coverage is that media do not seriously assess the issues behind "extremist" behavior. In 1968, the Kerner Commission (*Report of the National Advisory Commission on Civil Disorders,* 1968) concluded similarly: "The media failed to report adequately on the causes and consequences of civil disorders and on the underlying problems of race relations" (p. 20).

Given all the soul searching among professionals (Gilbert, 1968; Klein, 1968; Lyle, 1968) and the study by academics that followed earlier riots, has coverage improved? This chapter assesses media, particularly newspaper, coverage of the 1992 Los Angeles and related "riots." Specifically, it asks the following questions: (a) How much coverage, in terms of amount and prominence, did sample newspapers give to the riots? (b) What was the amount and nature of coverage given to causes of the riots? (c) Did the riot coverage change with time (across the four months)? (d) Did the riot coverage differ by newspaper?

METHOD

Content analysis was the method of study. The sample selection included purposive selection of four newspapers and systematic selection of stories from these papers. The four newspapers selected were the West Coast's *Los Angeles Times,* the East Coast's *New York Times,* the Midwest's *Chicago Tribune,* and the South's *Atlanta Constitution.* Newspaper selection, although limited by the availability of microfilms in the local library, was purposive in the following respects. All four newspapers are resource-rich, the type of newspapers particularly singled out for criticism by the Kerner Commission. They are also influential enough nationally or regionally to have a trickle-down effect on the content of smaller newspapers. Additionally, the *New York Times* is considered an elite newspaper of record. The circulation of these newspapers (morning edition) is as follows: the *Los Angeles Times*, 1,146,631; the *New York Times*, 1,145,890; the *Chicago Tribune*, 724,257; and the *Atlanta Constitution*, 302,616 (*Editor & Publisher International Yearbook*, 1993). The African American population in the respective cities is as follows: Los Angeles, 14%; New York City, 28.7%; Chicago, 39.1%; and Atlanta, 67.1% (Slater & Hall, 1993). Together, what these newspapers say matters, and given the African American populations in their cities, what the newspapers say about them matters even more. Geographically, the newspapers represent four regions of the United States; the inclusion of the *Los Angeles Times*, however, also provides a local dimension.

All relevant titles related to the riots (either in Los Angeles or in other communities as a result of the L.A. riots) were checked in the respective indexes of the newspapers. Once the appropriate title was located within each index, a systematic sample of 50% was selected using a random starting point and a skip interval of two. The sample dates were April 30, 1992 (first day of coverage of the riots) to July 31, 1992 (the number of stories had tapered off considerably by then). This selection process specified a total of 478 stories. The usable sample was 473 because of wrongly indexed items and missing microfilms.

Once each sample story was located on microfilm, it was coded for date, newspaper, length (in terms of number of lines and number of words), size (less or greater than one column length in number of words), page (front or otherwise), placement on page (above or below fold), story type (story, opinion, feature, other), byline (staff, wire, name, other), and topic (riot, law enforcement/government, reaction, consequence, cause, after riot, other).

Because the sample newspapers used differing column widths, inches were not used as a measure for length. Instead, measurement for length of story was standardized in the following manner. For each sample newspaper, the average number of words per line was calculated; this was used as a standard to calculate number of words in a story (by multiplying it by number of lines in the story). When a story changed column width, coders recalculated average number of words per line for that column width and used it in calculating number of words in that story. Similarly, for each newspaper, the number of words in a standard (full) column was calculated. This number was compared with the number of words in the story to determine whether the story was greater than one column length in size.

A story got a point each for being greater than one column length, appearing on the front page, and starting above the fold. The sum of these points was the prominence score for the story. Categories for story type, byline, and topic were derived from initial pretests on nonsample data. Within story type, news referred to hard news; opinion material included editorials, op-ed pieces, and letters; and features included news analysis, commentary, and features. Within byline, staff stories were those for which the writer could be clearly identified as a staff member; wire referred to wire stories; names referred to stories with signed names whose affiliation was not clear; and other was for unsigned material. For opinion materials, the names byline most probably indicated readers who wrote in; for features, it most likely designated freelancers; and for news stories, it most likely indicated stringers. Irrespective of this, the names byline indicated nonreliance on the wire services.

Within topic, riot included all stories focusing directly on the riots in Los Angeles and related riots in other cities. Law enforcement/ government stories included stories about the police, fire department, government officials, National Guard, and so on. Reaction stories were about reactions to the verdict or the riot. Cause stories looked into reasons for the riots, and consequence stories dealt with results of the riots. After-riot stories included reconstruction, rebuilding, follow-up, and so on. Given that the coding unit was each story and given that only the dominant topic was coded, the coding does not capture any crossover subtopics in each story.

Altogether, six coders were used. Intercoder reliability,[2] using Holsti's (1969) formula on 20 stories recoded by all the coders, was 90% for number of words, 91% for size, 92% for story type, 84% for byline, and 67% for topic. As microfilm copies of stories were used for the reliability test, it was not possible to code page and placement on page; these are not difficult coding decisions and as such can be expected to be made with high reliability.

The study has a few limitations. First, it used only the print medium, and within it only four newspapers. Many people get their information from television these days. Second, the paper used a large coding unit (each story); therefore, subthemes that differed in paragraphs within a story were not captured. Finally, the study equates riot coverage with African American coverage. The Los Angeles riots, after all, did take place in African American communities. A qualitative review of the stories abstracted in the relevant newspaper indexes also brought out the connection between the riots and the African American race.

Many riot stories were attached to the not-guilty verdict in the Rodney King incident. The incident was specifically covered as a racial event. The Reginald Denny beating that followed was also given a substantial racial focus.

Famous African American individuals created another racial link in many stories. For example, Reverend Jesse Jackson argued for racial and economic justice; Los Angeles Mayor Tom Bradley addressed issues of healing racial problems and rebuilding the inner city; Minister Louis Farrakhan compared all U.S. cities to the Los Angeles time bomb because of injustices; West Coast rappers Ice T and Ice Cube explained their views on black anger and the riots; and so on.

The connection was apparent in the number of stories that covered middle-class black reactions, the impact and assistance of black businesses, job opportunities or the lack thereof for African Americans, the assistance of black churches, the truce between two major black gangs, attacks on affirmative action and civil rights, and the previous Watts riots, among other topics.

The riot-race link was also clear from the stories that explored issues such as the inner city, South Central Los Angeles, police brutality, the ghetto, gangs, black youth, poverty, urban relations, race relations (particularly between African Americans and Koreans), racial harmony, racism, racial tension, race and income, and unemployment.

Finally, content apart, the language also established the connection. The riots were called black protests, black attacks, black unrest, and black violence. The words *race* and *racial* were used in many stories.

FINDINGS

Of the total sample of 473 stories, 111 (24%) received front page treatment, 316 (67%) were above the fold, and 265 (56%) were larger than one column length (Table 5.1). The mean prominence of these stories (based on these three measures) was 1.5 (the possible range was

TABLE 5.1 Distribution of Stories by Variables

	N	Percentage
Page		
front	111	24
other	362	77
Placement		
above fold	316	67
below fold	157	33
Size		
greater than one column	265	56
less than one column	208	44
Mean prominence		(1.5)
Mean size (words)		(1,002)
Byline		
staff	287	61
wire	11	2
name	135	29
other	40	9
Story type[a]		
news	350	74
editorial	44	9
features	77	16
Topic		
riot	50	11
law/government	92	20
reaction	95	20
consequence	47	10
cause	34	7
after riot	101	21
other	54	11

a. "Other" stories excluded.

0 to 3). The mean number of words in a story was 1,002 (larger than one column length for all newspapers). Overall, the riot stories seem to have provided a reasonable amount of coverage. Another indicator of the importance assigned to these stories was that a majority (61%) of the stories had a staff byline and very few (2%) were wire stories. In line with findings of past studies, and to answer the first research question, coverage of the 1992 riots was large.

Also, typical of riot coverage, most of the coverage (350 stories, 74%) was in the nature of hard news focusing on events and happenings of the immediate present (Table 5.1). There were 44 (9%) opinion

TABLE 5.2 Distribution of Topics by Byline

Topic	Staff		Name		Total	
	n	%	n	%	n	%
Riot	37	86	6	14	43	11
Law/government	73	84	14	16	87	23
Reaction	48	57	36	43	84	22
Consequence	36	84	7	16	43	11
Cause	6	23	20	77	26	7
After riot	59	63	35	37	94	25

NOTE: Topic "Other" and bylines "Wire" and "Other" excluded; chi-square = 51.81; p = .00.

pieces and 77 (16%) features. In terms of topic too, coverage followed patterns found in other studies. Stories about causes of the riot were the smallest in number (34 stories, 7%). After-riot stories were largest in number (101 stories, 21%) followed by reaction (95 stories, 20%) and law enforcement/government stories (92 stories, 20%).

Cause stories did not, however, differ in prominence from other topics. There was also no differential treatment of topics in terms of length (mean number of words). That is, cause stories were not smaller in prominence or length than other (topic) stories. Cause items were, however, seldom written by staff members (chi-square = 51.81; p = .00); they were generally signed (with names), indicating a more editorial nature (Table 5.2). On the other hand, stories about the riot itself and about law enforcement/government were more likely to be staff written.

The more editorial type of treatment of cause items was confirmed in the cross-tabulation of topic by type of story (chi-square = 52.44; p = .00). A larger percentage of editorials and, to some extent, features focused on discussing causes than other topics, while a smaller percentage of hard news stories focused on cause than other topics (Table 5.3).

The relegation of cause stories to the editorial arena, as well as the fact that they received smaller coverage, has implications. Although editorial materials receive high readership, they do not receive quite the attention that front page stories receive. This together with less coverage of cause stories might diminish their impact and leave the hard news stories to create impressions about the rioters. To answer the second research question, coverage tended not to focus on cause and, when it did, tended to give it an opinion orientation rather than a factual basis.

TABLE 5.3 Distribution of Topics by Story Type

Topic	Story		Opinion		Features		Total	
	n	%	*n*	%	*n*	%	*n*	%
Riot	42	84	3	6	5	10	50	11
Law/government	82	89	6	7	4	4	92	20
Reaction	61	64	8	8	26	27	95	20
Consequence	35	75	4	9	8	17	47	10
Cause	14	41	11	32	9	27	34	7
After riot	77	77	5	5	18	18	100	21
Other	39	74	7	13	7	13	53	11

NOTE: Story type "Other" excluded; chi-square = 52.44; p = .00.

It is possible, however, that, although the initial coverage of riots, given the news values of immediacy, impact, novelty, and so on, might focus more on hard news stories about the riots themselves and about law enforcement efforts, later coverage may be more reflective. An analysis of coverage by month did not, however, show any changes across months from the above patterns.[3] Hence, coverage did not get larger or smaller (mean length) or more or less prominent across the months; neither did the distribution of stories by bylines, story types, and topics change. That is, time did not influence the coverage to become more or less staff or wire written, more or less hard news or editorial/feature in nature, or more or less focused on the riots, law enforcement, or causes. To answer the third research question, the patterns of coverage found for the total sample were also true of each month; time did not make a difference.

Although time may not have made a difference in coverage, the particular newspaper did make a difference. The *Los Angeles Times* had the largest number of stories (61%) and the *Chicago Tribune* the least (7%) (chi-square = 365.27; p = .00) (Table 5.4). For the *Los Angeles Times*, this was a big, local story; hence, its coverage would be larger. The *Chicago Tribune,* although it had the least coverage, was really not far behind the *Atlanta Constitution*; the fact that there was some sporadic rioting in Atlanta and that Atlanta has a very large percentage of African Americans may account for its slightly larger coverage. The *New York Times* also gave the riots considerable coverage (it ranked second); given its status as a national newspaper and the fact that the

TABLE 5.4 Distribution of Stories by Month, Page, Placement, Size, Mean Prominence, Mean Size and Byline, Story Type, and Topic, by Newspaper

	LA Times n	LA Times %	NY Times n	NY Times %	Chicago Trib. n	Chicago Trib. %	Atlanta Cons. n	Atlanta Cons. %	Total n	Total %
Total	288	61	118	25	31	7	36	8	473	100
(chi-square = 365.27; p = .00)										
Month[a]										
April	3	1	1	1	2	7	0	0	6	1
May	262	91	101	86	28	90	36	100	427	90
June	23	8	11	9	1	3	0	0	35	7
July	0	0	5	4	0	0	0	0	5	1
Page										
front	78	27	18	15	9	29	6	17	111	24
other	210	73	100	85	22	71	30	83	362	77
(chi-square = 8.0; p = .046)										
Placement										
above fold	183	64	77	65	26	84	30	83	316	67
below fold	105	37	41	35	5	16	6	17	157	33
(chi-square = 10.02; p = .02)										
Size:										
greater than one column	172	60	56	48	21	68	16	44	265	56
less than one column	116	40	62	53	10	32	20	56	208	44
(chi-square = 8.8; p = .03)										
Mean prom	1.51		1.25		1.81		1.44		1.5	
(F = 3.94; p = .01)										
Mean size	1,111		876		917		626		1,002	
(F = 7.22; p = .00)										
Story type[b]										
story	238	83	83	72	12	39	17	47	350	74
editorial	9	3	16	14	10	32	9	25	44	9
features	41	14	17	15	9	29	10	28	77	16
Byline[c]										
staff	204	71	32	27	21	68	30	83	287	61
wire	0	0	7	6	3	10	1	3	11	2
name	67	23	57	48	6	19	5	14	135	29
other	17	6	22	19	1	3	0	0	40	9
Topic[d]										
riot	32	13	7	7	8	26	3	9	50	12
law/government	60	23	19	19	4	13	9	27	92	22
reaction	55	22	32	32	3	10	5	15	95	23
consequence	29	11	9	9	5	16	4	12	47	11
cause	15	6	12	12	5	16	2	6	34	8
after riot	65	25	20	20	6	19	10	30	101	24

a. Chi-square for month was done using only May and June because of expected cell frequency problems; it was nonsignificant.
b. Story type "Other" excluded; chi-square = 59.82; p = .00.
c. Chi-square for byline was done using only staff and name stories because of expected cell frequency problems; chi-square = 54.84; p = .00.
d. Topic "Other" excluded; chi-square = 25.69; p = .04.

riots story transcended local boundaries, this was not surprising. This pattern in amount of coverage by each newspaper did not change across months.

The *Chicago Tribune* and *Los Angeles Times* used more front page stories than did the *New York Times* and *Atlanta Constitution* (chi-square = 8.0; p = .046) and had a higher percentage of stories greater than one column length (chi-square = 8.8; p = .03) (Table 5.4). The *Chicago Tribune* and *Atlanta Constitution* placed a higher percentage of their stories above the fold than did the *Los Angeles Times* and *New York Times* (chi-square = 10.02; p = .02).

The story placement findings were reflected in the mean prominence scores, which differed by newspaper (F = 3.94; p = .01) (Table 5.4). Specifically, the *Chicago Tribune* and the *Los Angeles Times* differed from the *New York Times*; they gave the story more prominent coverage. The lower prominence given by the *New York Times* is consistent with this particular newspaper's reputation (lack of sensationalism) as well as design (quieter). The larger prominence given by the *Los Angeles Times* can be explained by proximity; it was a local story for this newspaper. Proximity may also explain results for length (number of words); the *Los Angeles Times* gave this story the largest coverage, differing from the *Atlanta Constitution* and the *New York Times* (F = 7.22; p = .00).

For byline, the *New York Times* used a much higher percentage of signed stories;[4] the other three newspapers had a higher percentage of staff-written stories (Table 5.4). The *Los Angeles Times* and *New York Times* had a much higher percentage of hard news stories, while the *Chicago Tribune* and *Atlanta Constitution* had a more even distribution across stories, opinion pieces, and features (chi-square = 59.82; p = .00). The smaller amount of overall coverage, fewer resources, and distance of the latter newspapers could all account for this difference, but their cities' larger African American populations probably were the most important reason.

Finally, the *Chicago Tribune* focused more on cause, consequence, and riot stories than any other newspaper (chi-square = 25.69; p = .04) (Table 5.4). The *Los Angeles Times* and *Atlanta Constitution* had more after-riot and law/government stories, and the *New York Times* had more reaction stories.

DISCUSSION

As would be expected, the "riot" story received the most attention in the *Los Angeles Times*. This paper had the largest number of stories, and these stories had high prominence and long length. Proximity has been shown to be an important variable in coverage. Shapiro and Williams (1984) found that proximal newspapers gave more information about a civil disturbance in Miami and tried to downplay violence. The *Los Angeles Times* also used more staff-written stories and more hard news (rather than editorial/feature material) and had the smallest percentage of cause stories.

The *New York Times* also gave the story substantial coverage. But the *New York Times* had less prominent coverage and short story length. Further, the *New York Times* was less heavily reliant on its own staff; it used signed stories more frequently. It also used hard news stories more and had the second largest percentage of cause stories.

Patterns in the *Chicago Tribune* and the *Atlanta Constitution* were mixed. The *Chicago Tribune* had few stories, but these were covered prominently. It used staff-written stories more but had an even distribution across content types in terms of hard news, opinion, and feature material. Its attention to cause stories was the largest in terms of percentage. The *Atlanta Constitution,* on the other hand, did not give the story much coverage or length. It used staff-written stories more but had a more even distribution of stories across hard, opinion, and feature materials. Finally, it did not cover cause stories much; given Atlanta's large African American population, this was surprising.

These differences in coverage by the newspapers, particularly the *Los Angeles Times* and the *New York Times*, may be attributed to geography and editorial policy. For the *Los Angeles Times*, the story was a local one, also probably contributing to larger, more prominent, and hard news-/event-oriented coverage mostly by its staff members. Its coverage of causes was small. The *New York Times*, in keeping with its reputation as an elite and serious "national" newspaper and being physically distant from the events, had a more evenhanded approach, giving the story some importance and focusing on hard news but having a more even distribution of stories by byline and focusing some attention on cause.

Fewer resources, geographical distance, and regional scope might also explain the smaller coverage of the story in the *Chicago Tribune* and the *Atlanta Constitution*. Distance might also be the reason for the less event-oriented, larger editorial/feature, and, in the case of the *Chicago Tribune*, cause-oriented coverage.

For the four newspapers together, it may be said that coverage was considerable. Although no comparative base was included in this study (for example, routine coverage of African Americans), it appears that the Los Angeles riot story did receive substantial attention at least in May. The Los Angeles riot story also seemed to have been prominently covered. At least a fourth of the time, the story was on the front page; two-thirds of the time, it was above the fold; and half the time, it was greater than one column length in size. Yet another indicator of the attention given to the story and the importance attached to it was the large use of staff stories (61%); only 2% of the stories were wire.

At the same time, attention given to the coverage of the cause of the riots was small, forming only 7% of the total stories; in fact, it was the smallest topic category. The largest percentage coverage of cause (in the *Chicago Tribune*) was only 16. On the other hand, actual riot, law enforcement, and after-riot stories dominated. This is also reflected in the large proportion of attention given to direct, hard news; features and editorials formed only a quarter of the stories.

Extensive coverage of less powerful groups when they engage in extremist behavior is a consistent media practice, as previously noted. Combined with the lack of routine coverage of these groups, this media practice tends to provide an unbalanced picture, which leaves the impression that the only activities or at least the large proportion of activities these groups partake in are of a violent, discordant nature. Further complicating the matter is the fact that protest coverage is often hard news, that is, event oriented. This has implications for blame assignment. A hard news format implies individual blame for events; by linking individuals to events, blame for events gets assigned to the individuals rather than to the system—that is, the society and its institutions at large. The individual's behavior is reported as a public safety threat, with a focus in coverage on law enforcement rather than on the behavior as a symptom of a problem (Johnson et al., 1971).

According to Nicholas Johnson (quoted in Gilbert, 1968): "A riot is a form of communication" (p. 13). Olien, Donohue, and Tichenor

(1984) add: "Social protest is not an aberration, but a time-honored part of the resolution of social problems in cases where the interests of various groups conflict with each other or with those of larger society" (p. 1). In other words, people participating in social protest are trying to send a message about and arrive at some solutions to their problems. For example, African Americans might regard protest activity as an effort to overcome invisibility by attracting attention to their legitimate grievances (over police relations, education, employment, housing, and so on). These problems, or causes for protest behavior, are generally societal or structural. A focus on them in news stories is more likely to imply system blame, that is, that the societal setup or system is responsible for the protests. In system blame, the social structure, framework, and historical factors, for example, "the degradation, misery, and hopelessness of living in the ghetto" (*Report of the National Advisory Commission on Civil Disorders,* 1968, p. 383), become the reason for the individual's behavior rather than some inherent flaw in the character of the individual. As noted, however, cause reportage, which would imply more system blame, was minuscule.

The implications of where the blame is assigned are twofold. First, solutions to a problem are based on the definition of that problem. If the problem itself is ill-defined, the solution cannot be useful. Second, and even more important, if the public is ill-informed, public policy cannot be just. A balance in reporting focus between event and cause, between individual and system blame, would generate long-term solutions that address root causes rather than manifest behaviors alone and would generate policy that is perceptive and fair.

For such changes to take place, however, a change is needed in the way news is made. Newspeople look for a news peg. They value immediacy. They have deadlines to meet. Event coverage satisfies these criteria. Issue coverage, on the other hand, is long term. It does not have neat beginnings and ends. Additionally, it raises uncomfortable questions about the personal values of news makers as well as about the established system of which news makers and their readers are a part. For the media not to heed the calls for change is irresponsible, given the important role they play in creating images and attitudes in people's minds and, in turn, policy.

NOTES

1. These increases have not, however, kept up with minority population increases (see Haws, 1991).

2. For the reliability test, coders counted number of lines. The researcher then used the established standards—number of words per line and per column for each newspaper—to do necessary calculations and check for agreement with the original coder on number of words and size, respectively. For nonstandard column widths, the researcher used the original coder's standard for number of words per line to make the calculations and check for agreement. A leeway of 50 words either way was allowed in calculating intercoder reliability for number of words. For story type, byline, and topic, the majority coding decision was used (except in the case of a tie) as the correct decision to check for agreement.

3. Most of these tests (exceptions are given below) were run using only May and June because April and July had very few stories and would present expected cell frequency problems in the chi-square analysis if included. For size and prominence of stories, all four months were included.

4. A call to the *New York Times* indicated that signed names without clear affiliations could refer to staff members. Hence, this particular difference could be artificial.

REFERENCES

Blanchard, E. D. (1968). The poor people and the "white press." *Columbia Journalism Review, 7*(3), 61-65.

Breen, M. A. (1968). Ten leading newspapers rated for coverage of 1967 Detroit riots. *Journalism Quarterly, 45,* 544-546.

Bridge, M. J. (1992). *The news, as if all people mattered.* Rosslyn, VA: Freedom Forum.

Carter, R. E., Jr. (1957). Segregation and the news: A regional content study. *Journalism Quarterly, 34,* 3-18.

Chaudhary, A. G. (1980). Press portrayal of black officials. *Journalism Quarterly, 57,* 636-646.

Chicago Commission on Race Relations. (1922). *The Negro in Chicago: A study of race relations and a race riot.* Chicago: University of Chicago Press.

Colle, R. D. (1968). Negro image in the mass media: A case study in social change. *Journalism Quarterly, 45,* 55-60.

Editor & Publisher international yearbook. (1993). New York: Editor and Publisher.

Gandy, O. H., Jr. (1994). Race: America's rawest nerve. *Media Studies Journal, 8*(3), 39-48.

Gilbert, B. W. (1968). Race coverage. *Bulletin of the American Society of Newspaper Editors, 515*(1-2), 13.

Gist, N. P. (1932). The Negro in the daily press. *Social Forces, 10,* 405-411.

Hartmann, P., & Husband, C. (1974). *Racism and the mass media.* Totowa, NJ: Rowman & Littlefield.

Haws, D. (1991). Minorities in the newsroom and community: A comparison. *Journalism Quarterly, 68,* 764-771.

Holsti, O. R. (1969). *Content analysis for the social sciences and humanities.* Reading, MA: Addison-Wesley.

Johnson, P. B., Sears, D. P., & McConahay, J. B. (1971). Black invisibility, the press, and the Los Angeles riot. *American Journal of Sociology, 76,* 698-721.

Klein, W. (1968). News media and race relations: A self-portrait. *Columbia Journalism Review, 7*(3), 42-49.

Lambert, V. (1965). Negro exposure in *Look*'s editorial content. *Journalism Quarterly, 42,* 657-659.

Lester, P., & Smith, R. (1990). African-American photo coverage in *Life, Newsweek* and *Time,* 1937-1988. *Journalism Quarterly, 67,* 128-136.

Lyle, J. (Ed.). (1968). *The black American and the press.* Los Angeles: Ward Ritchie Press.

Martindale, C. (1985). Coverage of black Americans in five newspapers since 1950. *Journalism Quarterly, 62,* 321-328.

Martindale, C. (1989). Selected newspaper coverage of causes of black protest. *Journalism Quarterly, 66,* 920-923, 964.

Midura, E. M. (Ed.). (1971). *Why aren't we getting through? The urban communication crisis.* Washington, DC: Acropolis.

Olien, C. N., Donohue, G. A., & Tichenor, P. T. (1984). Media and stage of social conflict. *Journalism Monographs, 99,* 1-31.

Paletz, D. L., & Dunn, R. (1969). Press coverage of civil disorders: A case study of Winston-Salem, 1967. *Public Opinion Quarterly, 33,* 328-345.

Report of the National Advisory Commission on Civil Disorders. (1968). New York: Bantam.

Roberts, C. (1975). The presentation of blacks in television network newscasts. *Journalism Quarterly, 52,* 50-55.

Rosenberg, H. (1992, May 6). It's time for more heart, less heat on TV. *Los Angeles Times,* p. F12.

Rosenthal, M. M. (1978). Riot news: The press, the spread of opinion, and demographic self-interest. *Communication Research, 5,* 177-201.

Rudwick, E. M. (1964). *Race riot at East St. Louis, July 2, 1917.* Carbondale: Southern Illinois University Press.

Sentman, M. A. (1983). Black and white: Disparity in coverage by *Life* magazine from 1937 to 1972. *Journalism Quarterly, 60,* 501-508.

Shapiro, M., & Williams, W., Jr. (1984). Civil disturbance in Miami: Proximity and conflict in newspaper coverage. *Newspaper Research Journal, 5*(3), 61-69.

Shoemaker, P. J., & Reese, S. D. (1991). *Mediating the message: Theories of influence on mass media content.* White Plains, NY: Longman.

Slater, C. M., & Hall, G. E. (1993). *Places, towns and townships.* Lanham, MD: Bernan.

Stempel, G. G., III. (1971). Visibility of blacks in news and news-picture magazines. *Journalism Quarterly, 48,* 337-339.

6

Entering the Twenty-First Century

Oppression and the African American Press

REGINALD OWENS

"Iabt's a miracle." That's how George McElroy, editor of the *Informer and Texas Freeman* in Houston, Texas, explained why the African American press survives despite what he calls inadequate community and local business support. "Back in the 40s and 50s, there was only one voice," said McElroy, who has been affiliated with the *Informer* for about 50 years. He explained, "It was the black newspaper. Back then, black businesses and black newspapers were thriving. After integration, when we made the so-called move, many middle and upper-middle class blacks moved out of the neighborhood."

McElroy remembers the time when the city's daily newspapers would only publish negative news about African Americans. Even though things have improved considerably, McElroy thinks the coverage of African Americans by the dailies is still inadequate.

Although the African American press does not get the level of support it received in its heyday of the segregation years, it still serves several important purposes for the African American community. One function is as a forum for issues important to African American leaders. "These ministers and politicians have access to the black press that does not exist in the major papers," said McElroy, who is also a retired professor of journalism.

It has been the African American press that has taken the lead on issues of particular concern to the community, he notes. African American newspapers in Houston are regularly the catalyst that awakens mainstream media and local politicians to critical issues in the community. "We're closer to problems and concerns in our community. We see it first," he explained.

The plight of African Americans ensures the survival of the *Informer*, which has been in business since 1893. McElroy said that as long as African Americans perceive they don't get fair coverage in the mainstream media or equal treatment in society, there will always be a need for black community newspapers like the *Informer.*

The *Informer*, and the social context in which it was born and exists, represents a microcosm of the conditions of the African American newspaper. It thrives and it struggles—all at the same time. The contradictions of American life for people of African descent is what keeps it alive. These same problems are what keeps it in constant turmoil with itself and its social environment. The African American newspaper is a signal symptom of oppression—the epitome of being a part of the system and being apart from the system.

This chapter examines the communication consequences of oppression and the concurrent development of the African American press. How do people react from a communication standpoint when faced with oppression? The argument starts with the premise that the African American newspaper grew out of a hostile social, political, and economic environment. The use of print media is just one communication response to the African American predicament in the United States. The current inquiry demands that a study of the African American press include an analysis of the press as a cultural product of—or response to—subordinate status within a dominant society.

Studies have failed to see the social, political, and economic impact of African American newspapers that goes beyond circulation statistics. More specifically, newspapers in this analysis are weapons of the African American elite in the war of cultural symbols and politics. In this context, African American publications take on greater importance in the African American and ultimately the larger U.S. social structure.

As such, they are not viewed in the narrow confines of commercial market success—namely, circulation.

SOCIAL ENVIRONMENT FOR DEVELOPMENT

Freedom's Journal, the first African American newspaper, was founded March 16, 1827, in New York City. This period in New York—the 1800s—were contentious times for African Americans. People of African descent were subjected to such indignities as brutal human captivity for millions in the southern United States and second-class treatment for the several hundred thousand free persons. Slavery, as a new economic force in the nation, had taken on industrial proportions as the rules of captivity on southern plantations became abusive. The result: African populations of the North, West, and Canada began to swell as captives escaped from southern bondage (Johnson, 1930; Woodson, 1916).

And the debate raged on about human captivity as abolitionists argued vehemently against it. Slavocracy advocates strengthened their moral arguments and enacted legislation to support continued captivity of Africans. These discussions created ideological divisions both within and outside of the African American social structure (Fortenberry, 1974; Kinshasa, 1988; Owens, 1993a).

This scene, with debates about human captivity, persecution of African Americans, and intense ideological disputes, set the stage for the founding of *Freedom's Journal.* Specifically, the refusal of a European American editor to print a letter rebutting negative articles about people of color in New York City prompted African American leaders to initiate the newspaper. Behind this immediate reason was another— the need for a voice for African Americans (Penn, 1891).

Prominent African Americans seized upon this newspaper incident as an opportunity to create a vehicle to publicly argue their point of view. *Freedom's Journal* became one of their means of placing items on the nation's civic agenda and creating for the first time a vehicle for developing a national African consciousness (Gross, 1932). Other issues on the minds of free African Americans to be addressed in a newspaper were African American colonization, improvement of the group's social, economic, and political status, and development of a unified consciousness (Tripp, 1992).

Freedom's Journal helped to pave the way for sympathetic European Americans such as William Lloyd Garrison, who was considered by many to be one of the most militant abolitionists of the time. It was not, however, until 1831, three years after publication of *Freedom's Journal*, and Garrison published the *Liberator* that a European American advocated immediate unconditional abolition of slavery—an idea long supported by free Africans (Finkle, 1975; Reid, 1988).

The first African American newspaper was born during a period of tremendous economic and social change. The nation was experiencing its first depression (since the Panic of 1819) while the growth of the textile industry in New England and England created unprecedented demand for cotton—elevating the economic importance of the system of southern agriculture (Harris, 1960).

From this social context, four concepts emerge to form the theoretical basis for a study of the African American press—social structure, oppression, group ideological diversity, and newspaper activity—in terms of formation and circulation. The thesis here is that African American newspapers experience the greatest activity during times of economic, social, and political uncertainty. During these periods, African American people face increased hostility as well as social and economic deprivation—defined in this study as oppression.

Several scholars have noted the inadequacies of European American-controlled media coverage of African Americans (Martindale, 1985, 1986) and the subsequent distorted images that result from that coverage (Dates & Barlow, 1990; Johnson, 1991; Omi, 1989). Johnson (1991) presents a careful argument that a pattern of bias exists in mainstream media coverage of African Americans. He notes:

> Indeed, some analysts warn that the power that once toppled a president works the equivalent on the black community, thwarting black social advancement by conveying the illusion of impartial reporting while applying vastly different standards to news coverage of whites and blacks. (p. 328)

The conditions that created African Americans' spirit of resistance also inspired the development of dual social systems even in the days of early African captivity (Blassingame, 1972). Wilson (1991) notes the parallel between how people of African descent communicated on the African continent and in their new environment. In the early history of the African American press, free Africans founded newspapers that fought for freedom, while those in captivity developed other communication systems (i.e., songs, chants, nonverbal signs, and so on) to maintain group unity.

Africans living in European-dominated societies both in captive and in colonial contexts have developed at least two ways of thinking about the world (DuBois, 1903; Fanon, 1968). One is shaped by experiences based on African descent in what historically has been a hostile social, political, and economic environment. Another existence is that of being African and living (functioning) in the more personal, primary circle of family and friends. This concept is applied to both U.S. and international examples. The dual reality of African American existence has produced a separate social structure that caters to the specific needs of the group, as a distinct group.

There are a number of previous definitions of oppression that are important for this discussion. African American oppression has been described in simple terms as "slavery unwilling to die" (Feagin, 1986, p. 173). Turner (1984) discusses oppression as a specific systematic action, but Baldwin (1980) focuses on psychological oppression—the battle for the spirit of a people and the natural inclination to resist. Dictionary definitions assert that *oppression* is the state of being overburdened, miserable, depressed, and feeling weighed down with physical or mental distress. These definitions, according to Dick (1979), imply two parts: a subjective element (to feel) and an objective element (to be). This is a valuable dichotomy for the current study, because Dick's scheme brings together two important ideas—the "to be" concept, which refers to the physical environment, and the "to feel" idea, which corresponds to the communication aspect.

Of the four social structural conditions suggested by Goldenberg (1978) that must be present before oppression can occur—containment (segregation), expendability, compartmentalization, and mind control through ideology—the final condition is most important to this discussion. Ideology defines a group's consciousness, hence its communication and other responses. Finally, Bay's (1981) broad definition also includes a useful concept for this discussion—emancipation, which he defined as all those processes aimed at reducing oppression and expanding freedom for the group. The emancipation concept underscores a major point in this study—people's natural desire to actively seek freedom from social and economic encumbrances. Bay noted that emancipation was achieved with knowledge through group-controlled communication systems and vehicles—in this discussion, newspapers.

Bay's concept of ideology, for reasons of oppression, raises the notion of an ideology of freedom. This is a reasonable assumption given that most definitions of oppression have a component that promotes group consciousness—an ideology that attempts to explain the group's existence and quest for freedom. As suggested in the last section, on each side of the oppression/emancipation dyad, a consciousness develops. This consciousness requires the creation not only of physical methods of consciousness development but also of broad philosophical frameworks from which to create content.

If there exists an ideology of oppression for the oppressor or a rationalization for their behavior, then an opposite consciousness exists for the oppressed—an ideology of freedom. Oppression, then, affects the character, content, type, and intensity of communication and often is the indirect impetus behind the establishment of African American newspapers (Owens, 1991).

One underlying assumption about the African American social condition has been the existence of a spirit of resistance—that enduring quality of the African American psyche developed during captivity and nurtured through years of oppression. With that backdrop, current research has been about that spirit of resistance and the development of the newspaper in a communication system designed to counter oppression.

A systems approach using qualitative and quantitative analyses gives us two valuable ways of explaining the character of the African American press. One method of observation can be used to confirm and explain the other. The systems approach gives the potential for a richer analysis of the social components, but a method that can handle this sociological complexity is needed. This systems view is necessary for two reasons. First, a long time period is needed to examine trends. Time can verify, for instance, that some social phenomena believed to be significant at one point may turn out to be sociological flukes when observed over time. Second, in this study, there are nine concrete variables that can be observed over a period of time. These quantitative data provide a systematic history of selected oppression indicators for newspaper formation/circulation.

The cornerstone of this chapter is a quantitative analysis of 91 years of circulation and formation figures for African American publications in the United States from 1900 to 1990. This analysis examined the impact of oppression indicators on circulation and formation during specified periods of time. In addition, African American newspaper circulation and formation were examined within the context of the prevailing social conditions.

Indicators for oppression of African Americans used in the study were lynchings (1900-1970), executions (1930-1968), murder executions (1930-1968), rape executions (1930-1970), infant mortality (1915-1968), maternal mortality (1915-1988), and male deaths (1900-1968). Unemployment figures for all groups in the nation also are used as an indicator of oppression.

The years for analysis were chosen based on the availability of consistently published U.S. census data for indicators of oppression. The U.S. government did not start compiling execution data until 1930. Infant and maternal mortality data were not published until 1915. Population figures for 1900 to 1990 are from census figures for census years and census estimates for intervening years.

Ownership and circulation figures for African American newspapers were taken from successive volumes of *N. W. Ayer National Directory of Newspapers* and *Gale's National Directory of Publications*. For each year, the publications list circulation as well as the total number of most African American newspapers listed in that directory. There is no complete and consistent directory with circulation and formation information for African American publications. Ayer's and Gale's directories provide the most consistent data on these publications. Magazines are listed in the figures here, including from two to five African Canadian publications in any given year.

THE ACTIVITY DECADES

An examination of circulation and formation trends reveals that the greatest number and magnitude of changes in newspaper activity occurred in circulation. The 1920s, 1940s, 1950s, and 1970s show the most dramatic changes in terms of both increases and decreases. (See Table 6.1.) The four periods are selected because they represent years of tremendous social and political change as well as activity for African Americans and African American newspapers.

TABLE 6.1 African American Newspaper Activity Changes: 1900 to 1990

Year	*Newspaper Rates	*Circulation Rates	Newspaper % Increase	Circulation % Increase
1900	.02	20.09		
1901	.03	22.63	7.66	8.80
1902	.03	22.91	2.22	3.31
1903	.03	26.44	21.30	17.51
1904	.03	26.99	−2.15	4.01
1905	.03	29.48	−1.83	11.41
1906	.03	29.58	9.93	2.30
1907	.03	29.16	−4.78	.37
1908	.03	30.95	.36	8.23
1909	.03	28.06	4.64	−7.53
1910	.03	26.10	4.78	−8.18
1911	.04	27.67	8.47	1.28
1912	.03	35.33	−5.41	29.66
1913	.03	30.21	−12.70	−12.77
1914	.03	31.85	−4.00	7.48
1915	.03	31.51	−3.79	.34
1916	.02	34.84	−6.69	12.13
1917	.02	36.84	1.27	7.09
1918	.02	38.76	−5.83	5.15
1919	.02	40.15	−5.75	4.90
1920	.02	31.38	1.41	−20.37
1921	.02	48.68	.95	58.04
1922	.02	56.78	.47	18.36
1923	.02	64.48	.94	15.51
1924	.02	62.22	−3.72	−1.64
1925	.02	56.02	−.97	6.07
1926	.02	76.70	−10.24	19.57
1927	.02	57.57	−1.63	−23.90
1928	.01	58.87	−3.31	3.52
1929	.01	85.93	.00	47.49
1930	.01	66.03	−10.29	−24.96
1931	.01	53.17	.00	−15.99
1932	.01	55.96	−22.29	5.91
1933	.01	55.98	9.02	.63
1934	.01	54.27	3.76	−2.44
1935	.01	50.56	−3.62	−6.19
1936	.01	46.92	4.51	−6.60
1937	.01	60.20	−7.19	30.18
1938	.01	64.41	6.98	6.91
1939	.01	59.76	−7.97	−6.46
1940	.01	68.38	22.83	12.47
1941	.01	75.03	.64	13.48
1942	.01	79.08	4.46	5.96
1943	.01	79.35	−6.10	.50
1944	.01	96.67	1.95	20.60

(continued)

TABLE 6.1   African American Newspaper Activity Changes: 1900 to 1990

Year	*Newspaper Rates	*Circulation Rates	Newspaper % Increase	Circulation % Increase
1945	.01	115.82	−.64	19.37
1946	.01	217.55	6.41	98.87
1947	.01	153.76	27.71	−27.56
1948	.02	186.96	9.91	23.86
1949	.02	187.44	−.43	1.98
1950	.02	208.75	−1.72	12.79
1951	.01	152.06	−3.07	−21.37
1952	.01	170.56	.98	14.75
1953	.01	158.24	−179	−5.06
1954	.01	153.83	5.48	−.39
1955	.01	172.69	−7.36	14.11
1956	.01	122.21	−11.21	−27.42
1957	.01	90.40	11.58	−24.06
1958	.01	161.30	−.47	82.92
1959	.01	147.83	−5.21	−5.83
1960	.01	137.22	−5.50	−6.83
1961	.01	135.14	−15.87	−2.12
1962	.01	138.35	3.14	2.95
1963	.01	132.15	−3.05	−3.95
1964	.01	137.59	2.52	8.75
1965	.01	149.07	−4.29	8.35
1966	.01	137.28	−.64	−5.08
1967	.01	166.42	−6.45	23.20
1968	.01	169.61	4.14	3.50
1969	.01	165.17	−.66	−1.00
1970	.01	205.28	5.33	24.79
1971	.01	173.87	3.16	−13.76
1972	.01	191.37	−20.86	11.68
1973	.01	461.71	26.36	144.67
1974	.01	485.75	.00	6.61
1975	.01	506.30	.00	5.63
1976	.01	529.06	1.84	5.92
1977	.01	345.11	−1.81	−33.84
1978	.01	283.34	.00	−16.77
1979	.01	275.29	−17.79	−2.13
1980	.01	340.02	5.22	27.53
1981	.01	327.27	8.51	−1.33
1982	.01	319.23	−7.19	−.89
1983	.01	215.18	5.63	−31.68
1984	.01	235.24	.00	11.09
1985	.01	224.36	4.00	−3.08
1986	.01	316.03	−3.85	−.78
1987	.00	215.66	−6.67	.00
1988	.00	207.72	−2.14	−2.16
1989	.01	231.27	18.25	13.06
1990	.01	345.53	53.70	51.69

*Per 100,000 African Americans.

THE 1920s

The era of the 1920s has been dubbed the "Negro Renaissance" or the "Harlem Renaissance." It was a period of intellectual and artistic development for African Americans—a time that saw the creation of books, poems, songs, and other creative and political literary works. This period of African American literary creativity has no other parallel in contemporary history. The intellectual development and conflict of social consciousness produced debates that found eager forums in the African American press (Franklin, 1979).

THE 1940s

The 1940s were war years for the United States. The nation was in the throes of World War II, and issues of African American liberation from an aparthiedlike existence—in both the military and society in general—were widely discussed. African American editors challenged the existence of segregation in the armed forces and even pressured the government to desegregate the services (Finkle, 1975; Washburn, 1986). Despite the question of contradictions raised by some of those fighting for rights overseas that many could not enjoy at home, African Americans were eager to read news of their sons and daughters in the African American press (Stevens, 1973).

In this decade, the nation was experiencing welcome economic prosperity because of the war industries. News about African Americans in these industries and in battle overseas was in demand. Many advertisers recognized the spending power of African Americans and began to appeal to this emerging consumer group. This prompted the development of publications such as *Ebony* magazine, which actively sought advertising revenues from national companies (Brooks, 1959; Giles, 1954).

THE 1950s

The decade of the civil rights movement, ironically, was not one of great growth for the African American newspaper in terms of circulation or formation. (See Table 6.1.) Although circulation made a tremendous percentage increase toward the end of the decade in 1958, overall circulation was down for seven of the years in the decade. The traditional African American press was roundly criticized during this period for its lackluster coverage of the more militant activist movements as the 1960s were beginning (Gilliam, 1972; O'Kelly, 1978, 1982; Palmer, 1970; Thompson, 1993). The decline in readership lasted into the late 1960s.

Another factor that contributed to the decline of importance of African American newspapers to their traditional audience was the advent of a more "integrated" society and an emerging broadcast media—television and radio. African Americans, for a variety of reasons, were depending less and less on their traditional friend—the African American newspaper.

THE 1970s

The decade of the 1970s deserves special note because it had the highest circulation figures per 100,000 population of any decade. (See Table 6.1.) The African American press experienced both the largest single-year increase in circulation in 1973 and the largest single-year circulation decline in 1977. Additionally, the 26% increase in the number of newspapers in 1973 was the second highest single-year increase. This decade was on the heels of the 1960s cultural revolution among African Americans. The desktop publishing/computer revolution in the printing industry also occurred during this period. Finally, a new attitude in corporate America created a favorable climate for advertising in such new national African American magazines as *Essence, Black Enterprise, Black Collegian,* and other publications.

VISUAL TREND ANALYSIS

Some of the most valuable information in this study came from a visual trend analysis of newspaper circulation and formation over the 91-year study period. Visual trend analysis shows in graphic detail the highs and lows of newspaper activity during the study's time period. For the current study, this graphic map was juxtaposed against a backdrop of African American social conditions and important events in the history of African Americans.

TABLE 6.2 African American Newspaper Formation, Circulation, and Indicators of Oppression

| | *Pearson Correlation Coefficients* | |
	Formation	*Circulation*
Formation	1.00	
Circulation	−.65	1.00
Lynchings	.87	−.73
Executions	.78	−.64
Murder executions	.53	−.53
Rape executions	.60	−.11
Infant mortality	.89	−.70
Maternal mortality	.77	−.71
Male death rate	.91	−.73

NOTE: All coefficients reported are significant. Newspaper formation and circulation coefficients reported here represent correlations of figures expressed in numbers per 1,000 African American population.
$p < .001$.

The next level of analysis—simple correlations—sought to discover a systematic understanding of the relationship between indicators of oppression and newspaper data. Correlations are reported that compare relationships between the number of newspapers and circulation with the seven indicators of African American oppression—lynchings, executions, murder executions, rape executions, infant mortality, maternal mortality, and male deaths.

To standardize the data for more reliable analysis, raw newspaper circulation and formation figures were converted to rates per 100,000 African Americans. All government oppression variables, except lynchings, were reported as rates *per 1,000* African Americans. In addition, a percentage of increase of these rates and a percentage of increase of the oppression indicators were calculated.

The strongest relationships were between the number of African American newspapers and the indices of oppression. (See Table 6.2.) All of these relationships were positive and significant. According to this data, high levels of oppression are correlated positively with high numbers of newspapers.

African American male deaths had the strongest association with the number of newspapers, with a correlation coefficient of .91. The second strongest variable was infant mortality, with a correlation coefficient of

.89. Lynching was third, with a correlation coefficient of .87. The other variables in descending order of strength were executions (.78), maternal mortality (.77), rape executions (.60), and murder executions (.53).

Circulation, on the other hand, correlated negatively with the indicators of oppression. The number of newspapers and circulation, as noted in Table 6.2, show up negatively correlated with a Pearson correlation coefficient of −.64. When these raw formation and circulation figures are differenced, however, they show a positive relationship with a significant correlation of .29. Therefore, an increase in the number of newspapers, according to the differenced data, is associated with an increase in circulation. Also, circulation generally continues to show a negative relationship with most oppression variables.

The ultimate research goal has always been to suggest some degree of cause and effect with large aggregates of data representing a specified system. The current data set attempts to construct such a system. Although simple correlations have suggested a causal link between indicators of oppression and African American newspaper activity, more sophisticated multivariate procedures were applied to further support conclusions of the correlations. Additional Box-Jenkins time-series transfer analyses show that changes in one side are accompanied by a change in the other—even after controlling for other factors (Owens, 1993b). Extensive discussion of this point, however, is beyond the scope of this chapter. Both procedures confirm the initial premise in this study that indicators of oppression have a significant impact on African American newspaper activity.

Further use of Box-Jenkins times-series analysis allowed the researcher to identify key years in the 91-year data set. Therefore, time-series intervention analyses were completed, taking into account potential problems with autocorrelation and nonstationarity. Intervention analysis takes a set of time data and determines significant years in the series of data. The intervention analysis compared the block of time before a designated year with the time period after that point to see if there is a statistically significant change in magnitude of circulation or newspaper formation before or after. This procedure is useful in augmenting qualitative analyses.

The procedure provides two types of interventions for analysis—step and pulse. Step intervention indicates the beginning of a sustained gradual change in newspaper circulation or formation that lasts for several years. The step intervention is considered important because it predicts the general direction of circulation or formation over the period. A pulse intervention indicates a one-time change that applies only to that year and assumes no predictive power. Its greatest power lies in its analytical potential.

For newspaper circulation, there were four pulse intervention years—1920, 1929, 1946, and 1957—and one step intervention year in 1973. African American newspaper circulation reached the 1 million mark in the pulse intervention year of 1929—the year of the stock market crash that preceded the decade of the Great Depression. This 1929 pulse intervention introduced a decade with mainly decreases in circulation. The 1946 pulse intervention occurred during the decade of the founding of several mass circulation magazines including *Ebony*, which pioneered mass marketing to the African American consumer.

The 1957 pulse intervention happened during a period of decline in circulation for African American newspapers. This period represented the height of the civil rights movement when African Americans were seeking news about the social movements of the day that European American newspapers were reluctant to report on with any depth.

The year of 1973 was a step intervention year—the beginning of a period of gradual and constant growth in African American circulation. There was a 144% increase in African American publication circulation in 1973 over 1972—the largest to date. This intervention occurred in the decade that saw several mass circulation magazines aimed at the African American consumer begin publication.

The intervention analysis identified four significant step intervention years for newspaper formation—1903, 1932, 1947, and 1990. The lone pulse intervention year for formation was 1972.

The decade of the first step intervention year of 1903 was basically one of growth for African American publications because there were only three years of negative growth in this period. This was a decade that witnessed an increase in lynchings of African Americans, great migrations to the urban centers of the United States, the widespread enactment of Jim Crow laws in the South, the growth of African American businesses, and the establishment of self-help and political activist institutions such as the NAACP in 1909 (Lemann, 1991; Stroman, 1981; Woodward, 1974).

The decade of the 1930s saw a decline in the number of both mainstream and African American newspapers nationwide; therefore,

TABLE 6.3 African American Newspaper Activity 1980 to 1995

Year	Circulation	Number of Newspapers
1980	9,006,382	141
1981	8,886,245	153
1982	8,807,258	142
1983	6,601,684	150
1984	6,684,429	150
1985	6,478,533	156
1986	6,427,978	150
1987	6,428,295	140
1988	6,289,634	137
1989	7,111,189	162
1990	10,786,752	249
1991	11,519,369	281
1992	12,357,926	278
1993	13,273,207	275
1994	13,283,613	284
1995	12,993,490	278

a step intervention in 1932 served as an omen for the decade of formation decline to come (Emery & Emery, 1978).

In 1947, a step intervention was identified for newspaper formation. This was a period of growth for African American newspapers in both formation and circulation. The final step intervention year for newspaper formation was 1990. The number of African American newspapers increased by 53% over the previous year—from 162 in 1989 to 249 in 1990.

THE TWENTY-FIRST CENTURY

As we enter the twenty-first century, there has been sustained growth in African American newspaper circulation and formation in the decade of the 1990s—a contrast to the 1980s, which showed a decline in both numbers and circulation. This could have been projected because this study has shown that increases often occur during times of oppression and in hostile social, political, and economic environments.

In the 1980s, there was talk about the demise of African American newspapers—and rightly so, for those looking only at short-term newspaper activity or single-year numbers. One cannot, however, make viable conclusions about African American newspapers by examining only short-term newspaper activity. Adequate analysis demands long-term, multivariate treatment, as demonstrated in this study. Our long-term multivariate approach has shown that African American publications have had their ups and downs—but also claim many ups against tremendous odds.

African American publications are persisting into the twentieth century. The social conditions of the 1980s without doubt have set the stage for this contemporary growth of the African American press both in circulation and in formation. During the 1980s, African Americans experienced what Shull (1993) calls "A Kinder, Gentler Racism." The Reagan-Bush civil rights agenda was very conservative in administrative and judicial actions, ending the trend toward greater government assistance and enforcement. Significant conservative nominations to the Supreme Court, Civil Rights Commission, and other agencies ultimately weakened earlier affirmative action policies. At the same time, there has been a continuous eroding of efforts toward equality in such areas as education, civil rights, employment, and criminal justice, which has led to a widening of economic and racial divisions in America. The 53% increase (see Table 6.1) in the number of African American publications in the last two years of the 1980s decade was certainly a prelude to the growth of the 1990s.

With this evidence, the prediction here is continued stability for the African American press into the twentieth century. The history of African Americans and their publications shows a strong relationship between social environment and newspaper activity. Periods of increased social and economic instability for the group are followed by a period of increased activity for the press. We are in such an era as the twenty-first century approaches.

The conservative trends of the 1990s have been compared with those of a similar period in the nation's history when there was an intense European American backlash against African American social and political gains of the Reconstruction Era of the last century following the Emancipation Proclamation. The 1895 *Plessy v. Ferguson* U.S. Supreme Court decision established the legal boundaries of racial segregation. The 1990s conservative movement—100 years later—with attacks on affirmative action and civil rights can be viewed in a similar manner. Conservative politics of the 1990s has spawned the growth of ideological diversity, both within and outside of the African American social structure.

The 30 years following *Plessy v. Ferguson* witnessed the unprecedented development of African American institutions (especially newspapers). A similar result is predicted with the current conservative movement, which has already ushered in the beginnings of a changing of the guard in the African American social structure. This means more competing ideologies—hence, more media outlets. Table 6.2 notes the growth in the number of publications during the decades of the 1980s and 1990s. This growth pattern in African American publications has been typified in other eras when there has been an influx of divergent ideologies.

In addition, findings from social indices that measure quality of life in the African American social structure have become problematic in the past decade—unemployment, crime, prison population, black male deaths, teenage pregnancy, and so on. As this study has shown, increases in these types of social measures (read: indicators of oppression) foretell increases in African American newspaper activity.

The communication issue, though, encompasses more than print publications; the issue is one of communicating under oppressive conditions. As the technology changes, so do the communication vehicles. This points to an increase in the use of other media vehicles including broadcast, cable, and computer/cyberspace.

As long as differential benefits of society can be discerned between various groups—whether because of race, culture, geographic origin, or whatever—there will be a need for separate social structures—hence, separate institutions including media vehicles. This chapter has established a relationship between indicators of oppression and African American newspaper circulation and formation. When African Americans were faced with economic, social, and political hard times, they turned inward and developed institutions to assist in achieving parity with other groups.

Two major factors have emerged that have an impact on whether African American media will continue to survive. The first comprises differential African American social conditions and the concurrent realization by African Americans of needs deemed to be unique to the group. Some African Americans believe that they "have arrived" in society and don't see the need for African American institutions such as newspapers. This conflict has been at the base of many internal ideological disputes and has provided the impetus for the development of new group media (La Brie & Zima, 1971; Putthammer & Worthy, 1958; Rudwick, 1958; Thornbrough, 1958). Second, increased marketing and editorial sophistication on the part of African American publishers is also necessary as media competition, in general, intensifies. This becomes even more critical when mainstream media renew their efforts to appeal specifically to African American market segments and advertisers realize the potential of African American dollars.

One of the paradoxes of this study has been the inverse relationship of African American publication circulation and formation. On all measures studied, circulation and formation have reacted in opposite ways through the years. Increases and decreases of both tend to come during periods of economic and/or social crisis for the nation. These periods are also characterized by internal conflict within the African American community, where emerging and conflicting ideologies develop. When this happens, leaders with divergent ideological stands form institutions and media outlets (especially newspapers) to promote their ideas.

This chapter shows that ideological differences are often fueled by uncontrollable social, political, and economic factors both within and outside of the African American social structure. The newspaper is a tool of African American leaders to inspire, inform, and create a sense of unity among people of African descent. The newspaper serves as a means of creating support and consensus both within and outside of the African American social structure. Where there were differences within the African American group, the newspaper was a tool of influence both for group members and for nonmembers. Evidence suggests that where there were major differences within the group, each faction had a publication to trumpet their views.

Time-series and other analyses show that circulation has generally been increasing. There have been more years of percentage increases of circulation than not, and the per 100,000 African American population rate of circulation has been steady. Although mainstream and other newspapers have been on the decline, the African American press has maintained a steady circulation base. Given the history of how African American newspapers have been distributed, circulation may not be the best measure of their effectiveness. In other words, the same assumptions that underlie the operation of mainstream newspapers may not be appropriate when analyzing the African American newspaper.

For the thousands of reporters and editors at African American publications and the millions of readers who depend on them, talk that the African American press is dying can be disturbing. To these legions of loyal supporters, the African American press is alive and real. It is not some abstract entity listed in the back of a newspaper directory or a footnote in a text about the "minority" mass media. For the thousands who work at the publications, it is a cause; they see their work as part of a struggle for a people. To the faithful readers, the African American press is a source of news that cannot be found anywhere else—a point of view that only the African American-owned media will publish. The dispossessed seek out a publication to fight unpopular battles and as a forum that no other media will allow. Many politicians look to such publications to get the pulse of an important segment of the African American community. Corporate advertisers spend millions to market their goods to an influential segment of the $350-plus billion African American consumer market.

This vitality flies in the face of suggestions that the African American press is ineffectual and dying as we move into the twenty-first century. These contradictions are what sparked the initial interest in the study of the African American press. The net results of this study reveal that the African American press is an active participant in its social environment. The questions posed in this inquiry, I hope, create a better understanding as to why, after more than 168 years, the African American press is still surviving when other remnants of a legally segregated society are long gone.

REFERENCES

Baldwin, J. A. (1980). The psychology of oppression. In M. Asante & A. S. Vandi (Eds.), *Contemporary black thought: Alternative analyses in social and behavioral science* (pp. 95-110). Beverly Hills, CA: Sage.

Bay, C. (1981). *Strategies of political emancipation.* Notre Dame: University of Notre Dame Press.

Blassingame, J. W. (1972). *The slave community: Plantation life in the antebellum South.* New York: Oxford University Press.

Brooks, M. R. (1959). *The Negro press re-examined.* Boston: Christopher.

Dates, J., & Barlow, W. (1990). *Split images: African-Americans in the mass media*. Washington, DC: Howard University Press.

Dick, J. C. (1979). *Violence and oppression*. Athens: University of Georgia Press.

DuBois, W. E. B. (1903). *Souls of black folk*. New York: Dodd, Mead.

Emery, E., & Emery, M. (1978). *The press and America: An interpretative history of the mass media*. Englewood Cliffs, NJ: Prentice Hall.

Fanon, F. (1968). *White masks, black faces* (C. Lam Markmann, Trans.). New York: Grove.

Feagin, J. (1986, December). Slavery unwilling to die: The background of black oppression in the 1980s. *Journal of Black Studies, 17*(2), 173-200.

Finkle, L. (1975). *Forum for protest: The black press during World War II*. Cranbury, NJ: Associated University Presses.

Fortenberry, L. (1974). Freedom's Journal: The first black medium. *Black Scholar, 7*(3), 32-37.

Franklin, J. H. (1979). *From slavery to freedom: A history of Negro Americans*. New York: Knopf.

Giles, R. C. (1954). *A study of editorial contents and policies of six Negro magazines*. Unpublished master of journalism thesis, University of Texas at Austin.

Gilliam, D. (1972). What do black journalists want? *Columbia Journalism Review, 11*, 41-52.

Goldenberg, I. (1978). *Oppression and social intervention essays on the human condition and the problems of change*. Chicago: Nelson-Hall.

Gross, B. (1932). *Freedom's Journal* and the rights of all. *Journal of Negro History, 17*(3), 245.

Harris, S. E. (1960). *American economic history*. New York: McGraw-Hill.

Johnson, C. S. (1930). *The Negro in American civilization: A study of Negro life and race relations in light of social research*. New York: Holt.

Johnson, K. (1991). Objective news and other myths: The poisoning of young black minds. *Journal of Negro Education, 60*, 328-321.

Kinshasa, K. M. (1988). *Emigration vs. assimilation: The debate in the African-American press, 1827-1861*. Jefferson, NC: McFarland.

La Brie, H. G., & Zima, W. J. (1971). Directional quandaries of the black press in the United States. *Journalism Quarterly, 48*, 640-644.

Lemann, N. (1991). *The promised land: The great black migration and how it changed America*. New York: Knopf.

Martindale, C. (1985). Coverage of black Americans in five newspapers since 1950. *Journalism Quarterly, 62*, 321-329.

Martindale, C. (1986). *The white press and black America*. New York: Greenwood.

O'Kelly, C. G. (1978). The black press: Conservative or radical, reformist or revolutionary? *Journalism History, 4*(4), 114-116.

O'Kelly, C. G. (1982). Black newspapers and the black protest movement: Their historical relationship, 1827-1945. *Phylon, 43*(1), 1-14.

Omi, M. (1989). In living color: Race and American culture. In I. Angus & S. Jhally (Eds.), *Cultural politics in contemporary America* (pp. 111-122). New York: Routledge.

Owens, R. (1991, May 21-25). *Ideological disputes in the African-American press and social structure*. Paper presented to the Political Communication Division of the International Communication Association Convention, Miami, FL.

Owens, R. (1993a, August 11-14). *The African-American press: Counter ideology and the revolutionary process*. Unpublished paper presented to Qualitative Studies Division at the AEJMC Conference in Kansas City, MO.

Owens, R. (1993b). *The African-American press as response to oppression: Trends in circulation and formation.* Unpublished doctoral dissertation, University of Texas, Austin.

Palmer, L. F., Jr. (1970). The black press in transition. *Columbia Journalism Review, 9,* 31-36.

Penn, I. G. (1891). *The Afro-American press and its editors.* Springfield, MA: Wiley.

Puttkammer, C. W., & Worthy, R. (1958). William Monroe Trotter, 1872-1934. *Journal of Negro History, 43,* 299-316.

Reid, J. Z. (1988). *An historical analysis of* Freedom's Journal, *1827-1829.* Unpublished master of journalism thesis, Texas Southern University, Houston.

Rudwick, E. M. (1958). W. E. B. DuBois in the role of crisis editor. *Journal of Negro History, 43*(3), 214-240.

Shull, S. A. (1993). *A kinder, gentler racism? The Reagan-Bush civil rights legacy.* New York: M. E. Sharpe.

Stevens, J. D. (1973, February). From the back of the foxhole: Black correspondents in World War II. *Journalism Monographs,* p. 27.

Stroman, C. (1981). The *Chicago Defender* and the mass migration of blacks, 1916-1918. *Journal of Popular Culture, 15*(2), 73-79.

Thompson, J. E. (1993). *The black press in Mississippi: 1865-1985.* Gainesville: University of Florida Press.

Thornbrough, E. L. (1958). More light on Booker T. Washington and the New York age. *Journal of Negro History, 43,* 34-39.

Tripp, B. (1992). *Origins of the black press: New York, 1827-1847.* Northport, AL: Vision.

Turner, J. H. (1984). *Oppression: A socio-history of black-white relations in America.* Chicago: Nelson-Hall.

Washburn, P. S. (1986). *A question of sedition: The federal government's investigation of the black press during World War II.* New York: Oxford University Press.

Wilson, C. C. (1991). *Black journalists in paradox: Historical perspectives and current dilemmas.* New York: Greenwood.

Woodson, C. G. (1916). The attitude of the free Negro toward African colonization. *Journal of Negro History, 1,* 276-299.

Woodward, C. Van. (1974). *The strange career of Jim Crow* (3rd ed.). New York: Oxford University Press.

7

Carol Moseley-Braun

Black Women's Political Images in the Media

CARMEN L. MANNING-MILLER

For over two decades, political communication research has suggested that the construction of a political image in the press
includes the manipulation of the salience of both issues and
personal attributes (Barber & Gandy, 1990). In the election year of
1992, women of color assertively made their presence realized in many
jurisdictions of the American political arena. The unprecedented number of women who joined these ranks waged aggressive election
campaigns in response to an alliance with the courageous stance of
Anita Hill during the Clarence Thomas hearings.

Moreover, these candidates functioned in a political milieu where
women of color charged media with distorting and silencing their
voices. One of the most visible outcomes of this movement is the
election victory of Carol Moseley-Braun to the U.S. Senate (D-Illinois).
In this context, news coverage of Braun's election campaign and her
tenure in office provides an opportunity for case study that has at least
three distinct advantages.

An examination of election coverage of women candidates of color
may further our understanding of how media continue to define the
social and political positions of women of color. Second, it provides an

117

explanatory frame that permits an exploration of the complexities of African American women's political imagery and an appreciation of the unique character of this imagery. Third, such an analysis explores ways in which oppressive forces influence the election campaign experiences of women of color. The generation of this kind of knowledge can enable women of color to develop strategies to improve upon their campaign practices.

This analysis examines press portrayals of Senator Carol Moseley-Braun's election campaign, drawing upon perspectives on race, gender, and journalistic objectivity. The discussion concludes with a consideration of the impact of such coverage on future political activity and related research on women candidates of color.

STUDYING AFRICAN AMERICAN
WOMEN AND POLITICS

Historically, women of color did not have a significant voice in systems of governance. The role that they played in the political process was frequently behind the scenes (Rhodes, 1992, p. 112). Throughout American history, African American women have always participated in nontraditional political activities. Prestage (1991) notes:

> In litigation challenging state laws requiring segregation and discrimi-nation in a variety of areas, including voter registration, and in lobbying for legislative remedies at the national level, African-American women played prominent roles. . . . When the "outside of the courtroom" dimension of the movement emerged in the late 1950s and early 1960s, women again played significant roles in grassroots organizations in local communities, in national coordination structures, and in confrontations with hostile police officers and anti-integration groups and individuals. (p. 96)

Yet, scholars concur that silence and invisibility are the hallmarks of African American women of such status (see, for example, Collins, 1989; Rhodes, 1992). Painter (1992) contends that typically the roles available for black women in American popular culture are mammy, jezebel, and welfare queen, considering variations and reconstructions of these images over time. Communication scholar Marsha Houston has raised a flag. Houston (1988) writes: "I believe our continued exclusion perpetuates the myth that women's communication experiences are the same in every social and ethnic group" (p. 28). Hence, the political imagery of African American women in politics consists of symbols that are not traditionally or readily recognized by most Americans.

Gender research in political communication is often criticized because media studies have simply found differences in press portrayals of men and women in politics. This leaves unexplored the significance of the depiction of women's opportunities, particularly women of color, and their chances for long-range success in politics.

Most political communication research on race has not made a distinction between men and women politicians of color. Hence, studies are needed to determine what issues are particularly relevant to women candidates of color. Although research demonstrates that apparent biases exist, social implications have not been fully explored.

One important exception is a study by Jewel Prestage (1991). She finds that, currently, African American women are prime users of the ballot, hold a higher percentage of their race's elective offices than do white women, and as officeholders exhibit higher levels of women's organization membership than do white women and are highly supportive of women's issues. In spite of this level of political participation, Barber and Gandy (1990) find that newspapers differentiate the way they present African American political candidates and white political incumbents. They contend that African Americans were coded as effective leaders less frequently than white legislators, and African Americans were less likely than whites to be identified as moral.

Media studies also show that the press spend most of their time discussing "horse-race" aspects of election campaigns (Clarke & Evans, 1983; Weaver, Graber, McCombs, & Eyal, 1981). These aspects of campaign coverage pose special problems for women candidates. Historically, women have been perceived as less viable than their male counterparts because of women's lack of political experience and their typical challenger status (Jacobson, 1987; Trafton, 1984). Also, women candidates have lagged behind their male counterparts in terms of campaign finances and other organizational resources, as campaign resources act as commanding benchmarks for a candidate's visibility potential (Abramowitz, 1989; Burrell, 1985; Cox & Munger, 1989;

Goldenberg & Traugott, 1987; Hershey, 1989; Nice, 1984). These resources influence the candidate's relationships with the media (Clarke & Evans, 1983; Weaver et al., 1981).

A content analysis of local newspaper coverage of women Senate candidates found that viability issues are emphasized more in the coverage of female incumbents, female challengers, and females in open races than in the coverage of their male counterparts (Kahn & Goldenberg, 1991). Research findings suggest that coverage of policy issues is also particularly constraining for female candidates. The results of studies on voters' perceptions of female candidates and male candidates, as well as studies on sex stereotyping and issue coverage, offer compelling evidence.

Studies on voters' perceptions of candidate competency find that male candidates are perceived to be more competent in policy areas related to foreign policy, defense, economics, and agriculture. Women candidates are perceived by voters to be more competent in policy areas such as minority rights, environment, abortion, and social programs (Kahn & Goldenberg, 1991; Sapiro, 1981-1982).

Barber and Gandy (1990) find that this is not the case for African American men and women, and note the following differences: African American legislators were more likely to be quoted on local and racial affairs, whereas whites were more likely to be quoted on congressional, international, national, and county affairs.

An analysis of newspaper coverage of those issues shows that in local newspaper coverage of women Senate candidates, the perceived-female issues were discussed more frequently than perceived-male issues. The authors noted, however, that the presence of a woman in the race seemed to encourage greater discussion of perceived-female issues— even for male candidates (Kahn & Goldenberg, 1991).

Based on this prior research and criticism, the discussion is guided by the following assumptions. During the 1992 election campaign period, Senator Moseley-Braun's campaign was trivialized by the media. This differential treatment can be measured and interpreted by assessing the media's analysis of her campaign's viability, the media's use of traditional stereotypes to construct her political image, and the media's use of quotations and sources in story coverage.

Most of what has been written about African American women politicians has followed traditional humanistic and social scientific methods with little attention paid to the environment in which they communicate. African American women politicians across the United States are certainly not available in conveniently large groups (Houston, 1988). If women of color are not to remain invisible in political communication studies, scholars must consider the value of research methods that illuminate processes that clarify how society maintains notions of gender and race, with its separations and its discrepancies in power.

The media industry and social commentators argue about the effects of news: whether or not it makes people behave in certain ways or believe in certain things. The most important media effects can be explained in terms of the manner in which the news media require people to generate meanings preferred by the media. These are meanings that create identities for people and things and sustain the system of representation, even if those meanings and those identities are rejected by voters and the members of the media audience. The effect ensures that certain meanings—such as the connections between the subordination of women of color and group domination and/or racial inequality and group domination—will never become "unthinkable" (see, for example, Rakow, 1992).

A critical analysis of the news discourse allows an interpretation of the structures of text that function within specific contexts to imply negative representations of African American women. We now understand that the connection between gender, race, politics, and meaning is complex. First, women of color have different political and cultural relationships to systems of representation than do men. Second, women of color are forced to be participants in the cultural circulation of meanings preferred by news media, even those we object to, without opportunity to generate our own meaning. Third, gender and race are not only represented in texts such as news reports, they are a broader system of media representation.

This study of news as discourse is not dependent upon Senator Moseley-Braun's viability as a political candidate, or an election outcome, or her political behavior. This study analyzes the way meanings are constructed and/or the ways that public discourse is influenced by activating salient and preexisting narratives that explain underlying cognitions of knowledge, attitudes, norms, values, and ideologies. One does not have to see Moseley-Braun as a lawyer, or Illinois state official, or U.S. Senator, to think about, or recognize, or examine the ways in which media discourse fuels certain cultural politics.

This analysis is an interpretive study of national press coverage of Senator Moseley-Braun's campaign. The *Chicago Tribune* and the *Washington Post* were selected because of their national readership, because they are acknowledged as leading papers, and because they cover a range of political issues. Also, Senator Moseley-Braun's election campaign took place in Illinois and, with her success, she would ultimately affect congressional issues in Washington, D.C. Articles were analyzed from Moseley-Braun's announcement in December 1991 to Election Day in November 1992. This analysis of news content considers the news stories to be narrative constructions—the means by which sense is made of political and social reality. The coverage functions to foster shared and common understanding of gender and race in our world. As media products are political narrative, the media do not necessarily or consciously make absent certain narrative by presenting others, but construct reality in such a way that what we see and read comes to be what we believe—in this case about political candidates.

Teun A. van Dijk (1993) asserts that critical analysis of the meanings of news discourse focuses on various types of *implications*, which are defined as meanings that are not explicitly expressed in the text but may be inferred from words or sentences as well as from the mental models constructed during understanding. In news reports, the use of quotations as a means of implication is particularly powerful.

Then, too, the use of sources is equally powerful. The underrepresentation of women of color in the public sphere does not give news media a ready-made justification for their absence in news reports. Critics claim that journalistic routines, particularly those that require the use of official sources, overwhelm diversity in the marketplace of ideas. Elite sources, who tend to be white, are favored by reporters because they provide regular coverage. As racial and gender diversity increases in the public realm, however, source diversity should be valued as a reporting objective.

Also, it is argued that news reflects the views of publishers, writers, and editors in that they each make choices about what to include, exclude, emphasize, or ignore on the basis of political ideologies. These gatekeepers make choices in the long run that tend to reflect particular ideological perspectives. Dates and Gandy (1985) note that as news organizations cover political campaigns, decisions about coverage, emphasis, avoidance, or other presentation of content result in the publication of implicit or explicit assertions about a candidate. Thus, media are seen to help "set the agenda" of the campaign by influencing the salience of particular characteristics or attributes of candidates and their campaign activities when the media market these as either important or irrelevant through such coverage. These constructs of the news media are potentially formidable for women of color, and their full incorporation into the decision-making practices of the official public sphere may be challenged.

CAMPAIGN COVERAGE ANALYSIS

Senator Moseley-Braun raised more money than any other Senate challenger in Illinois during the nomination period and at one point led in the campaign by 35 percentage points. The ongoing media discussion of Moseley-Braun's viability and personal attributes, however, occurred at the expense of underreporting of policy issues and her campaign platform. Consider the following: One *Washington Post* article depicted Moseley-Braun as unfit to serve as U.S. Senator. Quoting a close friend of Moseley-Braun, the article stated: "Carol from time to time was viewed as a tad unmanageable" (Walsh, 1992, p. C4). The article also suggested that her demeanor had blocked her chances to run for Lieutenant Governor in Illinois: "Perhaps that's why when Ronan and others pushed her as the Democratic candidate for lieutenant governor in 1986, Washington blocked the move" (Walsh, 1992, p. C4).

These statements present relevant implications, for example, that Moseley-Braun is uncontrollable, even out of control, too independent and brash, suggesting that these are not positive attributes for successful women candidates in society. This double standard underlies the "feminine" ideal (see, for example, Morris, 1992). The double standard is one that says men are acceptably aggressive and women are shrill. The patriarchal order suggests that men, not women, achieve identity by breaking loose of structures, by demonstrating that they can get what they want through power, and by being critical, demanding, and free from the constraints of others. These traits run as themes throughout the popular culture, where power—either over women or over other men—is acceptable for men.

A *Chicago Tribune* commentary affirmed the spirit of an opponent's negative radio campaign, agreeing with the opposing camp that "she should have trouble defending her record to certain voters." Without further explanation of Moseley-Braun's record, the article highlighted Moseley-Braun's opponent's assessment, labeling her a "sleazy hack": "Williamson recently assailed Moseley-Braun as a 'sleazy hack,' but at least did so himself and didn't enlist an eager surrogate" (Hardy, 1992, p. C4).

In connection with a controversy involving her mother's finances, Moseley-Braun under press interrogation about the issue cried in public. The coverage framed her emotional state as significant and worthy of elaborate description: "Other media have recounted the fact as if it were the prelude to a nervous breakdown. . . . Some men in the room saw a woman who cracked under pressure" (Schmich, 1992, p. 2C).

One story led with a stereotypical account that trivialized her political image and her gender:

> Carol Moseley-Braun is a celebrity with a problem. . . . But at this particular moment she is preoccupied with a more mundane matter—searching through the supply of NO Nonsense panty hose at a hotel gift shop for a replacement for the pair that has developed a run. (Hardy, 1992, p. C4)

The descriptions of Moseley-Braun's emotional state during a press conference and her selection of hosiery in a hotel shop are gendered narratives. News media use double standards in interpreting the tearful displays of political candidates and what they do in their leisure time. President Bill Clinton's unrestrained crying on his inauguration day was interpreted in media reports as a show of humanity and warmth, not mental instability. The reference to Moseley-Braun's shopping gave too much information that was irrelevant to the description of campaign events. Are the hosiery preferences of male politicians reported?

The quotations of some spokespersons associated with Moseley-Braun's campaign staff expressed opinions that were seemingly consistent with a white ethnic consensus. Most sources suggested that Moseley-Braun's persona and competence didn't have anything at all to do with the success of Moseley-Braun's campaign. The story created the image of two independent campaigns. One campaign was headed by Moseley-Braun, with staff whom she managed. The other campaign was projected as a campaign of white feminists who used Moseley-Braun as a figurehead to further their political goals. The financial success, as well as the delivery of the vote, was attributed to this white female political apparatus, which deemed the political and monetary support of the African American community unnecessary.

Hardy's (1992) article read: "During the primary contest her organization appeared continually on the verge of collapse. . . . The campaign is a disaster and the problem is she thinks she won because of the campaign," said a friend of Moseley-Braun's (p. C4).

Alton Miller, Moseley-Braun's former press secretary, who left after clashing with campaign manager Kgosei Matthews, said that since the primary, a myth has begun to form around Moseley-Braun that women are going to elect her "despite anything. She can stay home and win" (Hardy, 1992, p. C4).

A *Chicago Tribune* story about a fund-raiser said that Carol Hodge-West, assistant comptroller and a new EMILY's List member, was enthusiastic but noted that aside from Moseley-Braun and her campaign aide, she didn't see a single black person at the fund-raiser other than herself. They need to diversify, she said, adding that minority businesswomen could be an important source of donations (Brotman, 1992, p. 4).

The use of these quotations and sources suggests that the bulk of the coverage highlighted white elite opinions about candidate Moseley-Braun's campaign's viability and her personal attributes. In the campaign coverage, sources not associated with Moseley-Braun's campaign were quoted most extensively and most credibly. In some situations, Moseley-Braun supporters were allowed to tell about their experience, but very few reflected positively on the campaign. The implications presented in quotation patterns presented Moseley-Braun's campaign as fatalistic and problematic. Other stylistic strategies further reinforced the gendered narrative that differentiated men politicians from women politicians, based on issues of stamina and personal behavior.

A NEW RESEARCH AGENDA

If women of color continue to take democratic avenues, such as the electoral arena, to effect change in their communities, practitioners and those of us who do political communication research should improvise a shift in method as well as in our conceptualizations of political communication theory.

This case study supports previous findings about the representations of women of color. First, the representations that emerged in this study were similar to the images of women of color in popular culture. As women of color emerge in the public sphere, depictions of unmanageable, deviant, politically incompetent individuals emerge as well. The narrative attempted to obscure Moseley-Braun's strengths and to silence the power of her voice as an African American woman. By defining the campaign as a vehicle for voices of white women, and as a campaign that succeeded because of the financial clout of Democratic white women's networks, Moseley-Braun's political and cultural identity faded. Her political image was constructed as a homogenizing force, totally eliminating issues of race and cultural identification in the campaign. This kind of coverage will endure short of major political and economic reformation in the United States. What is wrong is not necessarily the presence of this narrative but the increasingly felt absence of any competing set of political and cultural messages and values.

Until now, lacking access to the means of mass communication, black women have not been able to use their political presence as a corrective to stereotypes of race and gender. But as these opportunities arise, a number of interesting questions are posed related to research on women of color. As campaign financing remains a barrier for women in politics and causes of color, fund-raising and marketing issues become relevant. Most marketing research on populations is focused on the economic goals of organizations outside the African American community. Very little research is done on intraracial marketing, on how African Americans interact politically with each other, or on how African American women interact politically with each other.

National African American political and social organizations are an untapped database for case studies of fund-raising and agenda-building. Civil rights organizations and African American sororities and fraternities offer fascinating histories of campaign financing and agenda-building in the African American community—ranging from the most sophisticated use of information technology to simple grassroots approaches that measure financial success one fish dinner at a time. Scholarly research in the area of political advertising is nonexistent. Women of color have no tradition of political imagery that has been recognized and analyzed. We have not explored in any systematic way our perceived strengths or the potential of those strengths to change public perceptions and construct positive political images that have the possibility of capturing the national imagination in terms of our viability for governorships and even the U.S. presidency.

Political advertising research questions could also explore appropriate content for rebuttals to negative political ads. What kinds of messages and strategies are perceived as effective in negative political environments? What advertising strategies evoke voter backlash and negative voter perceptions? Are these strategies seemingly race- and gender-specific? Research questions are also interesting in the area of politics and new technology. Issues of access, ownership, and expense are critical to the democratic participation of marginalized populations. Superhighways of information will change the way we manage and access information. Political advertising and political news coverage will be more individualized and personalized. As the notion of a mass media and a mass media audience changes, the cost (financially and politically) of access to communication environments may become even more prohibitive and our voices will be silenced in new and even more profound ways.

Scholars should continue to document and articulate the ways that news coverage functions and the meanings it generates about difference—gendered and racial. Scholars should advocate concrete policy changes in media structure and in election campaigning. They should also continue to connect the theoretical developments in the nature and function of news with theoretical developments about women of color in other areas of mass media. Scholars should demonstrate that women of color are harmed by this kind of negative political imagery—and, hence, the democratic process is harmed. Finally, scholars should find the value in beginning theory-building with the premise that women of color have the right to communicate their own meanings about their political experiences.

REFERENCES

Abramowitz, A. (1989). Campaign spending in U.S. Senate elections. *Legislative Studies Quarterly, 4*(4), 487-509.

Barber, J., & Gandy, O. (1990). Press portrayal of African-American and white United States representatives. *Howard Journal of Communications, 2*(2), 213-225.

Brotman, B. (1992, October 25). Women using checkbooks to make voices heard. *Chicago Tribune*, pp. 1, 4.

Burrell, B. C. (1985). Women's and men's campaigns for the U.S. House of Representatives, 1972-1982. *American Politics Quarterly, 13,* 251-272.

Clarke, P., & Evans, S. (1983). *Covering campaigns: Journalism in congressional elections.* Stanford, CA: Stanford University Press.

Collins, P. H. (1989). The social construction of black feminist thought. *Signs, 14*(4), 745-773.

Cox, G., & Munger, M. (1989). Closeness, expenditures, and turnout in the 1982 U.S. House elections. *American Political Science Review, 83*(1), 217-233.

Dates, J., & Gandy, O. (1985). How ideological constraints affected coverage of the Jesse Jackson campaign. *Journalism Quarterly, 62*(3), 595-600.

Goldenberg, E., & Traugott, M. (1987). Mass media in U.S. congressional elections. *Legislative Studies Quarterly, 12,* 317-339.

Hardy, T. (1992, July 26). Comments. *Chicago Tribune,* p. C4.

Hershey, M. (1989). The campaign and the media. In G. M. Pomper (Ed.), *The election of 1988* (pp. 73-102). Chatham, NJ: Chatham House.

Houston, M. (1988). What makes scholarship about black women and communication feminist communication scholarship? *Women's Studies in Communication, 11*(1), 28-31.

Jacobson, G. (1987). The marginals never vanished: Incumbency and competition in elections to the U.S. House Representatives, 1952-1982. *American Journal of Political Science, 31,* 126-141.

Kahn, K., & Goldenberg, E. (1991). Women candidates in the news: An examination of gender differences in U.S. Senate campaign coverage. *Public Opinion Quarterly, 55,* 180-199.

Morris, C. (1992). *Storming the statehouse.* New York: Scribner.

Nice, D. (1984). Political equality and campaign finance in the American states. *Social Science Quarterly, 65,* 1104-1111.

Painter, N. (1992). Hill, Thomas and the use of racial stereotypes. In T. Morrison (Ed.), *Race-ing justice, en-gendering power* (pp. 200-214). New York: Pantheon.

Prestage, J. (1991). In quest of African-American political women. *Annals of the American Academy of Political and Social Science, 515,* 88-103.

Rakow, L. (1992). Don't hate me because I'm beautiful: Feminist resistance to advertising's irresistible meanings. *Southern Communication Journal, 57,* 132-142.

Rhodes, J. (1992). Mary Ann Shadd Cary and the legacy of African-American women journalists. In L. Rakow (Ed.), *Women making meaning* (pp. 210-224). Westport, CT: Greenwood.

Sapiro, V. (1981-1982). If U.S. Senator Baker were a woman: An experimental study of candidate images. *Political Psychology, 2,* 61-83.

Schmich, M. (1992, October 9). [Editorial]. *Chicago Tribune,* p. 2C.

Trafton, B. (1984). *Women winning: How to run for office.* Cambridge, MA: Harvard Common Press.

van Dijk, T. A. (1993). *Elite discourse and racism.* Newbury Park, CA: Sage.

Walsh, E. (1992, April 4). Carol Braun's rocky road to history. *Washington Post,* p. C4.

Weaver, D., Graber, D., McCombs, M., & Eyal, C. (1981). *Media agenda-setting in a presidential election.* New York: Praeger.

PART III

Issues in Television/ Cable

8

Television, Black Americans, and the American Dream

HERMAN GRAY

W illiam F. Buckley Jr. has observed, "It is simply not correct . . . that race prejudice is increasing in America. How does one know this? Simple, by the ratings of Bill Cosby's television show and the sales of his books. A nation simply does not idolize members of a race which that nation despises" (Demeter, 1986, p. 67). Buckley seems to suggest that if racial prejudice exists at all in the United States, it does not figure significantly in the nature of American society, nor does this explain very much about social inequality based on race and characterized by racial discrimination, racial violence, and economic dislocation—and perhaps most interesting about Buckley's observation is his reliance on Bill Cosby's successful media presence as a barometer of American racial equality.

An open class structure, racial tolerance, economic mobility, the sanctity of individualism, and the availability of the American dream for black Americans are represented in a wide range of media. Representations of such success are available in the *The Cosby Show,* the box office power of Eddie Murphy, the international popularity of Michael

SOURCE: This chapter originally appeared in *Critical Studies in Mass Communication, 6,* 376-386; used and slightly modified by permission.

131

Jackson, and the visibility of Oprah Winfrey. Equally important to the contemporary ideology of American racial openness, however, are representations of deprivation and poverty such as those shown on network newscasts and documentaries. In media reports of urban crime, prisons overcrowded with black men, increased violence associated with drugs, and the growing ranks of the homeless are drawn the lines of success and failure.

As Buckley's observations demonstrate, the meanings of these representations are not given; rather, viewers define and use the representations differently and for different reasons. One message of these representations of success and failure is that middle-class blacks (and whites) succeed because they take advantage of available opportunities while poor blacks and other marginal members of our society fail because they do not (Glasgow, 1981; Lewis, 1984). These representations operate not just in terms of their relationship to the empirical realities of black life in America but also in relationship to other popular media constructions about black life. My interest here is in the relationship between representations of black life in fictional and nonfictional television and the ideological meanings of these representations when television is viewed as a complete ideological field (Fiske, 1987a). In the following section, I theoretically situate the problem. I then turn to a discussion of black failure as represented in the CBS News documentary *The Vanishing Family: Crisis in Black America* and the representation of upper-middle-class black affluence in the *The Cosby Show.*

THEORETICAL CONTEXT

To describe how television representations about race communicate and to examine their ideological meanings, I draw on Gramsci's notion of ideological hegemony (Gramsci, 1971; Hall, 1982). Media representations of black life (especially middle-class success and underclass failure) are routinely fractured, selectively assembled, and subsequently become a part of the storehouse of American racial memory. The social and racial meanings that result from these processes appear in the media as natural and given rather than as social and constructed. In *Ideology and the Image* (1981), Bill Nichols stated that "ideology uses the fabrication of images and processes of representation to persuade us that how things are is how they ought to be and that the place provided for us is the place we ought to have" (p. 1). I use *hegemony* to specify the material and symbolic processes by which these racial representations and understandings are produced and naturalized (Fiske, 1987a; Hall, 1982).

Media representations of black success and failure and the processes that produce them are ideological to the extent that the assumptions that organize the media discourses shift our understanding of racial inequality away from structured social processes to matters of individual choices. Such ideological representations appear natural and universal rather than as the result of social and political struggles over power.

The process of media selection and appropriation, however, is only one part of the play of hegemony. Mass media and popular culture are, according to Stuart Hall (1980), sites where struggles over meaning and the power to represent it are waged. Thus, even as the media and popular cultural forms present representations of race and racial (in)equality, the power of these meanings to register with the expression (common sense) of different segments of the population remains problematic. Meanings constantly shift and are available for negotiations. It is in this process of negotiations that different, alternative, even oppositional readings are possible (Fiske, 1987a; Hall, 1980). Because of this constantly shifting terrain of meaning and struggle, the representations of race and racial interaction in fictional and nonfictional television reveal both the elements of the dominant racial ideology as well as the limits to that ideology.

Within this broad struggle over meaning, Fredric Jameson (1979) shows how popular cultural forms such as film and television work symbolically to establish preferred, even dominant ideological meanings. In popular culture, ideology is secured through the psychological appeal to utopian values and aspirations and a simultaneous repression and displacement of critical sensibilities that identify the social and economic organization of American society as the source of inequality. In television representations of blacks, the historical realities of slavery, discrimination, and racism or persistent struggles against domination are displaced and translated into celebrations of black middle-class visibility and achievement. In this context, successful and highly visible stars such as Bill Cosby and Michael Jackson confirm the openness and pluralism of American society.

The commercial culture industry presents idealized representations of racial justice, social equality, and economic success. Idealized middle-class black Americans increasingly populate fictional television. They confirm a middle-class utopian imagination of racial pluralism (Gray, 1986). These idealized representations remain before us, driven, in the case of television, by the constant search for stable audiences and the centrality of advertising revenue as the basis for profits (Cantor, 1980; Gitlin, 1983).

As Jameson further notes, however, utopian possibilities are secured against the backdrop of reified nonfictional (and fictional) representations. In the case of racial representations, the black underclass appears as menace and a source of social disorganization in news accounts of black urban crime, gang violence, drug use, teenage pregnancy, riots, homelessness, and general aimlessness. In news accounts (and in Hollywood films such as *Colors*), poor blacks (and Hispanics) signify a social menace that must be contained. Poor urban blacks help to mark the boundaries of appropriate middle-class behavior as well as the acceptable routes to success. As a unity, these representations of black middle-class success and underclass failure are ideological because they are mutually reinforcing and their fractured and selective status allows them to be continuously renewed and secured. Furthermore, the meanings operate within a frame that privileges representations of middle-class racial pluralism while marginalizing those of racial inequality. This constant quest for legitimacy and the need to quell and displace fears at the same time as calling them forth are part of the complex ideological work that takes place in television representations of race.

The representations of black American success and failure in both fictional and nonfictional television, and the assumptions that organize them, are socially constructed according to commercial, professional, and aesthetic conventions that guide producers and consumers of television (Gray, 1986). These conventions guide personnel in the selection and presentation of images to ensure that they are aesthetically appealing, culturally meaningful, politically legitimate, and economically profitable.

Although fictional and nonfictional representations of blacks emanate from separate generic quarters of television, they activate meanings for viewers across these boundaries. That is, the representations make sense in terms of their intertextuality between and within programs (Fiske, 1987a; Fiske & Hartley, 1978; Williams, 1974). Television representations of black life in the late 1980s cannot be read in isolation but should be read in terms of their relationship to other television texts.

The meaning that these representations express and activate are also significant in terms of the broad social and historical context in which they operate. Fictional and nonfictional representations of black life appear at a time when political and intellectual debate continues over the role of the state in helping the black urban poor and whether or not affirmative action ought to remain an active component of public policy. Within the black political and activist community, sharp differences remain over the role of the black middle class and the efficacy of black-generated self-help programs to battle problems facing black communities. Increased racial violence and antagonisms (including those on college campuses), economic dislocation, a changing industrial base, ethnic and racial shifts in the demographic composition of the population, and the reelection of a conservative national administration help set the social context within which television representations of black life take on meaning.

Myriad community, institutional, social, political, and economic forces shape the broad public discourse on the conditions of blacks in contemporary American society. In the absence of effective social movements such as those for civil rights, students, women, and against the war, which, at the very least, helped ground and mediate media representations, these representations take on greater authority and find easier access to our common sense (Winston, 1983, p. 178). Under these conditions, the ideological potency of media representations remains quite strong.

Media representations of black success and failure occur within a kind of gerrymandered framework. Through production conventions, political sensibilities, commercial pressures, and requirements for social organization and efficiency, television news and entertainment selectively construct the boundaries within which representations about black life occur. The primacy of individual effort over collective possibilities, the centrality of individual values, morality, and initiative, and a benign (if not invisible) social structure are the key social terms that define television discourses about black success and failure.

REIFICATION AND THE UNDERCLASS

To explore the reification side of the Jameson formulation, I begin
with a discussion of the CBS News report about the black urban
underclass. The social report that aired in January 1985 is titled *The
Vanishing Family: Crisis in Black America*. CBS senior correspondent Bill
Moyers hosted the 90-minute documentary, which was filmed in New-
ark, New Jersey. Through interviews and narration by Moyers, the
report examines the lives of unwed mothers and fathers, detailing their
education, employment, welfare history (especially across generations),
hopes, frustrations, and disappointments.

The appearance of the terms *vanishing family* and *crisis* in the title of
the program implicitly suggests the normalcy of everyday life when
defined by stable nuclear families (Feuer, 1986; Fiske, 1987a). Missing
is recognition that families and communities throughout the country
are in the midst of significant transformation. Instead, the program title
suggests an abnormal condition that must be recognized and addressed.

In the report's opening segment, visual representations also help
frame the ideological terms of the report. Medium and long camera
shots are used to establish perspective on the daily life in the community.
Mothers are shown shopping for food and caring for children; groups
of boys and young men appear standing on street corners, playing
basketball, listening to music, and working out at the gym. Welfare
lines, couples arguing, the police, housing projects, and the streets are
also common images.

These shots tie the specific issues addressed in the story into a
broader discourse about race in America. Shots of black men and youth
standing on corners or blacks arrested for crimes are conventionally
used in newscasts to signify abnormalities and social problems. These
images operate at multiple levels, so even though they explicitly work
to frame the documentary, they also draw on and evoke images of crime,
drugs, riots, menace, and social problems. People and communities
who appear in these representations are labeled as problematic and
undesirable.

The documentary's four segments are organized around three major
themes, with each segment profiling unmarried couples. By the end of
the four segments, the dominant message of the report is evident;
self-help, individual responsibility, and community accountability are

required to survive the crisis. This conclusion is anticipated early in the report with a promotional tease from a black social worker. In a 30-second sound bite, the social worker notes that the problem in the black community is not racism or unemployment but the corruption of values, the absence of moral authority, and the lack of individual motivation. This dominant message is also reinforced in the introduction to the report by correspondent Moyers:

> A lot of white families are in trouble too. Single parent families are twice as common in America today as they were 20 years ago. But for the majority of white children, family still means a mother and a father. This is not true for most black children. For them things are getting worse. Today black teenagers have the highest pregnancy rate in the industrialized world and in the black inner city, practically no teenage mother gets married. That's no racist comment. What's happening goes far beyond race.

Because blacks dominate the visual representations that evoke images of crime, drugs, and social problems, little in the internal logic and organization of the documentary supports this contention. Even when voice-over data are used to address these issues among whites, it competes with rather than complements the dominance of the visual representations. Moyers's comment is also muted because the issues are examined primarily at the dramatic and personal level.

For example, the first segment considers the experience of urban single-parent families from the viewpoint of women. The opening piece profiles Clarinda and Darren, both young and poorly prepared emotionally or financially to care for an infant. Clarinda supports the baby with welfare and is also the baby's primary source of emotional nurturance. Darren occasionally sees his baby but takes little economic or emotional responsibility for her. On camera, he appears distant and frustrated.

The second segment focuses on Alice, 23, and Timothy, 26. They are older but financially no more prepared to raise a family than Clarinda and Darren. Unlike Darren, Timothy is emotionally available to Alice. (On camera, they confess their love for each other, and Timothy is present at a birthday party for one child and the delivery of another.) In the interview, Alice freely shows her frustration with Timothy, especially his lack of work and unwillingness to take responsibility for his family.

Timothy, on the other hand, lives in a world of male sexual myths and a code that celebrates male sexual conquest and virility (Glasgow, 1981). Although he confesses love for Alice and his kids, he avoids economic and parental responsibility for them, especially when his own pleasures and sexual conquests are considered.

The mothers in these segments are caring, responsible, and conscientious; they raise the children and provide for them. They are the social, economic, and emotional centers of their children's lives. As suggested in the interviews and visual footage, the fathers are absent, immature, selfish, irresponsible, and exploitative. Where women are shown at home with the children, the men are shown on street corners with other men. Where women talk of their children's futures, men speak in individual terms about their current frustration and unrealistic aspirations.

The dramatic and personal tone of these representations makes them compelling and helps draw in the viewer. These strategies of organization and presentation also help personalize the story and, to a limited extent, give the people texture and dimensions. Nevertheless, these representations are also mediated by a broader set of racial and class codes that continue to construct the people in the documentary as deviant and criminal, hence marginal. The members of the community are contained by these broader codes. They remain curious but distant "others."

The third segment features Bernard, a 15-year-old single male who still lives at home with Brenda, his 30-year-old single mother of three. This segment tells the story of life in this community from the young male point of view. The male voice takes on resonance and, in contrast to Darren and Timothy, we learn that the men in this community have feelings and hopes too. The segment shows Bernard's struggle to avoid the obstacles (drugs, educational failure, unemployment, homicide, jail) to his future. From Brenda's boyfriend (and roll model for Bernard), we learn about the generational persistence of these obstacles to young male futures.

In each of these segments, the dramatic dominates the analytic, the personal dominates the public, and the individual dominates the social. Individual mobility, character, and responsibility provide powerful explanations for the failures presented in the story. Indeed, by the final segment of the report, the theme of moral irresponsibility and individual behavior as explanations for the crisis of the underclass is fully developed. Moyers introduces the segment this way:

> There are successful strong black families in America. Families that affirm parental authority and the values of discipline, work, and achievement. But you won't find many who live around here. Still, not every girl in the inner city ends up a teenage mother, not every young man goes into crime. There are people who have stayed here. They're outnumbered by the con artists and pushers. It's not an even match, but they stand for morality and authority and give some of these kids a dose of unsentimental love.

As a major "actor" in the structure of this report, Moyers is central to the way that the preferred meanings of the report are conveyed. As an economically and professionally successful white male, Moyers's political and moral authority establishes the framework for identifying the conditions as trouble, for articulating the interest of the dominant society, and for demonstrating that in the continued openness of the social order there is hope. Through Moyers's position as a journalist, this report confirms the American dream even as it identifies casualties of the dream.

Moyers's authority in this story stems also from his position as an adult. During his interviews and stand-ups, Moyers represents adult common sense, disbelief, and concern. This adult authority remains throughout the report and is reinforced (and activated) later in the story when we hear from caring (and successful) black adults of the community who claim that the problems facing the community stem from poor motivation, unclear and unsound values, and the lack of personal discipline. Like Moyers, these adults—two social workers, a psychologist, and a police officer—do not identify complex social forces like racism, social organization, the changing economy, or the welfare state as the causes of the crisis in their community. They blame members of the black community for the erosion of values, morality, and authority. This is how Mrs. Wallace, the social worker, puts it:

> We are destroying ourselves. Now it [the crisis] might have been motivated and plotted and seeded with racism, but we are content to be in this well now. We're just content to be in this mud and we need to get out of it. There are not any great white people running around this block tearing up stuff. It's us. We've got to stop doing that.

When combined with the personal tone of the documentary and Moyers's professional (and adult) authority, this comment, coming as it does from an adult member of the community, legitimates the emphasis on personal attributes and a benign social structure.

At the ideological level of what Stuart Hall (1980) calls preferred readings, each segment of the documentary emphasizes individual personalities, aspirations, and struggles for improvement. These assumptions and analytic strategies are consistently privileged over social explanations, and they provide a compelling vantage point from which to read the documentary. This displacement of the social by the personal and the complex by the dramatic both draws viewers into the report and takes them away from explanations that criticize the social system. Viewers question individual coping mechanisms rather than the structural and political circumstances that create and sustain racial inequalities.

MIDDLE-CLASS UTOPIA

I consider the utopian side of the Jameson formulation by exploring the theme that media representations of black success and failure are ideological, precisely to the extent that they provide a way of seeing underclass failure through representations of middle-class success. Implicitly operating in this way of viewing the underclass (and the middle class) is the assumption that because America is an open racial and class order, then people who succeed (and fail) do so because of their individual abilities rather than their position in the social structure (Lewis, 1984).

In contrast to the blacks in the CBS documentary, successful blacks who populate prime time television are charming, unique, and attractive individuals who, we assume, reached their stations in life through hard work, skill, talent, discipline, and determination. Their very presence in formats from talk show (Bryant Gumbel, Arsenio Hall, Oprah Winfrey) to situation comedy (Bill Cosby) confirms the American value of individual success and mobility.

In the genre of situation comedy, programs such as *The Cosby Show, 227, Frank's Place,* and *Amen* all show successful middle-class black Americans who effectively negotiated their way through benign social institutions and environments (Gray, 1986). Their family-centered lives take place in attractive homes and offices. Rarely if ever do these characters venture into settings or interact with people like those in the CBS documentary. As doctors, lawyers, restaurateurs, ministers, contractors, and housewives, these are representations of black Americans who have surely realized the American dream. They are pleasant and competent social actors whose racial and cultural experiences are, for the most part, insignificant. Although black, their class position (signified by their occupations, tastes, language, and setting) distances them from the codes of crime, drugs, and social problems activated by the urban underclass. With the exception of the short-lived *Frank's Place,* the characters are never presented in situations where their racial identity matters. This representation of racial encounters further appeals to the utopian desire in blacks and whites for racial oneness and equality while displacing the persistent reality of racism and racial inequality or the kinds of social struggles and cooperation required to eliminate them. At the level of the show's dominant meanings, this strategy accounts in part for the success of *The Cosby Show* among blacks and whites.

In virtually any episode of *The Cosby Show,* the Huxtable children—Sandra, Denise, Vanessa, Theo, and Rudi—are given appropriate lessons in what appear to be universal values such as individual responsibility, parental trust, honesty, the value of money, the importance of family and tradition, peer group pressure, the value of education, the need for independence, and other important guides to successful living in America. In contrast to the experience of the young men in the CBS documentary, *Cosby*'s Theo learns and accepts lessons of responsibility, maintaining a household, the dangers of drugs, the value of money, and respect for women through the guidance of supportive parents. In Theo's relationship to his family, especially his father Cliff, the lessons of fatherhood and manhood are made explicit. Theo and his male peers talk about their aspirations and fears. They even exchange exaggerated tales of adolescent male conquest. Because similar discussions among the young men in the documentary are embedded within a larger set of codes about the urban black male menace, this kind of talk from Timothy, Darren, and Bernard signals their incompetence and irresponsibility at male roles. In the middle-class setting of *The Cosby Show,* for Theo and his peers, this same talk represents the ritual of adolescent male maturation. Together, these very opposite representations suggest a contemporary version of the culture of poverty thesis that attributes black male incompetence and irresponsibility to the absence of male role models, weak personal values, and a deficient cultural environment.

The strategy of imparting explicit lessons of responsibility to Theo (and to young black male viewers) is deliberate on the part of *Cosby*. This is not surprising given that the show enjoyed its greatest commercial success in the midst of increasing gang violence and epidemic teen pregnancy in urban black communities. The show's strategy illustrates its attempt to speak to a number of different audiences at a number of different levels (Fiske, 1987a; Hall, 1980).

Shows about middle-class black Americans revolve around specific characters, settings, and situations (Gitlin, 1983; Gray, 1986). The personal dimension of social life is privileged over, and in many cases displaces, broader social and structural factors. In singling out *The Cosby Show*, my aim is not to diminish the unique qualities, hard work, and sacrifices that these personal representations stress. Nevertheless, I do want to insist that the assumptions and framework that structure these representations often displace representations that would enable viewers to see that many individuals trapped in the underclass have the very same qualities but lack the options and opportunities to realize them. And in the world of television news and entertainment, where production conventions, rating wars, and cautious political sensibilities guide the aesthetic and journalistic decisions of networks, the hegemony of the personal and personable rules. Whether it is Bill Cosby, Phylicia Rashad, Darren, Alice, or Bill Moyers, the representation is of either deficient or gifted individuals.

Against fictional television representations of gifted and successful individuals, members of the urban underclass are deficient. They are unemployed, unskilled, menacing, unmotivated, ruthless, and irresponsible. They live differently and operate with different attitudes and moral codes than everyone else; they are set apart. Again, at television's preferred level of meaning, these assumptions—like the images they organize and legitimate—occupy our commonsense understandings of American racial inequality.

CONCLUSIONS

The assumptions that organize our understandings of black middle-class success and underclass failure are expressed and reinforced in the formal organization of television programming. Formally, where representations of the underclass are presented in the routine structure of network news programming, it is usually in relationship to extraordinary offenses such as drugs, homicide, and crime. In contrast, middle-class blacks are very much integrated into the programming mainstream of television. Successful shows about black life inhabit a format and genre that has a long tradition in television entertainment—the situation comedy. The rhythm, texture, and form of this type of show are comfortable and familiar to most viewers. Moreover, these programs are coupled with others that are similar. Thus, for instance, the Thursday evening schedule was built around *The Cosby Show* and *A Different World*. *227* fit snugly into the Saturday evening programming flow with *Golden Girls* and *Amen*. Still, even though representations of underclass and middle-class life are presented in the "bracketed" space of the news documentary and the situation comedy, at the level of decoding, the meanings of these shows circulate in the programming flow across programs and genres.

Surely, then, the failure of blacks in the urban underclass, as Mrs. Wallace suggested in the CBS documentary, is their own because they live in an isolated world where contemporary racism is no longer a significant factor in their lives. The success of blacks in the television middle class suggests as much. In the world of the urban underclass, unemployment, industrial relocation, ineffective social policies, power inequalities, and racism do not explain failure, just as affirmative action policies, political organization, collective social and cultural challenges to specific forms of racial domination, and the civil rights movement do not help explain the growth of the black middle class.

The nonfictional representations of the underclass and the fictionalized treatment of the middle class are significant in other ways. Contemporary television shows in general and shows about black life in particular have reclaimed the family; they are set either in the nuclear family of *The Cosby Show* and *227* or in the workplace family of *Frank's Place* and *Amen* (Feuer, 1987; Taylor, 1987). The idealized representations of family presented in these shows maintain the hope and possibility of a stable and rewarding family life. At the same time, this idealization displaces (but does not eliminate) possibilities for critical examination of the social roots of crisis in the American family (Jameson, 1979).

Family stresses such as alienation, estrangement, violence, divorce, and latchkey kids are typically ignored. When addressed in the television representations of black middle-class families, they are represented as the subject of periodic and temporary disagreements rather than as expressions of the social stresses and disruptive impulses that originate in the social organization of society and the conflicting ideologies that shape our understanding of the family as a social institution.

At the negotiated level of meaning (Hall, 1980), *The Cosby Show* effectively incorporates many progressive moments and impulses from recent social movements. The show presents Claire's independence, autonomy, and authority in the family without resorting to exaggeration and trivialization (Downing, 1988). Again, this utopian impulse is one of the reasons for the show's popular appeal. And yet it is also one of the ways the explicit critical possibilities of the show are contained and subverted. Claire's independence and autonomy are expressions of her own individual character; they are confined to the family and put in the service of running a smoother household. This claim on the family and the affirmation of female independence are especially appealing when seen against the crisis of the family dissolution, female-headed households, and teenage pregnancy presented in the CBS documentary. Ironically, this celebration of Claire's independence and agency within the family has its counterpart in the CBS documentary. In each case, black women are assertive and responsible within the contexts of their various households. Thus, even within the constraints of underclass poverty, this moment can be read as an appeal to the utopian ideal of strong and liberated black women.

Ideologically, representations of underclass failure still appeal and contribute to the notion of the black poor as menacing and threatening, especially to members of the white middle class. Such a menace must, of course, be contained, and through weekly visits to black middle-class homes and experiences, whites (and middle-class backs) are reasonably assured that the middle-class blacks with whom they interact are safe (Miller, 1986). Whites can take comfort in the fact that they have more in common with the Huxtables than with those representations of the family in crisis—Timothy, Clarinda, Darren, and Alice.

The twin representations of fictional and nonfictional television have become part of the public discourse about American race relations. Although, no doubt, both the fictional and the nonfictional representations of blacks are real, like all ideology, the realities are selected, partial, and incomplete. Where the television lens is trained, how wide, which angle, how long, and with whose voice—these shape much of what we see and how we understand it. As these fictional and nonfictional television representations indicate, television helps shape our understandings about racial (in)equality in America.

REFERENCES

Cantor, M. (1980). *Prime-time television: Content and control.* Beverly Hills, CA: Sage.

Demeter, J. (1986). Notes on the media and race. *Radical America, 20*(5), 63-71.

Downing, J. (1988). "The Cosby Show" and American racial discourse. In G. Smitherman-Donaldson & T. A. van Dijk (Eds.), *Discourse and discrimination* (pp. 46-74). Detroit, MI: Wayne State University Press.

Feuer, J. (1986). Narrative form in American television. In C. MacCabe (Ed.), *High theory/low culture: Analyzing popular television and film* (pp. 101-115). New York: St. Martin's.

Feuer, J. (1987). Genre study and television. In R. Allen (Ed.), *Channels of discourse* (pp. 113-134). Chapel Hill: University of North Carolina Press.

Fiske, J. (1987a). *Television culture.* London: Methuen.

Fiske, J. (1987b). British cultural studies and television. In R. Allen (Ed.), *Channels of discourse* (pp. 254-291). Chapel Hill: University of North Carolina Press.

Fiske, J., & Hartley, J. (1978). *Reading television.* London: Methuen.

Gitlin, T. (1983). *Inside prime time.* New York: Pantheon.

Glasgow, D. (1981). *The black underclass.* New York: Vintage.

Gramsci, A. (1971). *Selections from the prison notebooks.* New York: International Publishers.

Gray, H. (1986). Television and the new black man: Black male images in prime-time situation comedy. *Media, Culture, and Society, 8,* 223-242.

Hall, S. (1980). Encoding/decoding. In S. Hall, A. Lowe, & P. Willis (Eds.), *Culture, media, language* (pp. 128-139). London: Hutchinson.

Hall, S. (1982). The rediscovery of ideology: Return of the repressed in media studies. In M. Gurevitch, T. Bennett, J. Curran, & J. Woollocott (Eds.), *Culture, society, and the media* (pp. 56-91). London: Methuen.

Jameson, F. (1979). Reification and utopia in mass culture. *Social Text, 1,* 130-148.

Lewis, M. (1984). *The culture of inequality.* New York: American Library.

Miller, M. C. (1986). Deride and conquer. In T. Gitlin (Ed.), *Watching television* (pp. 183-229). New York: Pantheon.

Nichols, B. (1981). *Ideology and the image.* Bloomington: University of Indiana Press.

Taylor, E. (1987, October 5). TV families: Three generations of packaged dreams. *Boston Review of Books,* p. 5.

Williams, R. (1974). *Television: Technology and cultural form.* New York: Oxford University Press.

Winston, M. (1983). Racial consciousness and the evolution of mass communication in the United States. *Deadalus, 111,* 171-183.

9

Sex on the Soaps

An Analysis of Black, White, and Interracial Couple Intimacy

SHARON BRAMLETT-SOLOMON

TRICIA M. FARWELL

In 1966, soap opera television presented the first story line involving a nondomestic black character when black actress Micki Grant was cast as a nurse in *Another World*. In 1968, the first major black story line plot in daytime soap television history was presented to soap viewers when *One Life to Live* featured a romantic relationship and engagement between a black housekeeper's daughter (Carla Gray) who passed for white and a white doctor (Paul Scott). The story line also represented the first projection of interracial romance on daytime soaps, despite the fact that intimacy between the black and white couple hardly existed. Twenty years later, soap opera television, or "daytime drama," reached another milestone in the spring of 1988 when *General Hospital* featured the first interracial marriage in a daytime serial (Cassata & Skill, 1983, p. 34; Narine, 1988, p. 94).

Soap operas, so named for their sponsorship in the earliest decades of television by soap companies, are built on suspenseful plots that greatly focus on romance, intimacy, and sex. Researchers have noted sex as a staple of the daytime soap (Barbatis, 1983, p. 88; Greenberg, Abelman, & Neuendorf, 1981, p. 83; Lowry & Towles, 1989, p. 76).

Research studies of sexual behavior on network television can be traced back as far as two decades. In one of the earliest studies, Franzblau, Sprafkin, and Rubinstein's (1977) analysis of 61 prime time programs found sexual behavior quantity varied by program type. Studies that followed between 1977 and 1981 observed increased rates of implicit and explicit sexual behavior on prime time shows (Franzblau et al., 1977, p. 164; Greenberg, Graef, Fernandez-Collado, Korzenny, & Atkin, 1980, p. 211; Silverman, Sprafkin, & Rubinstein, 1979, p. 33; Sprafkin & Silverman, 1981, p. 34).

The examination of sexual behavior on television has extended beyond prime time network programs to daytime soap operas. Lowry, Love, and Kirby in 1981 found an average of more than six sexual behaviors in the soaps per hour, most prevalently reflected in erotic touching, verbal intimacy, and implied intercourse. Greenberg et al.'s (1981) study found that daytime soaps have more sexual content than prime time programs, although the types of intimacy portrayed are radically different.

Past studies of sexual behavior on soap operas have examined frequency of intimacy, patterns of intimacy, intimacy between married and unmarried couples, contraceptive use, and infidelity. A few of these studies have also focused on the uses and gratifications aspects of soap opera viewing and the role of soap operas in constructing a reality for viewers (Carveth & Alexander, 1985, p. 259; Compesi, 1980, p. 155; Fine, 1981, p. 97; Katzman, 1972, p. 200; Sutherland & Siniawsky, 1982, p. 67).

Although researchers have examined a variety of interests related to soap opera intimacy, they largely have focused only on intimacy between white couples and have not examined the intimacy variable by race. Past soap opera intimacy examinations have not paid attention to black couples or interracial couples. This study extends past research to include an examination of the quantity and type of intimacy among black, white, and interracial couples portrayed in the daytime soaps. The need for more focus on the media portrayal of ethnic minorities and sociocultural integration is well documented (Gates, 1989, sec. 2, p. 1; Metabane, 1988, p. 22; Potter, 1986, p. 160; Rosen, 1986, p. 44; Sanoff & Thorton, 1987, p. 56).

Examinations of television that use cultivation analysis show that the study of ethnic minority treatment is justified by television's potential influence on viewer conceptions of a variety of social and political topics, including viewers' ideas and perspectives regarding sociocultural and racial integration. Soap operas are particularly useful for examining sociocultural integration due to their inherent focus on interpersonal relationships, love interests, and selected social issues (Greenberg & Alessio, 1985, p. 309; Greenberg et al., 1981, p. 83; Larson, 1994, p. 44; Lowry et al., 1981, p. 90).

LITERATURE OVERVIEW

Television, due to its constancy and pervasiveness, is viewed as the medium with the greatest potential to influence people's ideas and perspectives about racial groups and cultures with which they have little experience and no contact (Gates, 1989, sec. 2, p. 1; Larson, 1994, p. 44; Potter, 1986, p. 159). Television presents explicit examples and implicit principles regarding sociocultural integration and race relations. For example, for many blacks and many whites residing in racially homogeneous communities such as urban black communities or all-white suburbs, television typically is the principal illustrator of black and white communication and race relations (Auletta & Hammerback, 1985, p. 301; Carter, 1988, p. 29; Metabane, 1988, p. 21).

Researchers focusing on television coverage of ethnic minorities often have used cultivation analysis in their studies. Cultivation theory posits that television affects our perceptions and beliefs about social phenomena to the extent of providing a conduit in which dominant values and ideology are transmitted to viewers (Buerkel-Rothfuss & Mayes, 1981, p. 108; Carveth & Alexander, 1985, p. 259; Metabane, 1988, p. 23; Perse, 1986, p. 175). Television may contribute to our perception of various racial groups in society and to our attitudes regarding sociocultural and racial integration (Auletta & Hammerback, 1985, p. 301; Carter, 1988, p. 29; Metabane, 1988, p. 21).

Research shows that more Americans get their views about the world from television than from any other medium, especially on subjects in which they have no direct experience (Carveth & Alexander, 1985, p. 259; Hughes, 1980, p. 287; Potter, 1986, p. 159). In media cultivation

studies, the socialization role of television soap operas and their growing popularity over the past two decades has been noted (Gerbner,
Gross, Morgan, & Signorielli, 1982, p. 102; Greenberg et al., 1981,
p. 83; Matelski, 1988, p. 4).

Television first demonstrated acceptance of story lines about racial
integration and interracial friendships in the mid-1960s with shows
such as *I Spy* and *Julia*. Although they allowed some acceptance of racial
integration and interracial mixing, television producers rarely if ever
presented story lines that showed interracial intimacy (Dates & Barlow,
1993, p. 288; Wilson & Gutiérrez, 1985, p. 3). Today, however,
statistics show increases in interracial couples in America over the
years—no doubt a result of greater social integration (Porterfield, 1982,
p. 18; Todd, 1992, p. 202). While television depiction of interracial
couple story lines is not extremely common, such story lines are not the
taboo today that they were in past decades, and are occasionally
portrayed.

In soap opera television, intimacy is a huge draw for viewers. Love,
romance, and sex draw millions of loyal viewers every day (Cantor,
1979, p. 71; Greenberg, 1980, p. 10; Matelski, 1988, p. 31; Townley,
1984, p. 15). According to Nielsen research, soap operas have an
audience of some 20 million viewers (*Nielsen National TV Ratings,*
1993, p. 12). The soap audience is a very large, multiracial entity that is
loyal and dedicated to watching television soaps (Alexander, 1985, p.
295; Clemmons, 1991, sec. G, p. 8; Compesi, 1980, p. 155; Matelski,
1988, p. 21; Townley, 1984, p. 25). The focus of soap operas is the
development of interpersonal, social, and romantic relationships (Rosen,
1986, p. 43; Townley, 1984, p. 15; Williams, 1992, p. 3). Nielsen research
shows that 12.7% of all black households view daytime dramas compared with 6.3% of all other television viewers. The dozen or so serials
reap a bounty of over $700 million annually for ABC, CBS, and NBC.
A big chunk of the profits are drawn from the buying power of black
viewers (Narine, 1988, p. 97; *Nielsen National TV Ratings,* 1993, p. 23).

Before the 1980s, African Americans and other ethnic minorities
rarely were portrayed on television soap operas, unless in peripheral
roles as butlers, maids, or similar domestics (Carter, 1988, p. 29; Dates
& Barlow, 1993, p. 53; Lowry et al., 1981, p. 90; Rosen, 1986, p. 43).
Of course, if television producers were cautious about social integration
during these years, they were even less likely to depict integrated

romance because they tend to avoid programs that ruffle sponsors and ostracize viewers (Dates & Barlow, 1993, p. 45; Wilson & Gutiérrez, 1985, p. 57).

Although black and white intimacy was taboo in 1960s television, in 1967 it was the theme of Stanley Kramer's very successful Hollywood film, *Guess Who's Coming to Dinner.* Starring Sidney Poitier and Katherine Houghton, Kramer's film was the first big box office draw to depict love between a black man and white woman on the American big screen (Crowther, 1967, p. 38; Hochman, 1992, p. B13). The film, which was a breakthrough Hollywood portrayal of black and white romance, was nominated for 10 Academy Awards and won two (Hochman, 1992, p. B13). By today's standards, such a film would probably not be a big deal, but in 1967 it reflected a rather bold stand, given existing racial attitudes and the fact that in 1967 statues opposing interracial marriages were on the books in 16 states (Clemmons, 1991, sec. G, p. 8; Porterfield, 1982, p. 17).

In 1968, what is considered to be daytime serials' first interracial couple story line made its way onto *One Life to Live* (Williams, 1992, p. 97). In this case, a young, very light-skinned black woman, Carla Gray, who passed as white, had an intimate affair with a white male on the show. The fact that she masked her ethnicity and was perceived as being white by her mate may have provided an interracial setup that did not alienate viewers, because the program's ratings remained high despite the interracial story line (Rosen, 1986, p. 43; Williams, 1992, p. 97). It was not until the late 1980s, however, that viewers began to see black couples and interracial couples integrated into daytime soap opera life. But these couples were not always received with enthusiasm, and due to viewer criticism, often had very short-lived story lines (Matelski, 1988, p. 9; Williams, 1992, p. 95).

Indeed, the soaps have come a long way from portraying black Americans simply as domestics, athletes, or musical talent. Most soap operas today include one or two black couples in an otherwise all-white community. Like Claire and Cliff Huxtable of the popular and long-running *Cosby Show,* the blacks who appear on soaps today are usually middle-class professionals who are well integrated into the white community and indistinguishable from their white counterparts, except for color.

A few years ago, David Poltrack, vice president for research at CBS, stated that television is now color blind (Sanoff & Thorton, 1987, p.

56). One could argue that the willingness of these programs to portray racial and interracial intimacy today is a step toward reflecting color blindness. A few scholars have discussed the issue of intimacy and race on daytime soaps. Matelski (1988) concluded that the depth in which risky issues such as interracial intimacy are tackled by a soap opera is directly tied to the audience reaction to the soap. Issues that are controversial or potentially disruptive are ignored or played down to avoid alienating viewers (p. 13). Williams (1992, p. 20) noted that safe and conservative choices are made by soap producers.

The study of black and interracial intimacy on daytime soap operas enables us to determine the images that television soap producers present to American viewers, and serves as a kind of barometer of changes in media portrayals of blacks and other Americans of color. Research on media portrayals of ethnic minorities in recent years often has indicated that the media are doing a better job today than in past decades of creating fairer and more realistic depictions of minority characters (Dates & Barlow, 1993, p. 81; Wilson & Gutiérrez, 1985, p. 56).

Soap Opera Magazine, however, has criticized daytime soap producers' treatment of interracial romance as being too coy and cautious. The magazine points out, for example, that in a past love scene between Dave, who is white, and Valerie, who is black, on *Days of Our Lives,* you see the couple facing each other whispering words of love and passion and then you see them stiffly embrace and walk away ("Soap Standings," 1994, p. 5).

Previous studies of sexual behavior on soap operas have focused only on white couples and have not examined the intimacy variable of nonwhite soap characters. The study described in this chapter examines the quantity and types of intimacy between black couples, white couples, and interracial couples on daytime soaps. The major questions addressed are as follows: (a) How often do the soaps portray intimacy between black couples, white couples, and interracial couples? (b) How often do the soaps portray verbal intimacy and erotic touching among these couples? (c) How often do the soaps portray verbal intimacy and erotic touching in the same scene among these couples?

Given a history of television daytime drama in which black couples and interracial couples did not exist in the soap opera world, the extent to which interracial intimacy is portrayed on daytime soap operas can be considered an indication of how far television producers have come in their willingness to present such depictions. Periodic content analyses of media treatment and portrayal of Americans of color are essential if we expect to reliably determine how the media portray blacks and other Americans of color and how these depictions affect viewers and race relations.

METHOD

The study data consisted of videotaped recordings over an eight-week period of the top hour-long daytime soap opera from each of the three networks: ABC, CBS, and NBC. The soaps were videotaped Monday through Friday directly off the air between September 14 and November 11, 1994. The three top soaps from each network were determined by averaging weekly Nielsen ratings for the month of August. The top soap operas were *All My Children* (ABC) with an average rating of 6.2, *The Young and the Restless* (CBS) with an average rating of 7.4, and *Days of Our Lives* (NBC) with an average rating of 5.6 ("Ratings Race," 1994a, 1994b, 1994c, 1994d). The top soaps were chosen because they reach the largest audience for each network and, therefore, have the greatest potential to be influential.

The sample consisted of 132 hours of soap programming videotaped over the eight-week study period. The soaps were content analyzed independently by trained coders. The coders examined each soap scene for intimacy between black couples, white couples, and interracial couples. The unit of analysis was the scene, defined as a continuous situation that takes place in the same setting. A scene ended only when interrupted by another scene or by a commercial break. The return to the same setting or situation after a commercial break was considered to be a new scene. For the purpose of this study, *interracial couple* refers to an intimate relationship between a black and a white partner.

Intimacy was defined as any verbal or physical act that is clearly sexual in nature or that has sexual, romantic, or erotic connotations. In this study, intimacy was classified as either verbal intimacy or erotic touching. Erotic touching consisted of kissing, romantic hugging, petting, and sensual body touching such as caressing a person's shoulders or neck. Verbal intimacy consisted of talking about love, sex, or sensuous feelings. The following are examples of verbal intimacy:

I want you in every way.
Make love to me.
Honey, you feel so good.
You turn me on like a faucet.
I need you to hold me.
I love you so much.
Last night you made me feel wonderful.

A scene was considered to have both verbal intimacy and erotic touching if at least one aspect of each occurred during the scene. Excluded from the coding were acts of rape because they are considered acts of violence and not intimacy. Discussions with third parties about intimate situations or feelings were not examined; only intimacy between partners or potential partners was coded. A 10-item coding sheet was designed for the content analysis. Each intimate scene was analyzed by the coders. Calculation of intercoder reliability resulted in .91 for average agreement between coders. The formula used was a Scott's Pi coefficient of reliability that calculated the ratio of coding agreements to the total number of coding decisions.

RESULTS

Examination of the top three network soap operas over the eight-week study period resulted in the analysis of 3,360 scenes, out of which 421 depicted intimacy. The calculation of 421 scenes over 132 hours of programming produced a frequency of 3.2 intimate behaviors per hour. Out of 421 intimate scenes, 88% or 372 depicted white couple intimacy compared with 12% or 49 that depicted black couple intimacy. No scenes depicting interracial intimacy were shown on the three soaps during the study period.

QUANTITY OF INTIMACY

Of the three soaps, *Days of Our Lives* had the most intimate scenes during the study period, as shown in Table 9.1, constituting over half of the total scenes analyzed (53% or 222). The findings show that this soap lived up to its reputation in *Soap Opera Digest* as the sexiest soap on television, the soap that gives viewers lots of steamy romance. As

TABLE 9.1 Intimate Scenes on Daytime Soap Operas Between Black, White, and Interracial Couples: A Frequency and Percentage Comparison ($n = 421$)

	White Couples	Black Couples	Interracial Couples	Totals
Days of Our Lives	187 (44%)	35 (8%)	—	222
The Young and the Restless	114 (27%)	13 (3%)	—	127
All My Children	71 (17%)	1 (1%)	—	72
Totals	372	49	—	421

shown in Table 9.1, the soap's intimacy was overwhelmingly between white couples (84% or 187) when compared with black couple intimacy (16% or 35). No scenes in this soap depicted intimacy between interracial couples.

The Young and the Restless had significantly fewer intimate scenes than the previous soap. As shown in Table 9.1, there were 127 intimate scenes, in which 90%, or 114, depicted white couples and 10%, or 13, depicted black couples. There were no scenes that showed interracial couples.

All My Children had 72 intimate scenes, the fewest number in all soaps examined. Of those scenes, 99%, or 71, depicted white couple intimacy, and only 1% (1) depicted black couple intimacy. There was no interracial couple intimacy, however, a finding somewhat surprising given that the soap's regular cast includes an interracial married couple, Tom and Olivia Cuddahy—a white male and black female.

TYPES OF INTIMACY

The dominant mode of presenting intimacy in the three soaps was erotic touching, which was portrayed in almost half the 421 scenes analyzed. Four times more erotic touching than verbal intimacy occurred in the three soaps. Erotic touching scenes constituted 48%, or 202, of the total scenes analyzed, while verbal intimacy scenes constituted only 10%, or 44, of the total scenes analyzed. When type of intimacy was cross-tabulated by race of couples, no significant differences were shown between black couples and white couples.

When the data were examined for the frequency of erotic touching and verbal intimacy in the same scene, results showed their occurrence in 42%, or 175, of the total scenes analyzed. These findings are consistent with Greenberg et al.'s (1981) observation that the most common type of sexual behavior on the soaps was physically explicit petting. But the findings differ from a 1985 study of soaps by Greenberg and Alessio, which found that talking about sex is far more prevalent than engaging in it.

DISCUSSION

Findings in this eight-week purposive sample show interesting patterns and trends regarding the three top soaps examined, although such findings cannot be generalized. Study results show that intimacy portrayal on the three soaps still largely follows television's long tradition of presenting a world in which white couple intimacy is predominantly depicted, while black couple intimacy is not commonly featured and interracial couple intimacy is rarely visible. The findings suggest that after decades of being taboo and unaccepted, black couple intimacy, and to some extent interracial couple intimacy, is moving into the soap opera world, but slowly and in very cautiously measured doses.

The data showed that erotic touching prevailed over verbal intimacy, with no significant differences shown when cross-tabulated by race. Also, in 42% of the scenes analyzed, both erotic touching and verbal intimacy occurred in the same scene. The findings suggest that although black characters have improved their standing in the soaps in terms of occupations portrayed and may have moved from servants to lawyers, they still are not commonly portrayed in scenes with intimacy. The few black couples and one interracial couple on the daytime soap operas examined give the audience the impression that television is including more blacks. This study, however, supports Carter's (1988, p. 33) notion that TV, for the most part, depicts life as lived by the majority of the white population. On the daytime soap operas examined, intimacy was depicted as something that white couples do, while black couples only occasionally partake in intimacy. The fact that no scenes depicted intimacy between interracial couples suggests that such portrayals on the soaps are minuscule and limited. This conclusion is supported by the fact that, months after completing this study, the researchers viewed one instance of interracial intimacy on *All My Children* between Noah and Julia.

If soap producers give viewers what they think viewers want to see, then it seems the producers still perceive the soap audience of today as the audience of the 1950s in which soaps were created to entertain white women, despite significant constituencies of Americans of color, teenagers, professionals, college students, and men.

These findings suggest that although television soaps have evolved from the days when black characters were featured simply as domestics and when neither black nor interracial romance existed, they have not advanced to the point of a social reality in which black couples and interracial couples are commonly seen. Therefore, despite the fact that *All My Children* now toys with another possible interracial relationship in 1995 between Julia and Noah, the results in this study indicate that soap opera television remains very far from being color blind.

REFERENCES

Alexander, A. (1985). Adolescents soap opera viewing, relational perceptions. *Journal of Broadcasting and Electronic Media, 29*(3), 295-308.

Auletta, G. S., & Hammerback, J. C. (1985). A relational model for interracial interactions on television. *Western Journal of Speech Communication, 49,* 301-321.

Barbatis, G. (1983). Soap opera as etiquette book: Advice for interpersonal relationships. *Journal of American Culture, 6*(3), 88-90.

Buerkel-Rothfuss, N. L., & Mayes, S. (1981). Soap opera viewing: The cultivation effect. *Journal of Communication, 31*(3), 108-115.

Cantor, M. G. (1979). Our days and our nights on TV. *Journal of Communication, 29*(4), 66-72.

Carter, R. G. (1988). TV's black comfort zone for whites. *Television Quarterly, 23*(4), 29-34.

Carveth, R., & Alexander, A. (1985). Soap opera viewing motivations and cultivation process. *Journal of Broadcasting and Electronic Media, 29*(3), 259-273.

Cassata, M., & Skill, T. (1983). *Life on daytime television.* Norwood, NJ: Ablex.

Clemmons, C. J. (1991, June 8). A fever pitch. *Dallas Times Herald,* sec. G, p. 8.

Compesi, R. J. (1980). Gratifications of daytime TV serial viewers. *Journalism Quarterly, 57,* 155-158.

Crowther, B. (1967, December 1). Screen: Guess Who's Coming to Dinner arrives. *Time,* p. 38.

Dates, J. L., & Barlow, W. (1993). *Split image: African-Americans in the mass media.* Washington, DC: Howard University Press.

Fine, M. G. (1981). Soap opera conversations: The talk that binds. *Journal of Communication, 31*(3), 97-107.

Franzblau, S., Sprafkin, J. N., & Rubinstein, E. A. (1977). Sex on TV: A content analysis. *Journal of Communication, 27*(2), 164-170.

Gates, L. H. (1989, November 12). TV's black world turns but stays unreal. *New York Times,* sec. 2, p. 1.

Gerbner, G., Gross, L., Morgan, M., & Signorielli, N. (1982). Charting the mainstream: Television's contribution to political orientations. *Journal of Communication, 32,* 100-126.

Greenberg, B. S. (1980). *Life on television: Content analyses of U.S. TV drama.* Norwood, NJ: Ablex.

Greenberg, B. S., Abelman, R., & Neuendorf, K. (1981). Sex and the soap opera: Afternoon delight. *Journal of Communication, 31*(3), 83-89.

Greenberg, B. S., & Alessio, D. (1985). Quantity and quality of sex in the soaps. *Journal of Broadcasting and Electronic Media, 29*(3), 309-321.

Greenberg, B. S., Graef, D., Fernandez-Collado, C., Korzenny, F., & Atkin, C. K. (1980). Sexual intimacy on commercial TV during prime time. *Journalism Quarterly, 57,* 211-215.

Hochman, A. (1992, March 22). Sex, race and the movies. *Oregonian,* p. B13.

Hughes, M. (1980). The fruits of cultivation analysis: A reexamination of some effects of television watching. *Public Opinion Quarterly, 44*(3), 287-302.

Katzman, N. (1972). Television soap operas: What's been going on anyway? *Public Opinion Quarterly, 36,* 200-212.

Larson, S. (1994). Black women on *All My Children. Journal of Popular Film and Television, 22*(1), 44-48.

Lowry, D., Love, G., & Kirby, M. (1981). Sex on the soap operas: Patterns of intimacy. *Journal of Communication, 31*(3), 90.

Lowry, D. T., & Towles, D. E. (1989). Soap opera portrayals of sex, contraception, and sexually transmitted diseases. *Journal of Communication, 39*(2), 76-83.

Matelski, M. (1988). *The soap opera evolution: America's enduring romance with daytime drama.* Jefferson, NC: McFarland.

Metabane, P. W. (1988). Television and the black audience: Cultivating moderate perspectives on racial integration. *Journal of Communication, 38,* 21-31.

Narine, D. (1988). Blacks on soaps: From domestics to interracial lovers. *Ebony, 44*(1), 94-98.

Nielsen national TV ratings. (1993, December). Northbrook, IL: A. C. Nielsen Inc.

Perse, E. M. (1986). Soap opera viewing patterns of college students and cultivation. *Journal of Broadcasting & Electronic Media, 30*(2), 175-193.

Porterfield, E. (1982). Black-American intermarriage in the United States. *Marriage and Family Review, 5,* 17-34.

Potter, J. W. (1986). Perceived reality and the cultivation hypothesis. *Journal of Broadcasting and Electronic Media, 30,* 159-174.

Ratings race. (1994a, September 13). *Soap Opera Digest,* p. 12.

Ratings race. (1994b, September 27). *Soap Opera Digest,* p. 12.

Ratings race. (1994c, October 11). *Soap Opera Digest,* p. 12.

Ratings race. (1994d, October 25). *Soap Opera Digest,* p. 12.

Rosen, R. (1986). Soap operas: Search for yesterday. In T. Gitlin (Ed.), *Watching television* (pp. 42-67). New York: Pantheon.

Sanoff, A. P., & Thorton, J. (1987, July 13). TV's disappearing colorline. *U.S. News and World Report,* pp. 56-57.

Silverman, L. T., Sprafkin, J. N., & Rubinstein, E. A. (1979). Physical contact and sexual behavior on prime time TV. *Journal of Communication, 29*(1), 33-43.

Soap standings. (1994, March 22). *Soap Opera Magazine,* p. 5.

Sprafkin, J. N., & Silverman, L. T. (1981). Update: Physically intimate and sexual behavior on prime time television. *Journal of Communication, 31*(1), 34-40.

Sutherland, J. C., & Siniawsky, S. J. (1982). The treatment and resolution of moral violations on soap operas. *Journal of Communication, 32,* 67-74.

Todd, J. (1992). Attitudes toward interracial dating: Effects of age, sex and race. *Journal of Multicultural Counseling and Development, 20*(4), 202.

Townley, R. (1984). *The year in soaps.* New York: Crown.

Williams, C. T. (1992). *It's time for my story.* Westport, CT: Praeger.

Wilson, C. C., & Gutiérrez, F. (1985). *Minorities and media: Diversity and the end of mass communication.* Beverly Hills, CA: Sage.

10

Broadcast TV News Coverage of the O. J. Simpson Murder Case

Racist or Starstruck?

EDDITH A. DASHIELL

In the 1970s, when O. J. "The Juice" Simpson made football history as a record-breaking running back for the Buffalo Bills, the television cameras were there. In the 1980s, after O. J. traded in his number "32" football jersey with the San Francisco 49ers for an acting and sports broadcasting career, the television cameras were there. In June 1994, when O. J. Simpson was arrested and charged with the stabbing deaths of Nicole Brown Simpson, his ex-wife, and Ronald Goldman, a Los Angeles waiter and actor, the television cameras were there as well.

Events leading up to the O. J. Simpson murder trial included all the ingredients of a sensational news story—violence, death, sex, celebrity, and race—and it sparked a media frenzy—live coverage of the slow police pursuit along the Los Angeles freeways, live coverage of preliminary hearings and trial, profiles of the victims, and interviews with

AUTHOR'S NOTE: I thank Joe Bernt, associate professor in the E. W. Scripps School of Journalism at Ohio University, for his patience and help in conducting this study. Dr. Bernt was instrumental in helping me test the coding instrument, write the computer program needed to analyze the data, and edit the manuscript.

family members. Along with the intense media coverage of the Simpson case came renewed accusations of racism against the news media.

The American news media have been criticized for portraying black America as poor, criminal, drug addicted, and dysfunctional and for presenting the most victimized and hurting segment of the black community as the norm (Raybon, 1989). According to a *USA Today*-CNN-Gallup poll, nearly two-thirds of African Americans said they got upset at least once a week by the way news organizations covered black issues, and many believed news coverage worsened race relations rather than improved them (Fitzgerald, 1994). Many African Americans believed media coverage of O. J. Simpson and the murder charges against him was typical of the predominantly white media coverage of any black man accused of a crime. Most critics believed the media coverage of Simpson's situation was an effort to fit Simpson back into the all-black-men-are-violent-and-need-to-be-feared stereotype ("The O. J. Simpson Case," 1994, p. 54).

For many African Americans, the Simpson case was much more than a story of marital trouble and murder, it was a story of interracial marriage and the belief that a black man marrying a white woman meant gaining social privilege. It was a story of a black man accused of killing two white people with one of the victims being a woman. After all, it had not been so long ago in American history that a black man would have been lynched for just looking at a white woman. Some African Americans believed that the Simpson case would not have received the media coverage it did if Nicole Brown Simpson had been a black woman (Blackstone, 1994; McNamara, 1994; Vargas, 1994).

Other African Americans expressed sorrow and anger that Simpson, one of their few positive black role models and heroes, had been taken away. O. J. Simpson grew up in a poor, inner-city San Francisco neighborhood but was able to become a football hero, sports commentator, and actor. Many African Americans believed there was the perception that no matter how far O. J. Simpson tried to distance himself from his rough, inner-city childhood, he was just another black man from the ghetto unable to avoid violent crime, and the news media only perpetuated that stereotype ("The O. J. Simpson Case," 1994).

But perceptions about racist news coverage against O. J. Simpson had clear racial boundaries. An NBC-*Wall Street Journal* poll found that nearly twice as many blacks as whites believed that the media were biased against Simpson (Roberts, 1994). A CNN-*USA Today*-Gallup poll revealed that two-thirds of the black respondents felt that the media had been too harsh on Simpson, compared with less than one-third of the white respondents (Vargas, 1994). CBS News polls found that blacks were twice as likely as whites to think the media were biased against Simpson (Threlkeld, 1994).

For many white respondents, race was not an issue in the Simpson case. These polls showed that whites believed it was Simpson's celebrity status—not the color of his skin—that attracted so much media attention. White respondents in these polls said they saw Simpson as an individual, "not a representative of all black men" (McNamara, 1994). The polls found that most whites believed O. J. Simpson had risen above the race barrier, becoming a "nonthreatening," successful African American male (Blackstone, 1994). *Newsweek* journalist Jonathan Alter (1994) said: "Many whites had invested considerable psychic energy in their illusion of a color-blind society. Their almost paternalistic admiration for Simpson had made them feel better, more broad-minded, and acknowledging the shadow of race threatened that sense of accomplishment" (p. 19). Some argued that any hint of racism was outweighed by the facts: (a) Nicole Brown Simpson and Ronald Goldman had been brutally murdered, and (b) there was evidence that linked Simpson to the crimes.

But despite denials that race was a critical element in the Simpson case, the racial angle did begin to surface: accusations of racism against *Time* magazine for darkening Simpson's mug shot on its cover, accusations of police racism against Simpson, concern about the racial makeup of the Simpson trial jury, and the division along racial lines of public opinion polls about the case.

This study sought to see just how the issue of race in the Simpson case was handled by the national broadcast news media by examining a sliver of that coverage—the national evening TV news programs of ABC, NBC, and CBS from the night the murders were first reported on June 13, 1994, through the beginning of jury selection in the Simpson murder trial on September 30, 1994. This study examines the extent of the evening broadcast TV news coverage of the Simpson case, how often race was the focus of that coverage, and whether the media perpetuated the racism and the racial stereotypes that African Americans believe still exist in the United States.

OVERVIEW

An early and frequently cited research study into the relationship between race and the media was conducted by the federal government in 1968 when President Lyndon B. Johnson appointed a national commission to investigate the underlying causes of the urban, race-related riots during the 1960s. The 1968 report of the National Advisory Commission on Civil Disorders, commonly known as the Kerner Commission report, criticized the American news media in four areas: (a) The media failed to adequately report race relations and urban problems; (b) the media were often biased or racist in their coverage of news about blacks; (c) the media had a dismal record of employing blacks; and (d) the news media treated blacks as if they were not part of American society. The report said: "By failing to portray the Negro as a matter of routine and in the context of the total society, the news media have, we believe, contributed to the black-white schism in this country" (National Advisory Commission on Civil Disorders, 1968, p. 211).

More recent research into news coverage of African Americans has supported the opinion that among African Americans the American news media often present biased, inaccurate, unbalanced, and negative stereotypes of black America. Johnson (1992) found that news coverage of the black community contained disturbing biases and patterns of misinformation that may hamper black social advancement, especially among young blacks. Abron (1990) concluded that the mainstream media continued to misrepresent African American life and culture, but the discrediting of blacks by today's media was more subtle than in the 1800s. Entman (1992) found that local television news coverage of crime encouraged modern white racism—hostility toward and rejection of blacks. A study conducted at San Francisco State University's Center for Integration and Improvement of Journalism (1994) concluded that racial stereotyping still exists in the American media. Although this study was not a statistical analysis of American journalism, it did provide provocative case studies and analyses of how well the news media handled news coverage of people of color in their newspapers and on their newscasts.

Research has also focused on the relationship of race and the media in terms of high-profile African Americans. Gibbons (1993) analyzed media coverage of Jesse Jackson's race for the Democratic nomination for the presidency in 1984. Gibbons concluded that the news coverage of the Jackson campaign revealed more about the media than Jackson, saying the news media—"predominantly a white male bastion"—were nothing more than the "arms of the ruling estate," mirroring the attitudes of the corporate world and its goal of maintaining the status quo (Gibbons, 1993, p. xii). Feagin (1992) examined the effects of the white-male-dominated media on the Anita Hill-Clarence Thomas hearings and concluded that the United States was in need of a serious media outlet or scholarly journal that would focus on the role of white racism in creating and perpetuating the bases for racial oppression and conflict in the United States. The Simpson case offers researchers another high-profile opportunity to study the interaction of mainstream media and its coverage of the African American community.

METHODS

This study addresses the role played by race as opposed to the role played by celebrity, a traditional factor in the definition of news, specifically in network news coverage of this high-profile arrest and trial. As a high-profile African American, did O. J. Simpson's race play a significant role in media coverage of the double murder charges against him? Were the news media racist in their coverage of Simpson, as many African Americans believed, or were they simply awed by the celebrity status of a former football star accused of murdering his ex-wife and her male friend?

This study was a content analysis of the transcripts of 342 O. J. Simpson stories that aired on the national evening TV news programs of the three broadcast networks (ABC, CBS, and NBC) from June 13 through September 30, 1994. Transcripts of the evening TV news programs from the three networks were retrieved from electronic (CD-ROM) databases published by Research Publications International and University Microfilms Incorporated. Video of the three network programs was not analyzed for this study.

Each story was coded for a variety of characteristics and content, such as format, story type, story length, story location, domestic violence, death penalty, Simpson's celebrity status, media leaks, descriptions of the crime scene, references to the defense and prosecution, and references to the judge. For the issue of race, the stories were coded for the following references: interracial marriage, O. J. Simpson's race, Nicole Simpson's race, the race of other participants, racial makeup of the jury, and police racism.

The coding instrument was tested by the author and another mass communication researcher on a random sample of 10 news stories from the selection analyzed in this study. Based on item-by-item analysis and percentage of agreement, intercoder reliability (Stempel & Westley, 1989) averaged 96% for all items, with the percentage of agreement at 75% for the item measuring references to the prosecution and the prosecution's strategies. All other coding for this study was completed by the author. Level of significance was set at .05.

RESULTS

Just the sheer number of stories that aired by the three broadcast networks from June through September reveals the massive amount of attention the media gave the Simpson case. In the first 80 days of media coverage of the case, the three broadcast networks aired 342 stories, and at least one story about the Simpson case aired on all but 14 nights of that 80-day period. Of the 342 stories that aired during this time period, most of the stories (39.2%) aired during the *CBS Evening News,* followed by ABC's nightly newscasts *(World News Tonight* with Peter Jennings, *World News Saturday,* and *World News Sunday)* with 31.3%, and *NBC Nightly News* with 29.5%.

Overall, there was very little difference among the three networks in how they covered the O. J. Simpson murder case during their evening news programs. The majority of the Simpson stories (69.9%) were hard news as opposed to feature stories (29.5%) or commentaries (.3%). Of the 342 stories, 66.1% were of medium length (between 100 to 500 words). The only statistically significant difference among the networks was the story length. A breakdown by network revealed that CBS did significantly more in-depth, longer stories than ABC or NBC. Of the stories that aired on CBS, 31% were more than 500 words, compared with the stories aired on NBC, 25.7% of which were more than 500 words; only 14% of ABC's stories were in the 500-plus word range.

Descriptions of the crime scene and references to strategies by the prosecution and the defense dominated broadcast TV news coverage of the Simpson case more than the race issue, but with no statistically significant difference among the three broadcast networks. The broadcast TV media referred to descriptions of the crime scene in 55% of their evening news stories. References to statements, decisions, or strategies of the prosecution appeared in 74% of the stories, and the broadcast TV media referred to the statements, decisions, or strategies of the defense in 76.9% of their evening news stories.

In terms of race, this study is only descriptive in nature because statistical tests of the data found no significant differences among the networks regarding how they handled the issue of race in their coverage of the Simpson murder case. According to the results of this study, race played a minor role in the broadcast evening news coverage of O. J. Simpson.

The media spent June covering the murders, Simpson's arrest, and the upcoming trial with little reference to race but gave the race factor more attention in July when the Simpson defense team suggested that a Los Angeles police detective was a racist and had planted evidence at Simpson's home to implicate him in the murders. One of the most common quotations used by all three networks in their coverage of accusations of police racism was an excerpt from the police detective's military psychiatric examination records in which he referred to blacks as "niggers." There were 46 references to accusations of police racism among the stories that aired during the national evening TV news. Those references occurred in only 5.4% of the stories, however, with no significant difference among the networks.

Of the 342 stories that aired from June through September about Simpson, there were only ten references to Simpson's race, nine of which appeared in the transcripts of the *CBS Evening News*. For example, CBS referred to Simpson's race in its coverage of defense accusations that a Los Angeles police detective was capable of "framing a black man for the murder of two white people" (Hughes, 1994a). Five of the nine references CBS made to Simpson's race appeared in one story about how public opinion concerning the Simpson case had definite racial divisions. In that story, a source being interviewed referred to Simpson as an "honorary white person" (Threlkeld, 1994). The tenth reference to Simpson's race appeared in a July 23 transcript from *ABC World News Tonight* in which the reporter referred to Simpson as a "black suspect" in a story about a meeting between Los Angeles District Attorney Gil Garcetti and black leaders concerned that Simpson would not receive fair treatment by the criminal justice system because of his race (Norris, 1994). There were no references to Simpson's race in the transcripts of the *NBC Nightly News*.

Nicole Brown Simpson's race was only referred to five times with four of those references coming from a July 15 *CBS Evening News* story.

Ironically, in that story, the references to Nicole Simpson's race were in terms of "not being a black woman" as opposed to being "white" (McNamara, 1994). References to Nicole Brown Simpson mainly focused on her being a murder victim (38.3%) and sometimes on being an abused spouse (6.1%).

The racial makeup of the jury also received some attention in the media, mentioned 31 times (3.8%), but not at a statistically significant level. On July 19, all three networks ran stories that quoted Los Angeles District Attorney Gil Garcetti saying that he was hopeful and confident that the court would find a "white, black, brown, every color juror there is, who will indeed be fair and impartial" (Hughes, 1994b; Lewis, 1994b; Redeker, 1994). A September 26 CBS story referred to how the court would be selecting the jury for the Simpson trial from "heavily Hispanic and African American central Los Angeles" (Whitaker, 1994).

Interracial marriage received very little attention in the TV evening news, receiving only three references, and those references were in relation to potential jurors' attitudes toward interracial marriage as part of the media's coverage of jury selection in the Simpson case. The national TV broadcast media also mentioned race when they aired stories about whether the Los Angeles District Attorney's Office would seek the death penalty in the Simpson case and about black leaders' concerns that the criminal justice system's use of the death penalty discriminated against blacks. In the July 19 NBC story that focused on jury selection in the Simpson trial, the reporter also cited a Field Organization poll that found 35% of the white respondents believed that, if found guilty, Simpson should receive the death penalty, compared with only 3% of the black respondents (Lewis, 1994b). Other references to race consisted of media coverage of various news polls that identified the respondents as black, white, Latino, or Hispanic; stories about a possible witness to the Simpson-Goldman murders who claimed he saw two white men leaving the scene of the crime; and reports that a hair found on Ronald Goldman's clothing came from a "black person" (Lewis, 1994a).

Although not at a statistically significant level, it did appear that CBS was more aggressive in tackling the issue of race as a legitimate news story than the other two broadcast networks. For example, on July 9, CBS produced a story focusing on African Americans' doubts about Simpson's ability to get a fair trial because of their belief that the criminal justice system was biased against him (Threlkeld, 1994). Also on July 21, CBS Evening News compared the Simpson case with another high-profile murder case with racial overtones—the Atlanta child killings of 1981 (Norville, 1994).

Although race entered into some of the coverage, the broadcast TV media referred more to Simpson's celebrity status than they did to his race. Among the three networks, there were 252 references to Simpson as a celebrity figure and no significant difference among the networks. Overall, references to Simpson's celebrity status among the three networks occurred in 21.9% of the stories while references to Simpson's race occurred in only 1.5% of the stories. References to his celebrity status included numerous statements about his football career, his acting career, and his being a hero and role model to children.

DISCUSSION

Based on the results of this study, race played an important—albeit a minor—role in the broadcast TV evening news coverage of the Simpson case, with no evidence of blatant racism on the part of the media. Although there were relatively few references to race in the transcripts of the network evening news programs, the findings do suggest that race was still very much a part of the consciousness of television news media. The fact that the media organizations conducted polls structured to find out Americans' opinions about the Simpson case based on the respondents' race indicated that the media considered the race issue of such potential news value that it needed to be addressed in their coverage of Simpson.

Although the media did address the issue of race in their coverage of O. J. Simpson, other issues dominated the coverage. The issue of race in the Simpson case had to compete with a variety of other elements associated with the Simpson case: domestic violence, Simpson's celebrity status, problematic jury selection, squabbles between the Simpson defense team and the prosecution, criticism of leaks to the media, and descriptions of the crime scene.

Broadcast TV news coverage of the Simpson case resembled the media coverage given to a political race or a sporting event with the media focusing mostly on the strategies of the defense and the prosecution in terms of judgments about how one decision or event helped or hurt O. J. Simpson. Each day, the broadcast media would report the latest development in the Simpson case in much the same way a sports commentator would describe a key play in a close ball game or a political analyst would determine the winner in a political debate. The complexity of the Simpson case tended to overshadow the race issue in most instances, even though the racial elements of the case were not completely ignored by the broadcast TV media during their evening news programs.

When the issue of race was addressed, it was mainly related to the racial makeup of the jury, public opinion polls that divided respondents based on their race, and accusations of police racism. Of the race-related issues, police racism and the racial makeup of the jury received the most attention, but not at a statistically significant level. It appeared that Simpson's celebrity status received more media attention than his race. There were no clear indications that the media used language that was racist against Simpson himself; they were reporting the issue of race as a legitimate news story.

This study was extremely limited in that it only looked at a sliver of the massive media coverage of a high-profile African American man charged with murder. It examined the clearly elite network evening news shows in which one would expect to find the most objective and professional treatment. The findings did not support other studies that have found that the American news media routinely present biased, inaccurate, unbalanced, and negative stereotypes of black America; however, this study does not imply that the previous studies were wrong. This study does not attempt to suggest that racism no longer exists in media coverage of African Americans.

This study did not examine all the media coverage of Simpson. It did not analyze newspaper coverage, magazine coverage, radio news coverage, or cable news coverage. This study did not examine all the national broadcast TV news coverage—the morning news programs, news magazine programs, or special reports—and it did not look at local broadcast TV news coverage. Nor did it examine the television and print tabloid coverage. It would be unfair, therefore, to generalize about how all media handled the race issue in the Simpson case based on the analysis of one small part of the extensive media coverage of Simpson.

Of the massive media coverage, moreover, this study only looked at the transcripts of an 80-day period covered by the TV network evening news programs, thus ignoring the omnipresent video images that appeared simultaneously of the clearly African American O. J. Simpson. Race was the background noise to all these transcripts. Although the transcripts rarely mentioned the race of O. J. Simpson, the fact that he is African American is well known. His race is clearly visible in the networks' video—video of Simpson sitting in the courtroom, video of Simpson with his children at Nicole Brown Simpson's funeral, video of Simpson after his arrest, file footage of Simpson in the Hertz rental car commercials, file footage of Simpson on the football field.

CONCLUSION

A future study that incorporates the video as well as the transcripts of this news coverage may come to different, stronger conclusions. A comprehensive study that includes all the media—national and local; print, radio, television, and cable—and covers the entire Simpson case from the night of the murders until a jury verdict may render different and more statistically significantly results. Video offers a more subtle form of signaling racial concerns than the most carefully crafted prose. Video has the potential to remind viewers of race in every story without actually mentioning race in the voice-overs, as is the case with broadcast TV news coverage of O. J. Simpson.

One important finding of this study is that during the first 80 days of what would become a media saturation of coverage of the O. J. Simpson murder trial, the media paid more attention to Simpson's celebrity status than his race. It appears that O. J. Simpson—like other African American celebrities—had been "sanitized" as a TV commodity. Sports or entertainment fame tends at times to erase the race factor. Americans tend to ignore the race of an individual if that person is a great athlete or celebrity. O. J. Simpson was both. As a famous and well-liked sports hero and well-known actor and broadcaster, the media attempted to focus on Simpson's celebrity status instead of his race. A study comparing media coverage of high-profile African Americans accused of crimes with media coverage of noncelebrity African Americans also facing criminal charges might illustrate how celebrity status influences the way the media cover crime stories involving African Americans.

This study only suggests that, initially, the role of race was *one* issue but not *the major* issue in the complicated murder case against O. J. Simpson. As media coverage of Simpson continued through the year-long trial, the issue of race became more pronounced with reports of the prosecution's key witness, former Los Angeles police detective Mark Fuhrman, using racial slurs in a taped interview. The O. J.

Simpson murder case ended on October 3, 1995, in much the same way that it began, with America being divided by race in its reaction to Simpson's acquittal of the murders of Nicole Brown Simpson and Ronald Goldman. Media polls indicated that most blacks agreed with the jury's not-guilty verdict while the majority of whites believed Simpson should have been convicted (Whitaker, 1995). While black America celebrated Simpson's acquittal, white America expressed outrage, saying justice had been mocked and the predominately black jury had allowed race to cloud their judgment. Black America argued all along that the Simpson murder case was also a race issue, but for many whites the issue was domestic abuse. Race did ultimately play a much larger role in the aftermath of the O. J. Simpson murder trial, but in analyzing the first 80 days of media coverage of the Simpson case, the national broadcast TV news media during their evening news programs tried—at least in their language—to cover race as a legitimate news story rather than slipping into racial stereotypes.

REFERENCES

Abron, J. M. (1990, March). The image of African-Americans in the U.S. press. *Black Scholar,* pp. 49-52.

Alter, J. (1994, August 1). Black & white & read all over. *Newsweek,* pp. 19-21.

Blackstone, J. (Reporter). (1994, July 8). The O. J. Simpson case: Issue of race plays ever-increasing role in the Simpson case, according to blacks in Los Angeles. *48 Hours.* CBS, Inc. (From ProQuest-CBS News Transcripts Ondisc, Vol. CBS-94-11 [October 1990 to September 1994]. Ann Arbor, MI: University Microfilms, Inc.)

Center for Integration and Improvement of Journalism. (1994). *News watch: A critical look at coverage of people of color.* San Francisco: San Francisco State University.

Entman, R. M. (1992). Blacks in the news: Television, modern racism and cultural change. *Journalism Quarterly, 69,* 341-361.

Feagin, J. R. (1992, September). On not taking gendered racism seriously: The failure of the mass media and the social sciences. *Journal of Applied Behavioral Science, 28,* 400-406.

Fitzgerald, M. (1994, August 6). Most blacks upset by news coverage. *Editor & Publisher,* p. 15.

Gibbons, A. (1993). *Race, politics and the white media: The Jesse Jackson campaigns.* New York: University Press of America.

Hughes, S. (Reporter). (1994a, July 18). Attorneys for O. J. Simpson may try to show he was framed for murders of his ex-wife and her friend. *CBS Evening News.* CBS, Inc. (From ProQuest-CBS News Transcripts Ondisc, Vol. CBS-94-11 [October 1990 to September 1994]. Ann Arbor, MI: University Microfilms, Inc.)

Hughes, S. (Reporter). (1994b, July 19). O. J. Simpson case could turn into issue of race. *CBS Evening News.* CBS, Inc. (From ProQuest-CBS News Transcripts Ondisc, Vol.

CBS-94-11 [October 1990 to September 1994]. Ann Arbor, MI: University Micro-films, Inc.)

Johnson, K. A. (1992, February). "Objective" news reporting can poison young black minds. *Education Digest*, pp. 65-68.

Lewis, G. (Reporter). (1994a, September 15). DNA tests indicate blood samples at crime scene to be O. J. Simpson's. *NBC Nightly News*. National Broadcasting Company, Inc. (From ProQuest-NBC News Transcripts Ondisc, Vol. NBC-94-11 [October 1990 to September 1994]. Ann Arbor, MI: University Microfilms, Inc.)

Lewis, G. (Reporter). (1994b, July 19). O. J. Simpson offers reward for the location of the killer of Nicole Brown Simpson and Ronald Goldman. *NBC Nightly News*. National Broadcasting Company, Inc. (From ProQuest-NBC News Transcripts Ondisc, Vol. NBC-94-11 [October 1990 to September 1994]. Ann Arbor, MI: University Microfilms, Inc.)

McNamara, B. (Reporter). (1994, July 15). O. J. Simpson murder case generates race debate among black and white Americans. *CBS Evening News*. CBS, Inc.

National Advisory Commission on Civil Disorders. (1968). *Report of the National Advisory Commission on Civil Disorders*. Washington, DC: Government Printing Office.

Norris, M. (Reporter). (1994, July 23). Race now a factor in Simpson case. *ABC World News*, Saturday ABC News. (From *Broadcast News*, Issue BN199410 [CD-ROM] [November 1993 to October 1994]. Woodbridge, CT: Research Publications International.)

Norville, D. (Reporter). (1994, September 26). A comparison of the publicity for Wayne Williams' murder cases in Atlanta and the Simpson case. *CBS Evening News*. CBS, Inc. (From ProQuest-CBS News Transcripts Ondisc, Vol. CBS-94-11 [October 1990 to September 1994]. Ann Arbor, MI: University Microfilms, Inc.)

The O. J. Simpson case: Prominent blacks discuss race, sex, crime and "the case of the century." (1994, September). *Ebony*, pp. 29-34, 140-141.

Raybon, P. (1989, October 2). A case of "severe bias." *Newsweek*, p. 11.

Redeker, B. (Reporter). (1994, July 19). Simpson defense playing up possible racial strategy. *World News Tonight* with Peter Jennings. ABC News. (From *Broadcast News*, Issue BN199410 [CD-ROM] [November 1993 to October 1994]. Woodbridge, CT: Research Publications International.)

Roberts, D. (Reporter). (1994, September 28). Case for race? Racially divisive murder trial of O. J. Simpson. *Dateline NBC*. National Broadcasting Company, Inc. (From ProQuest-NBC News Transcripts Ondisc, Vol. NBC-94-11 [October 1990 to September 1994]. Ann Arbor, MI: University Microfilms, Inc.)

Stempel, G. H., & Westley, B. H. (Eds.). (1989). *Research methods in mass communication*. Englewood Cliffs, NJ: Prentice Hall.

Threlkeld, R. (Reporter). (1994, July 9). Black Americans suspect court system's treatment of O. J. Simpson; feel ambivalence toward his plight. *CBS Evening News*. CBS, Inc. (From ProQuest-CBS News Transcripts Ondisc, Vol. CBS-94-11 [October 1990 to September 1994]. Ann Arbor, MI: University Microfilms, Inc.)

Vargas, E. (Cohost). (1994, July 11). Cathy Hughes and Larry Elder, radio talk show hosts, discuss whether bigotry is involved in the O. J. Simpson murder case. *Today*. National Broadcast Company, Inc. (From ProQuest-NBC News Transcripts Ondisc, Vol. NBC-94-11 [October 1990 to September 1994]. Ann Arbor, MI: University Microfilms, Inc.)

Whitaker, B. (Reporter). (1994, September 26). Jury selection begins in O. J. Simpson trial. *CBS Evening News*. CBS, Inc. (From ProQuest-CBS News Transcripts Ondisc, Vol. CBS-94-11 [October 1990 to September 1994]. Ann Arbor, MI: University Microfilms, Inc.)

Whitaker, M. (Reporter). (1995, October 16). White v. blacks. *Newsweek*, pp. 28-35.

11

Advertising Discourse and the Marketing of *I'll Fly Away*

KAREN M. SMITH

In September 1991, NBC debuted *I'll Fly Away (IEA)* as "a heart-warming new family drama."[1] A small media blitz, or at least a marketing thrust of print ads, trailers, and on-air promos, proffered this new drama series as "quality," a bright new spot in an otherwise vast wasteland. *Quality television* refers not only to shows created to appeal to a specific, *quality* audience but, perhaps most important, the texts themselves are developed, seen, and read as having greater psychological depth and are more complicated in expression than is typical for TV programming (Feuer, Kerr, & Vahimagi, 1984, pp. ix, x).[2]

Although *IEA* was arguably the most realistic depiction of race and class struggles in the American South, as well as the most realistic and dignified look at the life of a black maid, the network, in its own inimitable style, sabotaged the show from the beginning through stereotypical promotions. The advertising never quite gave this heart-warming new drama a chance to succeed. Through a textual analysis of trailers and print ads, I will argue that the network continually posited a stereotype.

Joshua Brand and John Falsey, the producers and creators of *IEA*, offered a revolutionary vision and image of a black woman, and particularly a black maid, on television. Yet viewing the advertisements for the show, one would be hard-pressed to detail its actual contents or context. The discourse surrounding these texts served to deter potential viewers, for the texts consistently and constantly posited the show's black female lead in a peripheral, subservient, mammylike position devoid of social, political, familial, or cultural connections.

Without exception, the early ads for the show picture the maid, Lily Harper, with her young charge on her back, in her lap, or in some other problematic context. The ads promised: "In a time of change, some values never go out of style." The *values* emphasized here are more than a little questionable and had little to do with the actual content of the show; they had more to do with what one advertising executive boasted was "a clever marketing strategy" (Viscera, 1993).

HISTORICAL OVERVIEW

The mammy character/stereotype is a distinctly American creation, born in the southern U.S. imagination. The image, created during slavery, was a caricature of the slave women who worked in the kitchens of plantation owners. It was created in response to the antislavery movement of the North during the antebellum era, serving to further dehumanize and subjugate blacks. It became a nostalgia item during Reconstruction, with reproductions cropping up in various forms, and the images later spread throughout the country.

Patricia Turner (1994, p. 46) argues that the American author Harriet Beecher Stowe, in her seminal text *Uncle Tom's Cabin*, is generally responsible for popularizing the image. Her Aunt Chloe character, described as round, shiny, and black, has been absorbed by legions of readers for Stowe's text is widely accepted as "the world's first best-seller." The "traditional" mammy character, widespread in nineteenth-century popular fiction, minstrel shows, and the like, was generally conceived of in these same terms; as well, she was ever vigilant in her employ as housekeeper and nursemaid for her white masters and mistresses. So the image of the big, black, bandanna-wearing servant/cook/maid became ingrained in many aspects of the culture.

Although there is no evidence that actual "mammies" existed, the image has become so deeply ingrained in the American social and cultural consciousness that the character is immediately recognizable in various incarnations. The mammy character is, however, neither a creation of Stowe's nor limited to fiction and theater, for with the advent of the twentieth century, the image would be re-created in various forms—postcards, advertisements, product packaging, films, and, later, television.

The history of television has been fraught with images of black women as maids in stereotypical representations: docile, desexualized, dumb darkies always happy in the employ of whites. They were never willing or able to transcend the race/gender bifurcation or their (our) traditional role in American society as servile nurturers. From Ethel Waters in *The Beulah Show* to Florida Evans in *Maude* and on to contemporary times with Nel Carter in *Gimme a Break*, Mamie in the daytime serial *The Young and the Restless*, and Idella in CBS's shelved pilot *Driving Miss Daisy*, black women who work as maids have traditionally been represented as didactic pariahs. She customarily serves to offer sage bits of wisdom to the employer/his children, yet is never wise enough (interested enough?) to escape her own meager lot in society and rarely if ever is positioned in a culture or community that is her own.

The content of *IFA* offered quite a different look at this overused stereotype, seeking to explode it, while simultaneously the text of the advertisements continued to exploit that image and construct an altogether different idea of what this show was.

CREATING *I'LL FLY AWAY*

With the arrival of *I'll Fly Away*, Brand-Falsey Productions were faced with a difficult task. According to John Falsey (1993), he and his partner Joshua Brand were primarily interested in creating a show that explored racial issues in the American South, the civil rights movement, and how these issues affected ordinary people. The show gave equal access to the lives of both the black and the white protagonists. They set the show in the civil rights era because "no other time in this country's history is as important . . . as the modern civil rights movement" (Falsey, 1993).

After the pilot was completed, network research began, as is customary, in an effort to find out whether the show was appealing, and, if so, to whom and why. They tested the show and found that the characters of Lily, the housekeeper, and John Morgan, the youngest child of her employers, tested extremely well with test audiences. The network then encouraged Brand-Falsey to "put a little more emphasis on them and on the family as opposed to other areas of the show" (Falsey, 1993). In effect, they were told to decenter race, racial politics, and/or the race question in lieu of white, middle-class family problems and events. In other words, the "random" audiences had responded well to Lily and John Morgan, thus the network decided it best to exploit this coupling to attract viewers. The network didn't appear to consider the fact that audience members might have responded to the content of the show itself and not just isolated characters. Falsey (1993) allows:

> I think what probably happened was that the powers that be turned and said, "Look, they loved the Lily-John Morgan [pairing] . . . play that up because that's what everyone really loved about the show." I don't think they took into account how those trailers . . . are little 30-second bites out of a two-hour movie [and how they] were coming across.

These trailers, however, did not reflect Harper's character as anything but servile, and only as caretaker. Within the series, she cannot be constructed as such.

As the first episode introduces the characters, Lily Harper claims an identity apart from faceless caretaker at the outset. She begins a job as a housekeeper for Forest Bedford and starts by articulating her position as a person when he hires her. He never asks her name as he seeks to fill the position. She politely and firmly introduces herself to him, in effect offering a face, a personality, a person in the body of the new caretaker. She also informs the teenaged Nathan Bedford that she realizes that he does not see her, forcing him to reckon with his own racist and sexist notions. She plants herself firmly within the realm of this reality as a prominent black character within this white household.

There is nothing about the pilot or subsequent episodes to indicate that Lily Harper wants to or becomes little John Morgan's dry nurse, as pictured in the ad campaigns. Lily has a child of her own, a daughter who is very much a part of her life. Her world is small town black America, and the viewer is made aware of that fact from the very first episode, contrary to what can be extrapolated from the trailers. Racial, and to some extent, class politics remained a foundation for the show, seemingly to the network's chagrin as well as to the personal and political delight of many of the shows viewers.

PROMOTING *I'LL FLY AWAY*

Within the advertising texts, the network wanted less emphasis on "other areas of the show," such as the burgeoning civil rights movement—of which Lily comes to play an active part—and more on the Bedford family, because family values are as important to NBC as they are to 1990s America. Notwithstanding, the network was clearly not interested in showcasing the two families—Harper's and Bedford's. Bedford's white, middle-class family was deemed the valuable one with Lily taking her ostensible place as servant. This served once again to construct vacuous, one-dimensional caricatures within the ads themselves and could have served the same purpose in the text of the show. Jim Viscera (1993), NBC's vice president of on-air promotions, said in a telephone interview, "Research showed that family values were important. . . . The promos should and did reflect those values."

What kind of and whose family did NBC feel compelled to promote? Although Viscera (1993) went on to say, "We never distorted the show . . . we [just] didn't always lay it out exactly the way it was," I would argue that the promos were a gross distortion and misrepresentation of the show itself. With respect to a number of the early ads, I would argue that one could hardly tell what the show was about by viewing them.

One ad depicted a close-knit, well-dressed white family comfortably ensconced in what could be read as loving beatitude. Slightly separated, but nonetheless still a part of this auspicious familial portrait, is a very plain, disparate black woman. She stands connected to the family but is clearly not a part of the family. Her position as domestic is evident, and the "old South" atmosphere—porch swing, magnolias in bloom, and "Tara"-like domicile hearkened back to a time most Americans remember quite vividly. This ad pictures a white family and their "help"; there is nothing about the image that informs a viewer that Lily is anything else.

Another ad proffered text that read, "In a time of change, some values never go out of style," along with an image of Lily carrying John Morgan on her back while Forest gazes approvingly. This image posits Lily as nursemaid, as plaything, and as mammy, and is again reminiscent of a nostalgic time when a mammy was the rule for southern whites. This ad also reads as a testament or, more specifically, as confirmation of the privilege, gaiety, and comfort that whites have because of their "help." Her conjectural smile is cause for suspicion on the part of spectators: Could she be comfortable with this child on her back? Is this a part of her normal and/or daily duties? The value of having a black woman as personal caregiver and playmate for a white child is reminiscent of a negative past that most black Americans would like to forget.

A third ad was as problematic as those mentioned above. Although the text critically acclaims the show as "the best new drama of the fall season," "a stunning and wonderful show," "the best new drama since L.A. Law," the contrasting image is of Lily resting in a porch swing with John Morgan snuggled in her lap in an embrace. Forest is pictured well dressed, seemingly well fed, and certainly satisfied as he rests easy in the knowledge that his child is secure, well cared for, and happy.

Lily's body, then, is constructed as playground, as vehicle of transport, as inanimate object, as nursemaid; her existence is for the sole pleasure of her young white charge, the young master of the house. She is dehumanized at the expense of attracting those who would revel in or celebrate NBC's alleged "family values." Conversely, ads like these that depict family values circa the nineteenth century could not, would not, and did not appeal to black spectators and even liberal whites, contrary to the network's belief.

These ads provide images that are at once pernicious and provocative; yet they have little to do with the actual content or context of the show. Although there is no disputing that Lily is employed by the Bedford family, she is hardly seen coddling, cuddling, or cooing for John Morgan. Attention is paid to Lily as a mother in *IFA*, but it is always with her daughter, Adlaine. Unfortunately, Adlaine herself never makes the ads as a part of the show or part of Lily's life.

REACTION TO *I'LL FLY AWAY*

In a newspaper article, Judith Michaelson (1991) examines how television is "adjusting" its take on race and society and how representations of blacks are changing because of an increase (and/or recent detection and tabulation) of black viewers. Those interviewed in the article, however, including black actors, executives, and social and political leaders, have a markedly different opinion about these "changing" or new images and what they see: mainly comedic buffoons, cops, ex-cons, pimps, or whores in serious programming. There was also resistance to the symbol of what has come to indicate a quintessential black female stereotype: the maid. Keenan Ivory Wayans laments, "How many housekeepers can I watch without wanting to rip my hair out?" (Michaelson, 1991, p. 80). One can ascertain from the subjects in this report that these new, adjusted images do not appeal to blacks for the images are still representative of old, worn stereotypes.

Scholars and journalists alike are all tackling this subject with equal aplomb. For most black women who deconstruct and critique such images, the ads serve a dual purpose. They offend us as blacks whose history is resplendent with racist imagery, and they offend us through sexist imagery as women: black women. These sexist, racist, desexualized, and dehumanized images serve as constant reminders of a not so distant past and an equally austere present.

Noted black feminist scholar Mary Helen Washington (1992) writes:

> Most black people I talk to have never heard of the NBC television series
> *I'll Fly Away* or refuse to watch it because the main black character is a
> maid. [They say] I don't want to see another mammy show, with a black
> woman doting on some little kid and ignoring her own. (p. 35)

Even as Washington seeks to critique and praise the show itself for presenting a woman with "grace and dignity . . who is no stereotype," ironically, accompanying the essay is a photograph of Lily and John Morgan that reads, "Lily Harper . . is nobody's mammy."

Black journalist Deborah Gregory (1992), writing in a black women's magazine, laments the character of the maid as mammy and its resurgence in network programming:

> While we've been busy taking 20 high heeled steps forward . . consider
> this: there haven't been this many black actresses playing *docile* maids
> since Ethel Waters portrayed Beulah in the 1950's television sitcom.
> Black actresses recently seen twirling a feather duster include Regina
> Taylor as the southern *"mammy"* [and] Lily Harper on NBC's *I'll Fly
> Away.* (italics added, p. 40)

Accompanying the text of Gregory's article is a problematic advertisement from Lorimar Television, the production company that produces *IEA*. These advertisements went beyond television to include magazines such as *Essence* and *Emerge* that reach well over 6 million readers, the overwhelming majority of whom are African American. So the power of this ad campaign and of the images that accompany these articles has served to deter would-be viewers.

In spite of this campaign and largely by word of mouth, *IEA* gained a small but fiercely loyal contingent of fans, a minority of whom were black. Many inaccurately assumed that because *IEA* has a black protagonist, it was targeted and marketed toward a black audience and/or enjoys a large black audience. As I have argued, that certainly was not the case with *IEA*.

According to the Nielsen ratings and Eric Cardinal (1993), vice president of research at NBC, blacks constituted less that 16% of the audience for *IEA*. Although blacks make up 12%-13% of the population, they often constitute more than 25% of the prime time viewing audience. It was "discovered" in 1990, as Nielsen began to pay closer attention to black viewership, that blacks watched more than 69 hours of television compared with just under 50 hours for whites. With the advent of that statistical information, the network began to target black audiences more than ever. With the 1992 television season, 11 new shows featuring black performers were aired. Almost without exception, they were situation comedies featuring black actors in trite, buffoonish roles. And even though there were offensive, stereotypical characterizations, the shows did attract black viewers. The difference is that these comedies were advertised consistently, on the radio, on television during prime time, and with a host of print ads that can often be read as humorous, tame, and even safe.

Blacks and liberal whites alike refused to tune in to a show that offered up images as troubling as a black woman with a white boy on her back, as evidenced by the show's low ratings. Viewers, I would argue, have been offended by and need to resist age-old images of the black maid/mammy in what appears to be the same old roles, for political as well as cultural reasons. Black audiences, however, are not deterred by other kinds of problematic images, particularly when they have been marketed to appeal to the funny bone.

For example, similar media promotions for such comedies as *Martin* and *Hangin' With Mr. Cooper* have helped to ensure their success. These shows were able to find and keep an audience. *IEA*, as a dramatic show, however, was never fortunate enough to benefit from this type of media savvy.[3] Not only did the network market the show in the above-mentioned problematic way, the show itself was also shuffled around into four different time slots in just under two seasons.

After building a slow but steady audience at 8 p.m. on Tuesday, the network decided to move it to Tuesday at 10 p.m., then to Friday at 10 p.m., and then Friday at 8 p.m. John Falsey (1993) says,

> The worst thing that could have happened happened . . they [changed the time] and we fell down to a 12 rating . . people thought the show was off [the air] . . the majority of letters we get are basically saying, "This is the best show on TV, but when the hell's it on?"

Brand-Falsey also complained to the network about the lack of ad time and promotional time for the show beyond the initial few hours. Falsey (1993) asserts that the network

> very quickly decided after about the 5th hour of the show that the show was never going to be a ratings smash. [But] we quote-unquote have to leave it on because it's too good and it would be too embarrassing to take this incredibly great series off the air . . . but at the same time, we're not going to waste valuable 30 second bites on a show that we don't think is going to profit from it.

In other words, the paradox of *IEA* is that the show couldn't be a ratings topper because it didn't draw an audience, but it couldn't draw an audience because the network did little to advertise it accurately and promote it appropriately.

NBC'S REACTION TO THE REACTION

With the onset of the second season, and after several complaints from *IEA*'s creators, NBC decided to try and attract a younger audience. The season's opener was the beginning of the "Nathan's a babe" campaign (Pannick, 1993), capitalizing on the older son's youth, handsomeness, and appeal. According to Viscera and Pannick, they needed to alter the campaign to attract new viewers, particularly young people. The network assumed that *IFA* had a core of loyal viewers, yet appeared to make one last-ditch effort to encourage a larger following. But it was too little, too late. With the constant time changes, preemptings, poor promotion, and lack of commitment by the network, *IFA* attracted few new viewers.

The few-second season premier ads had little effect on increasing the ratings. Even a seemingly desperate campaign, putting the onus on the viewer to "save *IFA*," had little, or no, effect. The viewer was encouraged to make a difference by casting a vote for quality television like *IFA*. Even guilt was too ineffective in rescuing *IFA* from cancellation after such a haphazard promotional life. One wonders how dedicated the network was even in this campaign, for the trailers were shown a meager few times, only twice in prime time.

Oddly enough, the "save *IFA*" trailer is one of only two ads, print or on-air, in the two seasons to reflect the actual composition of the show. There are scenes of Lily with her family, juxtaposed against the Bedford family. I would argue that this was the network's final attempt to correct misconceptions and appeal to black viewers. Again, by this time, there was no hope of saving the show.

CONCLUSION

In essence, I have argued that *IFA* was one of the most realistic depictions of a black woman, and certainly a black maid, in television history. Although the advertising discourse typically positioned Lily Harper as mammy, ever-loving nursemaid, and panderer, writers and directors and producers (many of whom are black) in conjunction with the creators of the show created a strong, fiercely proud, and determined woman who was mother, friend, lover, and budding revolutionary.

IFA's brilliance in positing a revolutionary vision was enhanced by a technique called "bookending." The show opened and closed each week with a voice-over from Lily offering an anecdote about her daughter or grandmother, or relaying some personal story or lesson learned. In a show aired the beginning of the second season, Lily decides that she must end a romantic relationship because it stifles her growth as a woman and as a political activist. Her partner cannot reconcile Lily's need to further her education and work for racial uplift in her small Virginia town when he has offered her a new life in the big city of Chicago.

As the pilot of the show opens, Lily relates a moment from the life of her daughter, whose innocent questions of time and flight weren't answered to her own intellectual satisfaction, so she changed the subject. In the opening voice-over, Lily remembers "wanting to understand about time and space . . . I remembered that feeling and envied it . . . the privilege of putting off the truth until you're ready to know" (*IEA* pilot, September 25, 1993). This anecdote sets up the paradox Lily faces in deciding what is important in her life, the life of her child, and the life of the movement.

In the closing voice-over, she relates another story, this time from her grandmother. Because her grandmother was a gardener, she taught Lily about growing things:

> Sometimes a seed is planted too deep and is lost .. but covered with too thin a blanket, it's lost to the wind. She knew from experience. I think of the first people who ever planted anything. What made them sit and hope? What caused them to believe in such fragile things? (*IEA* pilot, September 25, 1993)

Again, Lily serves to comment on life matters, personal as well as political, offering up her own brand of wisdom and proffering the spectator a succinct and poignant commentary.

What these voice-overs served to do was empower black women characters in a way that I have never before experienced, simultaneously imbuing female viewers, particularly black female spectators, with that same power. The bookending gave voice to generations of black women as wise, caring, sensitive, intelligent, and so on. They are, through the character of Lily Harper, able to articulate their (our) culturally based condition, both personally and politically. The voice-overs also serve to help her character (and also, I would argue, the viewer) endure the pain and especially the pleasure that being a black woman can bring.

The show, then, is Lily Harper's. She sets the scenes, she constructs or deconstructs the gender and racial politics and images, and she adds closure, making sense of it all. Falsey (1993) remembers: "Regina Taylor once said that if there was one thing she wanted to get across through the character, it was off with the bandanna!" This, of course, is a direct reference to the mammy character; her stellar performances along with the sterling writing and production offered spectators just that. Sadly, the network impeded these efforts with ill-advised, poorly planned, erroneous, misrepresentative promotions that helped to doom the show from the very start.

NOTES

1. This text is taken from an ad slick for *I'll Fly Away*. Carol Pannick, an assistant in NBC's print ad department, proffered several slicks for this chapter, some of which appeared in *TV Guide*. Unless otherwise noted, all advertisements came directly from the advertising department at NBC.

2. This text introduces the notion of "quality television"; although it refers specifically to MTM Enterprises, Feuer's theory can be and is applied to contemporary television programming including Tandem Productions.

3. It is important to note here that although the buffoon is no less offensive than the maid/mammy character, historically the buffoon has served as a vehicle to make Americans laugh. The humor in the buffoon's character has consistently been a part of American culture, certainly predating television, but especially as a part of television culture. The maid/mammy character has traditionally been somber, no-nonsense, dour even when imbued with a sense of humor or a wise-cracking persona. She has also traditionally been more a part of "serious programming" than the buffoon, who appears almost exclusively in comedies. I would argue that her position as caregiver and her positionality in the lives and homes of whites has augmented her character in a way that has escaped the buffoon. Advertisements for shows such as *Martin* and *Hangin' With Mr. Cooper* take advantage of these cultural images appealing to familiar notions already discussed.

REFERENCES

Cardinal, E. (1993, March 17). [Author telephone interview with vice president of research at NBC].

Falsey, J. (1993, March 19, 22). [Author telephone interview with cocreator, coproducer of *I'll Fly Away*].

Feuer, J., Kerr, P., & Vahimagi, T. (Eds.). (1984). *MTM: "Quality television."* London: BFI.

Gregory, D. (November, 1992). Maid to order. *Essence*, p. 40.

Michaelson, J. (1991, September 22). TV adjusts its mirror. *Los Angeles Times*, Calendar sec., pp. 5, 77-80.

Pannick, C. (1993, March 15). [Author telephone interview with advertising executive].

Turner, P. A. (1994). *Ceramic uncles and celluloid mammies*. New York: Anchor.

Viscera, J. (1993, March 17). [Author telephone interview with vice president of on-air promotions at NBC].

Washington, M. H. (1992, September). Rising up with *I'll Fly Away. Emerge*, p. 35.

12

Black Entertainment Television

Breaking New Ground and
Accepting New Responsibilities?

ALICE A. TAIT

JOHN T. BARBER

For more than two decades, political leaders, media critics, civil rights activists, and others have decried the domination of the media environment by whites who have discriminated against African Americans and other minorities in employment, programming, economic support, and other important areas of America's mass media industries. As the year 2000 approaches, however, noteworthy changes are taking place in the media marketplace. African Americans are making inroads into all aspects of the media and are gaining more control over and even ownership of significant mass media systems (*Black Enterprise*, 1994; Randolph, 1995).

Black Entertainment Television (BET) is playing a leading role in the new wave of African American ownership and control of the nation's mass media outlets. BET is examined here because this cable network maintains some 35 million subscribers nationwide and is probably the only African American-owned and -operated media organization of such magnitude in the history of American mass media.

This chapter speaks to the pioneering efforts that BET is undertaking and attempts to shed some light on its impact on the African American community and American society in general. Discussed here are the network's strategies for establishing and running a large, complex media organization; its methods for gaining advertising and other forms of economic support; its Afrocentric approach to programming the network; and the major economic successes it has enjoyed since its inception 15 years ago.

AFROCENTRIC MEDIA

Afrocentricity involves a systematic exploration of relationships, social codes, cultural and commercial customs, mythoforms, oral traditions, and proverbs of the peoples of Africa and the African diaspora. Afrocentricity is the belief in the centrality of Africans in postmodern history (Asante, 1989). The major concern of Afrocentricity is whether or not the issue is in the best interest of people of the African diaspora. For example, some would argue that *The Cosby Show*, although not explicating every avenue of African American life, represented a prototype of an Afrocentric television program as the images produced in the show were consistently reflective of contemporary African American culture. Conversely, a stereotypical program like the *Amos & Andy Show* might be recognized as the antithesis of Afrocentricity (Tait & Perry, 1994).

Asante's Afrocentricity, therefore, can be used as an effective tool to develop a holistic understanding of an African American media entity such as BET and its impact on the people of the African diaspora. BET embraces several of the major characteristics of *Njia*, the Afrocentric worldview, to further enhance its business and programming efforts. The major principles guiding Njia are a discussion of all concepts from a liberationist perspective and valuing collectivistic thought over individualism. This allows for the recognition that power rests in group solidarity, which is pertinent to the African experience. Specifically, Njia is composed of the following elements: (a) honoring ancestors; (b) enjoying poetry, music, and creativity; (c) using *nommo* or generative word power; (d) embracing affirmations; (e) learning teachings from Njia; and (f) offering libation to posterity.

THE BUSINESS OF BET

BET was launched by Robert Johnson in 1979 and began airing shows on cable in 1980 (Barchak, 1993). His goal was to use the narrowcasting approach of cable television to reach the African American community in America with programming that was relevant to African American people. To do this, Johnson made several key moves.

A former lobbyist with the National Cable Television Association, Johnson formed alliances in the media world to establish a new media powerhouse. In the early years, Johnson persuaded the USA Network to provide BET with some of its spare satellite time so that BET could go on the air ("Bob Johnson," 1982). Next, he succeeded in getting Tele-Communications, Inc. (TCI), and Taft Broadcasting to make financial investments that would allow him to develop his fledgling network. Then Johnson arranged for major cable systems operators across the nation such as Warner Cable, American Telecommunications Corp., TelePromter, and TCI to carry his programs (Barchak, 1993). He convinced Anheuser-Busch, Champale, PepsiCo, Sears-Roebuck, Kellogg, and Time, Inc., to provide advertising with a view toward increased African American viewership on the growing cable network. Cable subscribers at the time were charged only $.25 to receive BET.

Johnson continued to expand his programming time until he saw an opportunity to expand to 24-hour service (Barchak, 1993). This was achieved by changing to a satellite service that allowed BET to provide programs during prime time. Time-Warner's Home Box Office (HBO) was the owner of the transponder and accepted 16% ownership of BET instead of charging a lease fee for time on its satellite. At this point, TCI owned 20%, Taft owned 20%, and HBO controlled 16% of the BET network. Because this would have placed majority control of the network outside the hands of Johnson, TCI and Taft reduced their shares to 16% each and Johnson remained the majority shareholder. Time-Warner, Inc. (TWI), and Tele-Communications, Inc. (TCI), are still investment forces that provide Johnson with the economic clout to continue to run BET in a very competitive and white-male-dominated arena.

Johnson stands at the helm of BET Holdings, Inc. In 1995, he purchased back his three million shares from Time-Warner, but TCI and Taft are still part owners. For several years now, BET has had these major business goals (Black Entertainment Television, Inc., 1990): (a) to become the dominant medium used by advertisers to target the black consumer marketplace, (b) to become the dominant medium engaged in the production and distribution of quality black-oriented entertainment and information to cable television households in the nation, and (c) to use the power of the medium to contribute to the cultural and social enrichment of the network's viewing audience.

Examining how BET has gone about achieving these objectives provides insight into new relationships and arrangements that the African American community is forming with the electronic media in a new age that promises 500 or more media channels on the "information superhighway."

To maintain its economic prowess, BET uses a strategy of combining advertising and subscriber revenues. Advertisers are willing to advertise on the network because they can reach a wide African American audience as well as others who view the network to catch popular African American programming. Both advertising support and its paid subscriber base have been growing consistently on the network since its inception. In 1988, BET made a breakthrough with one of the largest media advertisers in the nation, Proctor & Gamble, Co. (P&G). Prior to that time, P&G had been under criticism from African American media executives for not spending much of its $1.5 billion advertising budget with African American-owned and -operated media entities (Donaton, 1988). P&G decided to make a commitment to buy substantial time on all of BET's dayparts after BET advertising executives helped them realize that the network reached users and potential users of various P&G products.

Donaton (1989) explains that BET approaches advertisers with a three-pronged pitch: African Americans watch more television than any other group in the nation; African Americans watch programming that features African Americans more than other types of programming; and BET is the tool for reaching African American consumers. In the late 1980s, according to Donaton (1989), key advertisers on BET were Amtrak, AT&T, Bristol-Myers, Campbell Soup Co., Coca-Cola Co., Ford Motor Co., General Food, General Mills, General Motors Corp., Lever Bros., RJR/Nabisco brands, Polaroid Corp., Proctor & Gamble Co., Ralston Purina, Revlon, Inc., Time, Inc., United Airlines, and

Wm. Wrigley and Son. By 1991, BET listed 124 advertisers that included some of the nation's largest corporations and institutions (Barchak, 1993). BET's ad revenues leaped from $5.5 million in 1986 to $10.2 million in 1988 (Beck, 1989).

BET will probably continue to gain advertising revenue as the African American population that advertisers seek to attract continues to subscribe to the network in larger numbers. Moreover, because a great percentage of non-African Americans view BET *for* African American entertainment programming, advertisers are able to reach the African American buyers as well as "crossover" consumers (Beck, 1989; Jones, 1990).

Increasing subscription revenues since its beginning have helped to bolster BET's financial success. By 1993, BET had over 35 million subscribers, which brought the network $7.7 million (Jeffrey, 1993). About 90% of the nation's African American cable households currently subscribe to BET (Katz, 1993). This configuration has allowed BET to concentrate more of its attention on attracting audiences other than African Americans. This effort is evidently working because recent analyses of BET audiences have shown that 60% of the BET audience is non-African American.

Johnson and BET use program-length paid commercials as another strategy for increasing income. Much of this is arranged by selling significant amounts of time to Synchronal, a company that pays $500,000 per month to the network to run "infomercials" (Beck, 1989).

Johnson's successes in gaining strong support from powerful investors, gaining major advertising dollars, obtaining "crossover" subscriptions, and selling significant amounts of infomercial time have all combined to put the network on the New York Stock Exchange (NYSE). In 1992, BET Holdings, Inc., broke new ground for African Americans by offering 4.2 million shares of BET stock for sale. This netted a profit of $72.3 million for Johnson and his investors (Williams, 1992). This move also helped other cable networks to boost the sale of their shares in the stock market, especially Liberty Media, which is owned by BET investor TCI ("Cable Network Stocks," 1991). Thus, BET became the first African American-owned and operated company to be listed on the NYSE and a major influence in the cable industry.

THE PROGRAMMING OF BET

BET relies heavily on music videos and paid programming as network staples. From the beginning until now, the bulk of BET programming has been syndicated, or "in the can" ("Bob Johnson," 1982).

During the early years, the network devoted much of its time to African American film classics of the 1930s and 1940s, more recent movie releases, made-for-television movies, and college basketball and football games (Barchak, 1993). Two of the network's longest running shows are *Bobby Jones Gospel* and *Video Soul*. It was not until the late 1980s that the network turned to public affairs programming aimed at airing important issues in the African American community. Such programs include *BET News* and *On the Line*. It also added a celebrity interview program, late-night talk shows, a sports talk show, and other programs designed for audience interaction (Barchak, 1993). In the 1990s, BET began to present major entertainment offerings including the CBS Emmy Award winning series *Frank's Place,* a British sitcom called *Desmond's,* and NBC's multiracial soap opera *Generations.*

As BET's income increased, it built a $10 million production studio and began producing several original programs, including *Conversations With Ed Gordon, For Black Men Only, Comic View, BET's Uptown Comedy Club, NBA off the Court,* and *BET on Jazz* (Katz, 1993).

Despite all of the successes mentioned thus far, several critical questions still remain: Is BET breaking new ground and accepting new responsibility? Have BET programs affected media images of the African American community? Do BET images differ from other images of African American people found in mainstream media? Is BET Afrocentric television programming?

Because 77% of BET's programming consists of music videos, an analysis of the relevancy or irrelevancy of these is necessary for BET's racially mixed audience. BET's audience breaks down as follows: 25% Anglo American, 25% African American, and approximately 60% non-African American. Most of these viewers are 18 to 24 years of age (Barchak, 1993). Although there is a tendency to dismiss music as superficial and inconsequential, a closer examination will place it at the forefront of African and African American cultural traditions.

West African oral traditions were the primary means of spiritual survival and dissemination in a largely illiterate (by European standards) slave and folk community. African American music is the primary historical link for different generations, which would not have survived without oral traditions (Lomax, 1968; Ottenheimer, 1987; Waterman, 1952). A brief historical analysis of the major African American music genres is necessary for a complete understanding of the cultural significance of music to BET's audience.

MUSICAL PROGRAMMING

BET is the only national network extensively showcasing one of Africans' America's great cultural traditions—black music. This art form reflects African American history, struggle, and culture. Music not only reflects the African American community's political dispositions, it reflects creativity in fashions, hairstyles, choreography, and composing. In these categories, the implications are endless. Music and cuisine appear to be the most effective cultural change agents. In that regard, BET's racially diverse viewers are exposed to the African American culture in a nonthreatening palatable mode. It will be BET's 18- to 24-year-old viewers who will either change or maintain social injustices. Perhaps videos will provide a platform for creating the collective consciousness necessary for their involvement. A variety of video shows make up the primary programming on BET.

Today's rap music, similar to the rhythm and blues and jazz genres in their infancies, has been surrounded by controversy. Rap has earned what some feel to be an undeserved negative reputation. Gangsta rap hits upon issues of misogyny, racism, and homophobia. If gangsta rap represents a real depiction of the urban African American community, as most rappers claim, this vehicle has been successfully used to express surprising and shocking phenomena to many Americans. The current state of urban black America, according to some gangsta rappers, can be blamed on problematic government and economic conditions (Kelley, 1992).

Rappers themselves range from former gang members to middle-class teens. Although it cannot be denied that rap music includes extreme macho boasting, significant cultural topics are prevalent. For example, negatives such as street violence, brutality, and drug sales are addressed, and clean-cut, sanitized rap urges kids to stay in school, avoid crime, and say no to drugs.

Berry (1993) and Baker (1993) argue that cultural politics within hard-core rap music is creating a powerful discourse concerning the African American experience in America from artists such as Public Enemy, NWA, KRS-One, Ice T, and Sister Souljah. Although seen as deviant and unacceptable to the mainstream, others who understand these frustrations see the presentation of this reality through the cultural and historical representation of knowledge and experience. Baker (1993) heralds rappers for their ingenious use of technology, techniques, strategies, and creativity. He further urges black studies programs to provide a platform for a better understanding and crystallization.

Black religious music videos are an important part of Sunday morning programming on BET. The black religious music tradition operates on two levels. The first level is psychological and emotional. The music locates a sense of heritage. Second, the music mobilizes and strengthens the resolve for struggle. Black sacred music is the primary reservoir of black people's historical context and an important factor in the process of social change.

Rhythm and blues is a term that originated in the 1940s as a description of a synthesis of black musical genres (gospel, blues, swing); this music represents American musical and socioeconomic changes. Later called rock 'n' roll to camouflage its black roots, R&B parented the offspring musical genres of soul, funk, disco, rap, and so on (George, 1988). The blues depicts "secular" black life and sings of such worldly issues as love and sex. The blues describes every aspect of men and women's feelings toward one another. Through the blues, black people could express their views about infidelity and sex (Cone, 1972). Contrary to popular opinion, the blues does not represent complete despair and utter hopelessness.

The power of African American music is grounded in the historical reality of the black experience and the belief that things will change. Black music is unifying and functional. It is unifying in that it confronts the individual with the truth of black existence, that black being is possible only in a communal context. It unites the joy and sorrow, love and hate, and hope and despair of black people and moves the people toward liberation. Black music is functional in that it tells us about the feeling and thinking of African people as well as the mental adjustments necessary for survival in an alien land.

OTHER PROGRAMMING

Lead Story is a 30-minute news program with African American journalists discussing news from an African American perspective. *Our Voices* is a talk show exploring issues from an African American perspective. *BET News* is a 30-minute news program presenting issues from an African American perspective. *Screen Scene* reflects a clear entertainment focus with an emphasis on African Americans in movies and videos. *The Color of Money* airs on Saturdays and explores financial issues from an African American perspective.

Situation comedies such as *Roc* and *Desmond's* are aired early mornings and late evenings. The problem with situation comedies is their tendency to frame important issues in the African American community in humor. There is an established historical trend in film and television in which African Americans have been continually placed in comedic roles. This trend is well documented (Bogle, 1974; Corea, 1990; Dates & Barlow, 1990; Leab, 1975; MacDonald, 1983; Mapp, 1972; Moore, 1980). According to Dates (1990), televised comedies help Americans to adjust to the social order as transmitted myths and stereotypical ideologies reinforce society's implicit rules and codes of behavior. Dates (1990, p. 261) suggests that most African American comedies pick up threads of the established pattern of white superiority and black servitude and weave them back into popular culture.

Finally, infomercials have come to occupy a great deal of BET's programming schedule. They advertise exercise machines, culinary equipment, psychic networks, and cosmetics usually appealing directly to African American females. It is obvious that more attention should be paid to these infomercials because some are problematic. For example, a broader range of hairstyle options for African Americans is important because the Perfect Hair infomercials promote Eurocentric hair as the ideal hair. Promoting "Perfect Hair" or "good hair" perpetuates an African American pathology: the unacceptance of nonprocessed African American hair and the African American females' and males' obsession with accepting and attempting to achieve the unachievable—Eurocentric beauty. The crime is not necessarily in processing one's hair, although hair loss, the inordinate amount of time spent at beauty shops, and low self-esteem are regrettable. The crime is the denial of and inability to accept and be comfortable with oneself and one's hair in its natural state.

BET'S IMPACT ON THE AFRICAN AMERICAN
COMMUNITY AND BEYOND: TWO PERSPECTIVES

Is BET breaking new ground and accepting new responsibility? Have BET programs affected media images of the African American community? Do those images differ from other images found in mainstream media? Is BET truly Afrocentric and culturally oriented television programming?

PERSPECTIVE 1

BET's programming strategies and lucrative business practices have not made it a strong African American voice in America's media forum. Johnson himself has addressed this point: "Our network is not a radical departure for TV. . . . We have not reinvented the wheel, only painted it black," Johnson said ("Bob Johnson," 1982, p. 87). Johnson has yet to achieve his goal of demonstrating that there is an alternative "way to make television for an audience that's been denied its culture in a real sense" (Beck, 1989, p. 38). Moreover, reaching his objective of using the power of the medium to contribute to the cultural enrichment of the lives of the viewing audience seems a bit remote because African Americans can get what BET offers at various other locations on the dial.

Johnson has certainly demonstrated that he can excel in running major media operations in a profitable manner. Some of BET's major accomplishments that affect the African American community and society include (a) becoming the first African American-controlled video network in America; (b) becoming the first African American-controlled corporation listed on the New York Stock Exchange; (c) constructing a $10 million studio to produce African American programming; (d) constructing a $2 million corporate headquarters in the nation's capital; (e) developing partnerships with some of the nation's largest media power brokers; (f) gaining advertising revenue from major corporations that were previously resistant to targeting African Americans through cable television; (g) gaining 35 million subscribers nationwide; (h) purchasing Mile-Hi Cablevision (Sturgis, 1993a); (i) acquiring a pay-per-view movie channel (Sturgis, 1993b). Furthermore, BET is planning expansions into several new areas, including direct marketing of its own products such as records and cosmetics (Smith, 1993) as well as cablecasting an all-jazz network (Weiser, 1994).

The African American owner and controller of BET and its parent company BET Holdings, Inc., Robert Johnson, is steadily increasing his influence in the media world in general and specifically in the cable industry. He is doing this not by providing an Afrocentric channel through which the African American community can voice its feelings and aspirations but by managing a successful capitalistic vehicle for reaching the African American consumer, whom many advertisers want to reach, and by effectively bringing more African Americans on board as cable subscribers.

PERSPECTIVE 2

Johnson created BET as a response to an admitted deficiency, that is, to serve an audience that had never been adequately or directly addressed before. BET has performed a necessary function quite effectively: documenting, exploring, and articulating African American political, economic, cultural issues.

BET's African American community images differ from and replicate images found in mainstream media. Viewers see more African Americans on BET than they have ever seen on any major network at any time in the history of television and any other medium. Viewers see African Americans in diverse roles: as musicians, newscasters, anchors, journalists, actors, comedians, professionals, dancers, criminals, and so on. Viewers cannot get this broad spectrum on any other cable channel, network, or communication medium. BET is undeniably Afrocentric. It embraces many of the characteristics of Afrocentricity. Music is the greatest Afrocentric expression. Moreover, the public affairs programs also do a fairly good job of issue exploration. *Our Voices*, in particular, is extremely effective in examining issues to determine their impact on African Americans. The program's set uses an African motif, and similar African motifs can sporadically be seen in commercials and other programs. The most unique characteristic of BET is that it uses African American images and ideas as primary sources.

BET's weekly newscasts sometimes appear limited and redundant. Perhaps BET might provide more news analysis and broaden the range of issues covered. There is a need to increase programming for children. One would expect that after reaching economic success, BET would be able to aggressively pursue its goal of presenting additional relevant and original African American programming, which so far has occurred only to a limited degree.

BET recognizes its responsibilities to the African American community but has a long way to go to fulfill its obligations in being a significant media channel that voices the feelings and aspirations of the African American population. It is also necessary that a stronger effort be made to show the African American community in a more positive light. Although BET has been a tremendous windfall for a young African American entrepreneur and his powerful white partners, the profits, gains, and benefits that BET provides to the larger African American community remain questionable.

CONCLUSION

In this analysis, a number of the identified Njia elements were found in BET. From the business side, despite its capitalistic nature, BET is liberational. It represents the potential for African Americans to progress and succeed not only with ownership but in employment and business opportunities. In its focus on black music and other culturally creative forms, it honors an important African ancestry. The cable network also provides crucial affirmation of black financial power through its ability to reach African American consumers nationwide. Finally, BET stands as a tribute and legacy to future generations of African Americans.

Other major elements are played out in the Afrocentric news, public affairs, and entertainment programming on BET. Nommo, or the use of generative word power, is found in the oral tradition. *Our Voices* performs the functions of activism (to change or improve conditions), liberation (from systematic and cultural oppression), and unification (through educating Africans on collective empowerment) quite well. The hostess effectively explores the role that African Americans, African American institutions, and other actors play in resolving African American problems. Topics and subjects explored are not usually discussed on other networks. Inversion (elimination or redefinition of certain terms due to their inherent racist and derogatory nature, denial of individual ethnic identity based on a Eurocentric basis for that identification, and disregard for a worldview in which persons of European descent are actually a "minority") is practiced on BET. Some improvement is needed, however. Much dissatisfaction exists over the use of such terms as *minorities*.

The collectivistic social, political, and geographic orientations include recognition of a common heritage and activities that are practiced by African Americans. BET's programming does not strongly reflect the collectivist action of African Americans. BET does not often enough relate to or discuss commonalities among the African American struggle and those of other people of African descent. BET does, however, perform the collectivist function better than the networks and other African American-inspired programs. BET's *Our Voices* is involved in exploration of issues of self-determination and self-definition.

As an African American male, Robert Johnson has accomplished a great deal in contemporary American society. Exposure to a variety of black musical genres is important to African American culture. BET's news and public affairs presentations take a step in the right direction toward voicing the concerns of the African American community. Finally, the cable network's economic success speaks to the financial power of African American culture.

REFERENCES

Asante, M. K. (1989). *Afrocentricity*. Trenton, NJ: Africa World Press.

Baker, H. A., Jr. (1993). *Black studies, rap, and the academy*. Chicago: University of Chicago Press.

Barchak, L. J. (1993). Black entertainment television. In R. G. Picard (Ed.), *The cable networks handbook* (pp. 15-22). Riverside, CA: Carpelan.

Beck, K. (1989, June). BET faces the music, comes up with talk. *Channels*, pp. 58-60.

Berry, V. (1993, August 24). *Hardcore rap and the revolution of cultural politics*. Paper presented at the AEJMC Conference, Kansas City, MO.

Black Enterprise. (1994, December). Top 50 Black entertainment powerbrokers. [Entire issue].

Black Entertainment Television, Inc. (1990, August). *Personnel policy manual: Welcome to BET*.

Bob Johnson: Making a BET on black programming. (1982, October). *Broadcasting*, p. 87.

Bogle, D. (1974). *Toms, coons, mulattoes, mammies and bucks*. New York: Bantam.

Cable network stocks reach for new highs. (1991, November). *Broadcasting*, p. 30.

Cone, J. H. (1972). *The spirituals and the blues.* New York: Seabury.

Corea, A. (1990). Racism and the American way of media. In J. Downing, A. Mohannadi, & A. Sreberny-Mohammadi (Eds.), *Questioning the media: A critical introduction* (pp. 255-266). Newbury Park, CA: Sage.

Dates, J., & Barlow, W. (1990). *Split image: African-Americans in the mass media.* Washington, DC: Howard University Press.

Donaton, S. (1988, August). P and G boosts ad buy on black TV. *Advertising Age,* pp. 3, 70.

Donaton, S. (1989, April). Johnson broadens the range for BET. *Advertising Age,* pp. 531-532.

George, N. (1988). *The death of rhythm and blues.* New York: Pantheon.

Jeffrey, D. (1993, March). Subscribers, ad revenue augment BET sales, profits. *Billboard,* p. 4.

Jones, F. G. (1990). The black audience and the BET channel. *Journal of Broadcasting and Electronic Media, 34,* 477-486.

Katz, R. (1993, June). Going beyond the hood. *Cablevision,* p. 12.

Kelley, R. D. G. (1992, June). Straight from underground. *Nation,* pp. 793-796.

Leab, D. (1975). *From Sambo to Superspade: The black experience in motion pictures.* Boston: Houghton Mifflin.

Lomax, A. (1968). *Folk song style and culture.* Washington, DC: American Association for the Advancement of Science.

Mapp, E. (1972). *Blacks in American films: Today and yesterday.* NJ: Scarecrow.

MacDonald, J. F. (1983). *Blacks and white TV: Afro-Americans in television since 1948.* Chicago: Nelson-Hall.

Moore, M., Jr. (1980). Blackface in prime time. In B. Rubin (Ed.), *Small voices and great trumpets: Minorities and the media* (pp. 117-140). New York: Praeger.

Ottenheimer, H. (1987). The bardic origins of the blues. *World and I, 11,* 492-503.

Randolph, L. B. (1995, January). Blacks in the fast lane of the information highway. *Ebony,* pp. 98B-98H.

Smith, D. (1993, July). BET making foray into direct marketing arena. *Billboard,* pp. 10, 113.

Sturgis, I. (1993a, January). Johnson to buy Mile-Hi. *Black Enterprise,* p. 17.

Sturgis, I. (1993b, September). BET expands into pay-per-view. *Black Enterprise,* p. 15.

Tait, A. A., & Perry, R. L. (1994). African-Americans in the television media: An Afrocentric analysis. *Western Journal of Black Studies, 18,* 195-200.

Waterman, R. (1952). African influence on the music of the Americas. In S. Tax (Ed.), *Acculturation in the Americas* (pp. 207-218). Chicago: University of Chicago Press.

Weiser, J. (1994, January). BET joins jazz/cable connection. *Downbeat,* p. 10.

Williams, T. (1992, January). Taking stock of the BET IPO. *Black Enterprise,* p. 11.

PART IV

Issues in
Radio/Music

13

Empowering Voices

KUCB and Black Liberation Radio

SHARON ALBERT-HONORE

M inority communities often feel that they have little or no voice in public affairs. Minorities often have concerns about racism and antihumanism and feel that their views are ignored by the public-at-large.[1] In particular, incidents involving O. J. Simpson ("Insider's View," 1995), Rodney King (Morrow, 1991), and Larry Milton (Alex & Carter, 1992) have brought about complaints that mainstream media reports on racism, police brutality, and excessive force are usually one-sided. Minorities have been frustrated for some time with the lack of choices open for them to express themselves.

As a result of the civil rights movement and the Kerner Commission appointed by the president, the government has recognized the need for a diversity of voices.[2] When the commission filed its report in 1967, it condemned the historical trend in news coverage by a press that "has too long basked in a white world, looking out of it, if at all, with white men's eyes and a white perspective" (*Report of the National Advisory Commission on Civil Disorders,*, 1968, p. 5). They noted that media priorities were based solely upon an event's significance to the white majority. The Kerner Commission's strong indictment of the mass media's role in perpetuating discrimination led to government intervention.

As the government agency that was established to regulate broadcasting, the Federal Communications Commission (FCC) has a responsibility to the public to ensure that the media adequately serve their diverse listening audience. Therefore, despite philosophical disagreements over minority preferences and affirmative action policies, the FCC has attempted to influence broadcast tone and content by increasing minority ownership of radio and television stations (*Commission Policy*, 1978). Ownership, however, does not necessarily affect programming, particularly on commercial stations, because investors may not find minority-oriented content profitable.

There are approximately 1,500 noncommercial radio stations in the United States (Goodman, 1993). The stations are labeled "public," "educational," and "community." For the purpose of this chapter, a *community* station is defined as one that is associated with a specific community group, maintaining strong identities and upholding public access as a guiding principle.

Minority community radio (Lewis, 1984) exists to present those alternative voices. Community radio is defined by Lewis as listener supported, autonomous, nonprofit, and an alternative for musical listening. The First Amendment values of self-fulfillment and maintaining the search for truth are thereby enhanced (Caristi, 1992). Many practitioners of community radio believe that their medium is the one best suited for offering minorities an opportunity to speak out and to provide additional perspectives on public issues (Long, 1992a). They agree with former Commissioner Nicholas Johnson (1968), who said: "Radio holds as much promise as any institution in our land for really reaching and serving and advancing the cause of the blacks in our country" (p. 4).

A presumption exists that when the ideas and opinions of minorities are generally suppressed, rational judgment becomes impossible and force may be substituted for reason. This context provides the basis for the theoretical stance that freedom of expression is essential for maintaining the balance between leverage and consensus (Franklin & Anderson, 1990). Consequently, because suppression promotes inflexibility, real problems confronting a society are concealed and public attention is diverted from the critical issues that exist in urban black communities. Community radio stations can be compared with the isolated colonies that Lohman says are being deliberately left underdeveloped and underfinanced by the federal government (Lohman, 1965).

By way of two case studies, this chapter examines minority voice as it exists within two black community radio stations. It addresses several crucial questions. How does community radio promote African American voice? What role does minority community radio play in the minority community? To what extent does community involvement help to maintain community radio? How do minority radio station personnel view the responsibility of the FCC? This chapter specifically examines two different stations owned and controlled by African Americans—KUCB in Des Moines, Iowa, and Black Liberation Radio in Springfield, Illinois. It explores the role that each station plays in providing voice to these otherwise voiceless communities.

KUCB RADIO, DES MOINES, IOWA

KUCB, 89.3 FM, is perceived by many community members to be the voice of the people and the "soul source" for the African American community in Des Moines, Iowa. Minorities compose only 7% of the total population in the state capital, a city of more than 500,000 (Iowa Department of Economic Development, 1992). Located in the heart of the African American community, the station structures much of its programming content around three distinct black social institutions: the church, community center, and high school.

From the beginning, KUCB has had an impact on the minority residents of Des Moines. In the late 1960s, more than 20 members of the Des Moines African American community pooled their resources and applied for a license to run a community radio station.[3] A researcher, Sleanora E. Tate, interviewed many of the founders of KUCB. She reported that the black community believed, prior to the establishment of KUCB, that there was no available medium to promote the minority voice in Des Moines. Comments she heard included the following: "Des Moines will make you struggle—or strangle—if you are black and poor." "Someone said this town is the biggest minimum security correctional facility in the land." Oppression and racism wear soft-soled shoes here. "Not many black folks in Des Moines know that they make up a 20,000-foot carpet" (Tate, 1988).

In the fall of 1978, KUCB aired its first broadcast. More than 20 years later, three original board members remain active. KUCB serves as an important vehicle to reflect the sentiment of a large segment of the Des Moines population that clearly feels they are still not being heard by mainstream media. In January 1992, AKO Adbul-Samad, KUCB board member, told the station's listeners: "We consider our-selves to be citizens of this country but we don't enjoy all the benefits. We have always been viewed as less than human" ("Police Brutality," 1992). In addition, station personnel note that audience members are encouraged to use the station as a tool to communicate their views and frustrations. This, in turn, allows the station to reflect a reality that is often excluded from mainstream reports.

There is a continuing feeling of oppression when talking with KUCB board members. "African-Americans have suffered significantly at the hands of the white man," Abdul-Samad explained. "The system of oppression is the cause of all the problems that we find ourselves up against" (Samad, 1992).

KUCB personnel are proponents of minority community radio and maintain that communication, education, and organization in the African American community are principal factors in achieving a stable and balanced society. They encourage programming that emphasizes black pride as well as black history. For example, Jamal Long, radio host and KUCB board member, says, "I try to encourage our people to feel good about themselves. I tell young people, there's nothing wrong with being black. There's nothing to be ashamed about. You should feel proud" (Long, 1992b).

Kalongi, a former general manager at KUCB, believes that the key role of the station is to educate the community and allow the station to be a forum for social issues. The programs often highlight contribu-tions by African Americans. These positive messages are repeated several times a day. Kalongi argues that continuous repetition is the most effective way to get the attention of the listeners and that KUCB is making a difference in Des Moines. "We have always felt that KUCB was on the cutting edge of social change," he argues. "Because, truth is the weapon of freedom: we communicate, educate and organize" (Kalongi, 1992).

Many KUCB staff members say that audience members perceive their messages as positive. Consequently, they note that the community responds conscientiously to the station's challenge to work together for changes in the community. Sister Haddasha, a program host and board member, says, "Our people are real clear on directions. All we do when we get on the air is articulate what the people are saying" (Haddasha, 1992). Many of the messages encourage African Americans to organize and unite against social, economic, and legal problems in the community.

During December 1991 and January 1992, KUCB devoted much of its airtime to the issue of police brutality. This was the result of the police beating of Larry Milton, a 35-year-old African American male. Milton said he was beaten, kicked, and choked by Des Moines policemen in an unprovoked attack. Among his many injuries was a head gash that required 22 staples. The incident caused a furor within the Des Moines black community and led to statewide media coverage. KUCB devoted "100 percent of its radio time to concerned listeners" (Kalongi, 1992). They aired many calls from irate members of the minority population during a radio broadcast by community leaders. During one broadcast that focused on the incident, a caller argued that the African American community in Des Moines was "not going to pacify this incident of police violence" (*Our Voices*, 1992a).

Many minorities consider the police department to be an extension of the white domination that has held black Americans in servitude for hundreds of years. Social historian Joseph Lohman (1965) argues that many minority groups view the law as a foreign power that does not act in their best interests. He also notes that minorities view police as an army of occupation. All of the KUCB staff members interviewed feel that there is a history of mistreatment of minorities by the Des Moines police. They say that incidents of abusive treatment have consistently been overlooked, or condoned, by the criminal justice system and mainstream media. Thus, KUCB personnel believe that they serve as a powerful and necessary voice for minorities in the community: a voice that assists the Des Moines minority community in dealing with their perceived hostile and tenuous relationship with the police department.

As a result of the Milton incident, KUCB used its airtime to investigate many issues and attitudes concerning the Des Moines police department. Community members formed an informal investigative committee to look into the deaths of African Americans since 1979 that involved police officers. They noted that more than 20 young African American men had died under suspicious circumstances while in the custody of Des Moines policemen during that time period (Brown, 1992).

Community meetings were held to discuss the findings, and KUCB continued to act as a forum for citizens to voice their opinions. KUCB, along with several African American groups, demanded that something be done. During a January 1992 broadcast, a KUCB editorial spokesperson said, "We call for the immediate dismissal of the three police officers involved in this [Milton] violence. We also call for the resignation of the police chief, William Moulder" (*Our Voices,* 1992b).

Most KUCB personnel feel that mainstream media are often negligent in their coverage of police incidents in the black community, and, therefore, the community looks to their station to give the issue viable coverage. They maintain that KUCB's pressure in the Milton beating has forced the issue of police brutality in Iowa to the forefront. Community members note that the timing of the incident (Christmas) coupled with public sentiment about excessive violence made the story "newsworthy."

Mainstream media, according to Sister Haddasha, are also highly critical of KUCB's format and programming style. Some station broadcasters have accused them of promoting violence and racial unrest. They complain that callers are allowed to say whatever they want without being censored before going on the air. A number of the local media, including the *Des Moines Register*, at times have been unsupportive of efforts by KUCB to allow citizens to express themselves. "A criticism of the station that we hear over and over again, is that we let people express their viewpoints," says Tasha Smith, a 16-year-old host and volunteer. "But we have a First Amendment that says whether you disagree or agree with what a person is saying they still have the right to express their viewpoint" (Smith, 1992).

On the other hand, KUCB personnel argue that mainstream stories about Milton's charges of police brutality, especially in the *Des Moines Register*, were undeniably "soft." Generally, the thrust of the reports was to cast doubt on Milton's story. They maintain that newspaper articles repeatedly described Milton as "injured" with no indication of how severe the injuries were, despite the fact that photographs accompanying the articles showed a man almost completely disfigured by his injuries. His face was severely battered with his eyes swollen shut, his mouth bloodied, and numerous cuts and bruises.

Furthermore, KUCB personnel accuse the mainstream media of diverting attention away from the critical issue of police violence in the minority community. They point to a particular story that ran in the *Des Moines Register* that preferenced the police department's version of what happened with comments by Police Chief Moulder. The article appeared on the front page with a bold sidebar quoting Moulder as saying: "You had an individual who fought with three officers. They were about to lose the battle with him. The force used was proper" (Alex & Carter, 1992, p. A1).

KUCB's operating license has been challenged by two minority groups in the Des Moines area. Local attorney Alfredo Parrish in Des Moines has agreed to represent KUCB before the FCC at no charge (Parrish, 1992). After hearing the appeal by representatives from KUCB to remain on the air, the FCC determined that their radio license should be revoked. That decision is under appeal by KUCB station personnel who have asked that a higher court review the case. Parrish estimates that a final determination concerning license renewal will not be rendered for many years. The fate of the station, for now, is uncertain.

BLACK LIBERATION RADIO, SPRINGFIELD, ILLINOIS

There are well over 15,000 African American citizens in the predominantly white community of Springfield, Illinois. One of them has a voice that has made a difference, Mbanna Kantako. Kantako, a "pirate" radio station operator, lives in one of the apartments in John Hay Homes, a 600-unit public housing development.

The neighborhood is neat and quiet, yet depressed and neglected. Paint is peeling off the door frames, but there are vegetable gardens planted in front of most apartments. The streets are nearly empty, except for a number of police cars that patrol the area. Outside Kantako's front door, a crayoned sign warns, "On the AIR, Go to Back door." Pasted on the back door is an old WTRA (Tenant Rights Association) sticker.

Kantako and his wife, Dia, live in a small three-bedroom apartment with their three children, Kadonni, 12; Mbanna, 10; and Ebony, 6. A large newspaper clipping with the headline, "Mbanna Kantako and His Microwatt Revolution," hangs over what appears to be a makeshift radio studio in the living room. On the wall is a black-and-white photograph next to an article and a laminated red-and-black plaque that reads "Black Liberation Radio, 107.1."

In the late 1960s, a group of concerned citizens decided that the voices of African Americans were not being heard in the city of Springfield. Kantako explains:

> In 1986 a group of us got involved in the community, looking for direction, a sense of purpose. More than 20 residents from John Hay Homes became involved in a Federal Voting Rights lawsuit. We disagreed with the final decision and filed as dissident plaintiffs. (Kantako, 1992b).

Kantako says when the group began to express their opinions, they were labeled by mainstream media as a "radical splinter group with militant ideology" (*Soundprint*, 1991). They decided to band together in an effort to have their voices heard.

Dissatisfied with the way mainstream media reported their issues, the group met to discuss alternative ways to communicate their ideas to other African Americans in Springfield. The plan was twofold: to combat negative publicity from mainstream media and to preach a positive message to the African American community. The decision to start a radio station was unanimous. Kantako recalls:

> We considered the most effective way of getting our message to the people. We discussed starting a newspaper, but we recognized that a large percentage of our people can't read. And a whole lot of them that can read, don't or can't comprehend what they are reading. (Kantako, 1992a)

Black Liberation Radio began broadcasting in 1986 under the name WTRA (Tenant Rights Association, which has been renamed the Human Rights Association). Several of the men had technical experience and connected a 1-watt transmitter so that the entire 600-unit housing project could receive the signal. Mbanna Kantako's living room served as the radio station and more than 20 people were involved. The cost of the equipment was less than $500. Kantako says: "The biggest lie that has ever been told is that it costs a lot to run a radio station" (Kantako, 1992b).

Kantako sees Black Liberation Radio as an instrument for educating the African American community. "In a real sense, our duty at Black

Liberation Radio is to bring information. We want to teach people to educate themselves" (Kantako, 1992b). Topics aired on the station include race discrimination, historical accounts of minorities in the United States, legal struggles, AIDS as a genocidal concept, and other health issues that affect people of color. Kantako states that all of the topics seek to raise the consciousness level of the audience members and make them think. He says:

> We need correct information. This is what we communicate to the people, 'Mind, know thyself.' Who are you Black man? Who are you Black woman? When people understand what they are capable of doing, they will aspire to be great. (Kantako, 1992b)

He admits that many of the subjects are controversial, but argues that debate is one of the best ways to get people to discuss these issues. "We know that there is evidence to prove that when given the proper information, our people [black community members] will act intelligently," he says. "So we would be unintelligent to cease giving them the proper information" (Kantako, 1992b).

Despite being blind, Mbanna Kantako chooses much of the subject matter that is read over the air. He says that Black Liberation Radio is the voice of the people in the community and sees his role as an untiring educator and teacher. Also describing himself as a deprogramming director, he says:

> Community members know this is their station, no matter what happens. I am sitting here in 1992, and I have to convince my brother [black man] that he's a man. I have to convince my sister [black woman] that she's a woman. I have to convince my people that they are human beings. (Kantako, 1992a)

Black Liberation Radio is a small operation and Kantako involves his family in his efforts to educate the African American community of Springfield. His wife, Dia, and daughter, Kadonni, frequently read historical accounts by minority authors on the air. Kantako says it is important to "break open the books for our people [African Americans]. They will do great things when they know. They just don't know" (Kantako, 1992b). In March 1992, for instance, excerpts from *A Century Dishonored* by Harriet Ward and the COINTELPRO papers

(1976) were read over the air. Reading from Ward's book, Kadonni Kantako compared the white majority's treatment of Native Americans with the suffering in African Americans' experience. Dia Kantako explained to her listening audience that the program COINTELPRO was the acronym for the FBI efforts to destroy American political movements of which the FBI disapproved. "Members of the Civil Rights Movement were primary targets of the Senate investigation," says Dia Kantako. "According to Hinds (1978), a memorandum dated March, 1968, outlined 5 long-range goals of the committee against Blacks" (*Freedom Found Books*, 1991). After the readings, listeners called in to voice their opinions. Six-year-old Eboni Kantako has a listening audience of children. They tune in to hear her read *Goodnight, Gear Bear* (Baum, 1988). The Kantako children are taught at home and the grading criteria for their homework assignments is based partly on their interpretation of the reading material and their broadcast performance.

The diversity of his listening audience is a tribute to the success of the station. Mbanna Kantako says community members range in age from 6 to 60. "The other day, two older ladies stopped me outside and told me how much they liked the show," he says. "They didn't want me to mention their names on the air, but they told me that they listened to the station every day" (Kantako, 1992b).

Kantako operates this illegal radio station seven days a week, 24 hours a day. He has defied an order from the FCC in 1989 to shut down his operation and has refused to pay the $750 fine. Kantako argues that he has a constitutional right to voice community opinion over the airwaves without being sanctioned by the FCC. "We don't believe the FCC is GOD," said one station supporter in a recent broadcast. "We came on the air because we weren't being represented and our concerns weren't being addressed and we can't let them push us off the air" (*Free to Speak*, 1991).

According to the creators of Black Liberation Radio, the FCC should not have regulatory control. "It's not something that we figure a group of people can give us the 'right' to do," Mbanna Kantako says. "We're human beings. We have the right to communicate" (Kantako, 1992b). In addition, he says the regulatory system is a sham: "It is ridiculous when you think about it. Someone could come and give us a piece of paper and we would just abandon our position and stop broadcasting" (Kantako, 1992b).

In 1987, Kantako was contacted about forming a loose association with a station in Fresno, California—Zoom Black Magic Radio. The operator of Zoom was under scrutiny by the FCC and was also broadcasting without a license. After several months, due to ideological differences, Kantako decided to disassociate his operations and re-named his station Black Liberation Radio.

About this time, the programming content also changed, and Kantako began addressing the issue of police brutality. "In January 1989, people started bringing us cases of police brutality, and we started airing those cases," he says. Eight months later, the FCC came to visit Kantako's apartment and determined that Black Liberation Radio was in violation of the federal regulatory guidelines regarding licensing. The FCC fined the station $750 and ordered him to shut down. "The FCC showed up and told us we were illegally using the air," says Kantako. "I said that the air has to belong to somebody for us to be illegally using it" (Kantako, 1992a). Despite the formal warning by the FCC, Black Liberation Radio has continued to broadcast.

Kantako directly attributes the intervention of the federal agency to complaints from the police department in Springfield, which had criticized his show. He says:

> The FCC wanted to meet with a group who were involved in this station, but we wouldn't tell them at first where we were broadcasting from. We agreed to meet them somewhere. When we got to the designated location they called about half a dozen police. So we had to bring them back to the station. Those who represent the U.S. government have proven historically that when it comes to morality they are bankrupt. (Kantako, 1992b)

Kantakok says serious problems began for Black Liberation Radio when the station continued to broadcast issues of excessive police actions after being warned by the local police to broadcast on other issues.

> In March 1979 it got deep when FEMA (Federal Emergency Management Agency) brought in about a hundred white boys with masks and everything, and shot down a brother [black man] and two sisters [black women]. They alleged that the brother was holding these sisters hostages. But it wasn't nothing like that. (Kantako, 1992a)

Kantako explained that the police overreacted to a domestic situation and were responsible for the unprompted deaths of three people. Black Liberation Radio was on the scene reporting the events as they happened and Kantako says the reports given by his station and the ones by mainstream media were very different. "We reported the event all day," he says.

> We told the people something was going to go down and sure enough, they [the police] shot every one of them. There was a clear contradiction in what actually happened and the way the story was reported in mainstream media. (Kantako, 1992b)

During a broadcast in April 1989, Black Liberation Radio aired a show that dealt with several minority members' perceptions of the police. Audience members were encouraged to call in and voice their opinions about violence, harassment, and intervention on the part of policemen in the United States. Mbanna Kantako focused on specific incidents in the Springfield area and compared policemen to swine. When introducing a segment of the show, he said,

> The following ninety minutes will be uninterrupted so we can air a secretly recorded meeting at the police station in Springfield, Illinois. Oink, Oink, Oink, Oink, squeal, squeal, . . . A pig's a pig to me. They are all symbols of the state. (Cokely, 1990; *Notes,* 1990)

Kantako believes that the radio station is an important instrument for reporting incidents of police brutality in Springfield. Furthermore, he says that residents are penalized for defending the station: "We had been receiving reports from brothers and sisters that they would go down to the jail, and the police would brutalize them, and then say, 'Now, go and tell your radio station that' " (Kantako, 1992b). Gary Caveno, producer of a recently aired radio broadcast, verified Kantako's perception of the relationship that exists between the police and Springfield's African American residents: "The relationship between the poor black community in Springfield and the police is a tense one. Black residents complain about being harassed on the street, roughed up, sometimes even shaken down for their money" (*Soundprint,* 1991).

Kantako also believes that the radio station is a lifeline for residents because unnecessary force can sometimes be eliminated when a strong communication vehicle is available. He tells the story of a retarded boy who died in jail during a period in which the radio station was off the air. "In July 1989, the police beat a brother to death in the county jail and it hit me especially hard," he explains. "They said he had a heart attack, but the family had pictures of his mangled body. I thought, 'Maybe if we had been on the air, this wouldn't have gone down like that' " (Kantako, 1992b).

Alleging police brutality has often been futile for the African American residents of Springfield. "A move to establish an independent review commission to investigate complaints against the police was defeated by Springfield's overwhelmingly white city council," Caveno says, "The vote on the review commission came after a series of violent incidents, which included beatings, the death of a prisoner in the city jail, and controversial large-scale drug raids" (*Soundprint,* 1991).

Mbanna Kantako maintains that the FCC does not have the authority to regulate airwaves and that the public is guaranteed a right to expression. He argues that the rules of the FCC violate his constitutional right to freedom of expression:

> If we wanted to look for backup to what we are saying we would look to the United Nations Universal Declaration of Human Rights, Article, 19,[4] which basically says, that every people have a right to communicate in the interest of their people. (Kantako, 1992b)

On January 20, 1995, U.S. District Judge Claudia Wilken apparently agreed with this idea when she ruled in favor of another pirate station in Berkeley, California. Anarchist Stephen Dunifer explained that he got the idea for his station from Mbanna Kantako. The FCC was seeking an injunction to shut down his operation after they levied a fine of $20,000 for 24 illegal broadcasts over a 13-month period. After making her ruling, Judge Wilken said she had a serious question about the constitutionality of ending the operation of Free Radio Berkeley.

DISCUSSION

As this description of minority-owned and operated community radio stations shows, the stations serve as vehicles to reflect a reality that is often ignored. The stations act as tools to communicate views and frustrations within a community because the mainstream media tend to exclude minority issues when presenting the news and are often biased in their presentation of subjects. Community stations such as KUCB and Black Liberation Radio are necessary to focus on topics of interest to their particular listening audiences and make sure such views and opinions are presented.

Studies show that although the policy of exclusion of ethnic minorities in news coverage may seem benign, it has a significant impact on the development of race relations (Hacker, 1991). The lack of coverage of minorities in white news media indicates the lack of status of minorities in a society, and in broadcast news this presents a powerful social and psychological message. Exclusion from news media coverage signifies exclusion from American society because a primary function of news is to reflect social reality.

KUCB and Black Liberation Radio represent alternative vehicles for minority voice. A prevalent theme at both stations is to use oral communication to educate minority community members and to help them organize against inequality and oppression. Both stations encourage the listening audience to speak out on topics that affect many African Americans. Specifically, issues have centered on the problematic relationship between the police and the African American community.

Mainstream media have accused both stations of advocating violence and promoting racial dissention. Kantako (Black Liberation Radio) and Kalongi (KUCB) have been described as *angry* and *militant*—two terms that are highly subjective. In private discussions, interviews, and observations of community interaction, the conclusions are much different: Both men have been described by their communities and colleagues as self-assured and confident in their efforts and opinions.

Much of what has been written about the stations by the mainstream press is also incorrect and sensational. For example, Mbanna Kantako does not have a white publicist; his wife's name is Dia, not Barbara; and he has not been arrested by the Springfield police for drug offenses (Harrison, 1990; "Mbanna Kantako and His Microwatt Revolution," 1992; Rodriguez, 1991). It seems that the African American community generally does not pay attention to the negative publicity and is protective of the image of their community stations.

In the two case studies, each station indicated a general distrust of FCC authorities. Jamal Long (KUCB) and Mbanna Kantako regard the agency as a symbol of domination and control. Kalongi (KUCB) and Dia Kantako (Black Liberation Radio) believe that the FCC is more interested in discrediting individuals and shutting down the stations than it is in improving the quality of programs and upgrading the facilities. At both locations, people are suspicious and distrustful of rules and regulations set forth by the commission. They believe the FCC is concerned with policing rather than correcting and assisting. Furthermore, they argue that the FCC has not been successful in achieving its stated goal of increasing minority ownership.

Community radio does provide a forum for minority voices, but two questions involving the continuation of community radio need and deserve attention. First, if the FCC is concerned with increasing minority stations and creating a diversity of voices, and if the policies they have in place are not working, alternative measures must be considered. Second, if community involvement plays a significant role in maintaining community radio, it is important for the FCC to consider the wants and needs of the community.

Minority community stations and the FCC might consider dialogue as a step toward increasing diversity of ownership. The FCC has legitimate concerns. The minority community radio stations and their listeners also have legitimate arguments. Lines of communication must be established between the FCC and the community to maintain what Ralph Nader argues are two basic principles: ownership and the right to develop a community intelligence as a consequence of that ownership. Nader (1991) writes:

> The people are the landlords of the public airwaves, and the broadcast companies are the tenants. Under the present, inverted system the FCC ignores both who owns the airwaves and the public interest standard that this agency is supposed to enforce. (p. 24)

KUCB and Black Liberation Radio are examples of the need in our society for a diversity of voices. The ability to speak out for truth and against injustice is necessary, yet not always possible in mainstream media. Jamal Long, board member at KUCB radio, says that community radio stations serve as critical vehicles to help minorities band together and accomplish positive goals. "If we give people direction then they can move by themselves. If you set people on the right course they can walk on down the road by themselves" (Long, 1992b).

NOTES

1. Mbanna Kantako, operator of Black Liberation Radio in Springfield, Illinois, says the term *antihumanism* refers to anyone who stands in the way of a people's right to food, clothing, shelter, and education for development ("Senseia Kankowi on Black Liberation Radio," Springfield, January, 30 1992). For the purpose of this chapter, *minority* is defined as "those of Black, Hispanic Surnamed, American Eskimo, Aleut, American Indian and Asiatic American extraction" (see Minority Ownership of Broadcasting Facilities, 68 F.C.C. 2d 979, 980 n. 8, 1978).

2. The National Commission on Civil Disorders, commonly known as the Kerner commission, was established by an Executive Order of President Lyndon Johnson, to investigate and make recommendations about the origins of race riots in the 1960s and methods and techniques to averting and controlling such riots (see Executive Order no. 11365, 1967).

3. The license was granted to the Center for Study and Application of Black Economic Development (License file no. BLED-841029CY, Permit No. BPED-830919A0).

4. Adopted on December 10, 1949, this statement of principle by the United Nations asserts the rights of each individual in the world to know, to impart, and to discuss. The main part of the declaration's goals are contained in Article 19, which says: "Everybody has the right to freedom of opinion and expression; this right includes freedom to hold opinions without interference, and to seek, receive and impart information and ideas through media and regardless of frontiers."

REFERENCES

Alex, K., & Carter, T. (1992, January). Injured man accuses D.M. police. *Des Moines Register*, p. A1.

Baum, S. (1988). *Goodnight, gear bear.* New York: Grosset & Dunlap.

Brown, D. (1992, February 25). [Telephone interview with author]. KUCB Radio, Des Moines, IA.

Caristi, D. (1992). *Expanding free expression in the marketplace: Broadcasting and the public forum.* New York: Quorum.

Cokely, S. (1990, February 19). *Eye of the storm.* Black Liberation Radio, Springfield, IL.

COINTELPRO: The FBI's covert action programs against American citizens. (1976). *Supplementary detailed staff reports on intelligence activities and the rights of Americans: Final report of the Select Committee to Study Governmental Operations with Respect to Intelligence Activities.* Washington, DC: Government Printing Office.

Commission policy. (1978). Regarding the advancement of minority ownership in broadcasting facilities (68. F.C.C. 2d.). Washington, DC: Federal Communications Commission.

Franklin, M., & Anderson, D. (1990). *Mass media law: Case and material* (4th ed.). New York: Foundation Press.

Freedom found books. (1991, September 14). [Radio program]. Black Liberation Radio, Springfield, IL.

Free to speak. (1991, July 18). [Radio program]. Black Liberation Radio, Springfield, IL.

Goodman, R. A. (1993, May-June). Uneasy listening: What happened to the public part of public radio? *UTNE Reader,* p. 105.

Hacker, A. (1992). *Two nations: Black and white, separate, hostile, unequal.* New York: Scribner.

Haddasha, S. (1992, February 16). [Interview by author]. KUCB Radio, Des Moines, IA.

Harrison, E. (1990, November 19). Out of the night, from a corner. *Los Angeles Times,* p. B1.

Hinds, L. (1978). *Illusions of justice: Human rights violations in the United States.* Iowa City: University of Iowa Press.

Insider's view. (1995, February). *Emerge Magazine,* p. 28.

Iowa Department of Economic Development. (1992). *Community quick reference.* Des Moines, IA: Author.

Johnson, N. (1968, August 17). Remarks prepared for delivery to the Annual Convention of the National Association of Television and Radio Announcers, Sheraton Town Ambassador Hotel, Miami, FL (Special Collections, University of Iowa Library, University of Iowa, Iowa City).

Kalongi, S. (1992, February 16). [Interview by author]. KUCB Radio, Des Moines, IA.

Kantako, M. (1992a, January 15). [Interview]. KUCB Radio, Des Moines, IA.

Kantako, M. (1992b, March 8). [Interview by author]. Black Liberation Radio, Springfield, IL.

Mbanna Kantako and his microwatt movement. (1992, February). *Spin Magazine,* p. 43.

Lewis, P. (1984). Community radio: The Montreal conference and after. *Media Culture and Society, 6,* 137.

Lohman, J. (1965). *The San Francisco report.* Berkeley: University of California, School of Criminology.

Long, J. (1992a, February 12). [Interview by author]. KUCB Radio, Des Moines, IA.

Long, J. (1992b, February 16). [Interview by author]. KUCB Radio, Des Moines, IA.

Morrow, L. (1991, April 1). Rough justice: After the outrage in Los Angeles. *Time, 137*(13), 16.

Nader, R. (1991, March-April). Clean reception: Nader's nineties. *Mother Jones, 16*(2), 24.

Notes on the devil's news. (1990, October 13). Black Liberation Radio, Springfield, IL.

Our voices. (1992a, January 1). KUCB Radio Program, Des Moines, IA.

Our voices. (1992b, January 3). KUCB Radio Program, Des Moines, IA.

Parrish, A. (1992, March 26). [Telephone interview by author]. Des Moines, IA.

Police brutality. (1992, January 1). KUCB Radio, Des Moines, IA.

Report of the National Advisory Commission on Civil Disorders. (1968). New York: Bantam.

Rodriguez, L. (1991, August 12). Rappin in the hood, rebel radio. *Nation, 253,* 192.

Samad, A. (1992, January 2). [Interview by author]. KUCB Radio, Des Moines, IA.

Smith, T. (1992, February 16). [Interview by author]. KUCB Radio, Des Moines, IA.

Soundprint. (1991, December 1). KSUI Radio, Iowa City, IA.

Tate, S. E. (1988, January 1). Joeanna Coleman [Photocopy]. KUCB Radio, Des Moines, IA, p. 6.

14

"Pride and Profit" in Black Radio Promotions

Celebrating Family Days and Business Partnerships

PHYLIS JOHNSON
THOMAS A. BIRK

There are over 360 "black/urban" commercial radio stations in the United States (*Broadcast Yearbook,* 1993). It is difficult to define black/urban programming, in that there is much format diversification, such as rhythm and blues, jazz, dance, rap, gospel, and Motown as well as an incorporation of a significant proportion of the music into urban contemporary and contemporary hit stations. Urban contemporary stations, although not necessarily black owned or managed (e.g., Philadelphia's WUSL-FM), have established community ties with their urban audiences. Black/urban radio, a composite of black and urban contemporary formats, has often localized its programming to fit the needs of the African American community, engaging in block programming and offering primarily a variety of musical styles, talk shows, and promotional activity.

AUTHORS' NOTE: Mark Newman (1988) first coined the term *pride and profit* in his book *Entrepreneurs of Profit and Pride*.

E. Steven Collins, promotion director of WDAS-AM/FM in Phila-delphia, offered this expanded definition of black/urban radio:

The overall sense and direction, philosophy, sound, image, position, of a radio station, any radio station is not just its music format. It's its commentaries, its editorials, its news, its public affairs, its public service announcements, its commercials for that matter. . . . Clearly at black radio, music is maybe 51 percent of concern, but 49 percent really is what else we do; it can't just be music. It has to be more. It can't just be spoken more. It has to be action. We have to be in the community. (Collins, personal communication, July 25, 1992)

Black/urban radio, at many stations, has created coalitions within the community and generated community participation. Black/urban radio is distinguished from other formats by its unique commitment to the African American community, although this degree of commitment varies market by market and station by station (Love, 1990c; Settel, 1967).

This chapter will examine the social and economic success of two partnerships between black/urban commercial radio stations and their communities: WDAS's Unity Weekend in Philadelphia and WTLC's Indiana Black Expo in Indianapolis. The activities surrounding Unity Weekend 1992 and Indiana Black Expo 1993, the role of management, and the success of these events were all documented through an examination of promotional materials, media reports, and interview transcripts as well as observation.

PRIDE AND UNITY

Norman W. Spaulding (1981) pointed out that the African American church had a direct influence on black radio, and that "choral groups and church choirs appeared more frequently on Chicago radio than any other form of black/urban programming from the 1920s until World War II" (p. 34). Approximately 56 hours of African American radio programming (including religious programming) were broadcast weekly by commercial radio stations in the mid-1940s, and this figure grew to more than 400 hours a week in the 1950s (p. 47).

Beginning as early as the 1940s, WDIA-AM and, to a lesser extent, KWEM-AM (later KWAM) were instrumental in programming black gospel music as well as other black-oriented music on Memphis radio (Lornell, 1988). In 1949, however, when WDIA debuted the first all-black format in the nation, it strengthened its involvement with the African American community in Memphis and the surrounding regions. The station became famous for its Goodwill Announcements, which aired "announcements about missing persons, lost personal property, church meetings, and socials; it answered appeals for blood donors, helped reunite families, assisted listeners in getting jobs, and even found occasional lost animals" (Cantor, 1992, p. 197). By organizing religious and popular music events, such as the "Goodwill Revue," "Star-Lite Revue," and "Hallelujah Jubilee Caravan," WDIA raised money to construct a school for physically challenged children, helped bus students to the school, and used some of the proceeds for college scholarships (Cantor, 1992).

As early as the 1950s, Alex Haley praised black radio for promoting church activities and community service events (George, 1988). With this type of commitment continuing into the 1990s, black/urban radio and black gospel radio, specifically those stations addressing African American concerns, have sponsored fund-raising promotions for local police departments, social agencies, schools, and a number of nonprofit organizations such as the YMCA, Big Brother, Big Sister, United Negro College Fund, March of Dimes, American Cancer Society, and National Civil Rights Museum (Love, 1991d).

Today it is difficult to define black gospel programming, in that it has become fragmented and often incorporated into other formats like rhythm and blues, jazz, dance, rap, and Motown. Black gospel radio has localized its programming to fit the needs of the community, and what sets it apart from white gospel radio is its artists' commitment to church values and the African American experience (Cusic, 1990). Whereas only 2% of the nation's total radio audience listens to gospel music, the impact of black gospel music, in particular, has provided inspiration and guidance in areas other than spiritual matters, such as education, family unification, voter registration, and minority-owned businesses.

For decades, the black church has given its parishioners an emotional and economic support system, meeting the "basic needs of the church family" (Scott & Black, 1989, p. 22; also see Smith, 1988-1989). Many black/urban stations with secular formats but Christian messages promote family unity and acknowledge cultural traditions unique to the African American:

> The black church not only teaches familistic values, it also ritualizes family values. It promotes activities wherein individuals are called upon to actually carry out the requirements of their faith such as visiting the shut-in and giving time and talents . . . [T]he church dramatizes the value of physical survival and ritualizes the process by which that can occur— by communally giving one to the other. (Scott & Black, 1989, p. 22)

Toni St. James, KJMS-FM/KWAM-AM program director, has implemented promotions that touch the everyday lives of listeners; an example is KJMS's Pillsbury Church Bus Giveaway:

> Something that is pretty unique to black/urban radio is it's very community-oriented, and if it's not you see those that are having problems reaching their audiences. For some reason, according to some research that I've seen in Arbitron, our listeners tend to listen longer . . . [making] them feel the station is basically part of their everyday life. (St. James, personal communication, February 11, 1992)

Indeed, a 1992 national survey conducted by the authors (Johnson & Birk, 1993) found that almost all black-owned commercial radio stations engaged in community service activities. Education, drug awareness, and voting registration topped the list for types of promotional activities conducted during 1991.

During the annual Unity Weekend, cosponsored by WDAS-AM/FM and the City of Philadelphia, several themes or issues are promoted: education, employment, spirituality, and the family (E. S. Collins, personal communication, July 25, 1992). WDAS's Unity Day (expanded to Unity Weekend in 1992) began in 1978 when the "need for family reunification became a pressing concern" (Collins, July 25, 1992). Family celebrations by WOKS-AM/WFXE-FM (Columbus, Georgia), WQUE-FM (New Orleans), KJMS-FM (Memphis), WJLB-FM (Detroit), and WDAS-AM/FM (Philadelphia) have attracted from 5,000 to over a half million listeners ("Day of Music," 1991).

Black radio's emphasis on education is not so surprising when one considers that a number of the early African American broadcasters were well educated (Newman, 1988; Spaulding, 1981).[2] Black radio has provided "culturally specific programming" as a source for African American history and pride, and has especially promoted "black achievement in education" (Ghee, 1990, p. 87). According to Roy Wood Sr.,[3] news director of WAGG-AM/WENN-FM: "Black radio has the obligation to be in the forefront of educating us about our history. It's not taught in high school. . . . The only way [youth] have to learn our history is through communication channels like Black Radio" (cited in Love, 1990a, p. 50).

Recent education research, in an effort to provide support for at-risk children, has focused on the bonding of families, businesses, social agencies, and media into inner-city community partnerships (Hale-Benson, 1986; Johnson, 1992; Kozma & Croninger, 1992). The National Urban League, identifying the family as "the primary educator," called for participation in education through "intensive mobilization and coalition-building activity" within the African American community (Jacob, 1987-1988, p. 16). A number of researchers have suggested an alliance between African American parents, civic groups, business leaders, politicians, inner-city churches, and schools to help at-risk African American youth overcome social and educational inequities (e.g., Chapman, 1991; Hare, 1988-1989; Hilliard, 1987-1988; Slaughter & Kuehne, 1987-1988). A 1986 study conducted by Pennsylvania State University concluded: "Ethnic identity increases as blacks' education and income rise, and is strongest among blacks earning $30,000+ per year" ("Black Consumer," 1991, p. 20). African Americans between 27 to 54 years old are more likely to join culturally specific organizations than other African Americans ("Black Consumer," 1991). The role of education, particularly in secondary and higher education, in the African American community has been as a means to "social mobility and of equality" (Thompson & Cusella, 1974, p. 331).

THE CASE OF WDAS-AM/FM

The black church has been "the major staying rock" of the African American community and black/urban radio in Philadelphia:

In the fifties and sixties, the surge of black consciousness, the Dr. King era, Elijah Mohammed era, and all those things that prompted the black community to seek political empowerment, economic empowerment, needed a place to be aired (e.g., talk shows, news programs, news and information) and a recognition on the part of the black community that black radio was its best media friend. (E. S. Collins, personal communication, July 25, 1992)

WDAS is an African American-owned radio station licensed in Philadelphia, Pennsylvania, owned by Unity Broadcasting. Chairman of the Board Eugene D. Jackson explained the mission of his company from its inception:

I formed the company about 20 years ago. Unity is the parent name, and I believed at that time unity was the number one thing we needed in America, and so we named our company Unity Broadcasting. And we continue to want to build a unity relationship in America through our radio station and broadcast opportunities. Philadelphia, the City of Brotherly Love, expresses that so substantially, and today is symptomatic of what it is we need to be doing—everybody joined together to make everything happen positive for all of Philadelphia. (*Unity Promotional*, 1991)

WDAS-AM is a gospel format station that has served the Philadelphia area for almost a half century and has evolved into a community center radio station. WDAS-FM airs black adult contemporary music. Both stations work together in hosting a number of local and national events. In addition to setting up a gospel stage during Unity Weekend in August, the stations sponsor a number of events throughout the year: "Black Family Reunion," "Father's Day Rally," Martin Luther King Jr. celebrations, live broadcasts from area black churches such as the "Impact of Black Churches Historically on Evolution" and the "United Negro College Telethon" hosted by WDAS personalities (*Unity Weekend*, 1992). Some of these promotions are especially relevant to the African American community, in that the black church has been criticized for failing to adequately address the needs of African American fathers, in particular adolescent fathers, in the inner city (Smith, 1988-1989).

Unity Weekend is an event now cosponsored by the city of Philadelphia and WDAS-AM/FM. Cody Anderson, WDAS's former general manager, wanted to do something specifically to promote "unity in the family, in the neighborhood, in the community," and with Unity

Broadcasting as the new owner, "it seemed to be the appropriate time to initiate Unity Day" (E. S. Collins, personal communication, June 24, 1992).

In 1978, Unity Day began as a simple community gathering: "The agenda was to have a softball game, to have some entertainment," according to Collins (June 24, 1992), the executive producer, "and basically rededicate ourselves to being together as a unit, as a community." The event began as a family-oriented picnic on Belmont Plateau, with over 50,000 people attending Unity '78. And over the years, it found its way to the Benjamin Franklin Parkway, which is a bigger area in town. At that point, "I believe 300,000 people showed up, and it was just outstanding," said Collins.

Then, a decade later, when Kernie Anderson (not related to Cody Anderson) became the new general manager, he decided to expand the event. Anderson said:

> I think Unity Weekend, the whole experience, is something that is . . . relevant to the African American community. And so I think when you're dealing with a management team that has lived in the African American community, a lot of the ideas, a lot of the expansion, a lot of the adjustments, they tend to come out of our experiences and by the same token, any modifications, additions, tend to come out of analyses of the past events. (Anderson, personal communication, August 6, 1992)

Surpassing WDAS's wildest dreams, the 1991 Unity Day drew over 800,000 people into the heart of Philadelphia. The festivities included informational, political, and culturally specific events as well as entertainment:

> Most of the entertainment is directed specifically to family oriented audiences, everything that day, the whole day is laid out to attract the elderly, the young, teenagers, moms and dads, clergy, everything. There are millions of things that we build in so that there's something for everybody. And people usually come out. . . . It speaks volumes to black management and the cooperation that . . . city government has given us. (E. S. Collins, personal communication, June 24, 1992)

Unity Day is actually one element of a "five-day festival called Unity Weekend" ("Unity Weekend," 1992). The name Unity Weekend was introduced in 1992. The theme of Unity '92 was "Claim Your Future," which was adopted from WDAS commentator Karen Warrington, who uses the phrase on the WDAS Arts Review and Commentary program ("Unity Weekend," 1992). Every year there is a new theme; some of the former themes have been "Claim Your Culture," "The Dream Lives," "Striving Towards Excellence," and "Free South Africa":

> So it could be political, it could be entertainment, it could be any number of different things, but it has to mean something, and we try to find something or some person who is the embodiment of the theme. The year we had "Free South Africa," we had Harry Belafonte as our host of the day; "Striving Towards Excellence"we had Julius Irving [and] this year we're attempting to secure Quincy Jones, who epitomizes culture and really mastering culture. (E. S. Collins, personal communication, June 24, 1992)

Other honorary hosts and speakers have included the Reverend Jesse Jackson, Spike Lee, and Dick Gregory.

Collins explained the purpose of the annual celebration as the "need to bring our community together around family-oriented issues [such as] the importance of going to church, being respectful, sharing, fellowship, giving and love" (Love, 1990b, p. 97). Collins said it brings everybody together:

> Policemen who ordinarily look at the black community with a lot of fear, and the black community who look at the police with a lot of fear—on Unity Day, after five minutes, they're talking to each other. The cop loosens his tie and puts his hat back, and he has a Coca-Cola. And he sees people who he thinks are OK—like the old days. It's wonderful.

Events include a youth downtown street sweep, panel discussions, a number of community service booths, education and health exhibits, a softball game, family events, and even "a new thing called the science factory, where 50 companies encourage inner city youth primarily, but people generally, to be in the sciences":

> If one kid becomes a chemist because of Unity Day, we've done something really good. And there's thousands of opportunities because there's so many hundreds of thousands of young people and other people who'll be there that day. So the sky is the limit on what we could do, and each year we try to increase it, make it better, make it bigger, make it stronger,

make it more meaningful, and good things happen every year. (E. S. Collins, personal communication, June 24, 1992)

At Unity '92, staging areas set up specifically for educational issues included a mini-science pavilion presented by the Philadelphia Gas Works, storytelling at the McDonald's Children's Stage, as well as booths and displays by Temple University, the Free Library of Philadelphia, Eastern College, Delta Sigma Theta, and Zeta Phi Beta. The African-American Historical and Cultural Museum was a focal point of the Unity Weekend proclamation from the mayor of Philadelphia, Edward G. Rendell.

A total of over 200 vendors, ranging from the Philadelphia 76ers to Temple University, participated in the event as did such corporate sponsors as AT&T (with the AT&T We Mean Business Pavilion), the *Philadelphia Tribune,* the United Bank of Philadelphia, Coca-Cola (Philadelphia bottler), McDonald's, Atlantic Bell, and 11 health organizations, including eight Philadelphia area hospitals, which participated in the Health Partners Health Pavilion (*Vendor List,* 1992).

Vehicles and personnel from many different city departments and agencies were present, and the radio station's general manager indicated that negotiating for city services was one of the monumental tasks in the management of this event: "People from license inspection to the police department, fire department, health department, sanitation, the city manager's office—it's maybe around 12 to 15 departments we interact with" (K. Anderson, personal communication, August 6, 1992).

With hundreds of vendors and organizations, tens of thousands of spectators, recording artists El DeBarge and Chaka Khan, and rain that continued to alter events and timetables, this event was a major undertaking—one that takes months to prepare and significant dedication from the broadcasters involved. According to General Manager Kernie Anderson (personal communication, August 6, 1992):

We look at our planning process as almost year-round. We are doing something relevant to Unity Weekend just about every week beginning the day after Unity. So it's a year-round planning process because we are always adding more to it and just tightening up the logistics of it.

One of the recent additions has been an expansion of the Cultural Stage, continued Anderson:

I have demanded that we really put emphasis on having various ethnic groups there. So I'm really looking forward to that stage. While it will still have a strong R & B base to it, there will be a significant number of groups from other ethnic communities, the Asian community, the American Indian community, the Irish community, I think we have a Yiddish group. And I think that we're such a factor in the market that we have the responsibility [to] expose this huge crowd to the various cultures.

WDAS management has a keen sensitivity to the issues facing the urban community, although they do not do a lot of formal research. The key technique used to assess community needs is observation from personal experience. Collins and Anderson both agreed that it is more important to be aware of what's going on in the community than to conduct formal research. Collins explained why this ability to tap into an audience's needs is so essential to the success of a radio station:

Much like a significant amount of things that are done in black radio and definitely here at 'DAS, it's a response. That's the research. No one has to tell us that we need to promote voter registration, we don't need to see the numbers (we know people aren't registered to vote) to get serious about it. There's no one really that has to say that we need to understand infant mortality figures, we know we need to promote, "take advantage of," these programs . . . and so on and so forth. So there's not a lot of research. But it's clear to us the kind of things that a city this big [needs], with this large amount of African American people.

The success of the events is measured in a number of ways: the number of people that attend, the number of community service organizations that participate, the number of pavilions Unity Weekend is able to expand to focus on myriad issues relevant to the community, the media publicity, letters, telephone calls, and some on-site measurement: "You're up and down the parkway, you're there, and you talk to people," said Anderson (personal communication, August 6, 1992).

Unity Weekend is a symbol of African American management at its best. Collins said it is "a statement of black management," and added:

Advertisers sing our praises. It's one thing to have big ratings in a major market in a major country like America, but when you can bring people out and show them different things, it says something about how much the station cares, and how much real power the station has in the community.

Anderson summarized his management philosophy as a general manager of a commercial radio station and as a role model to the African American community:

> Everybody in this radio station knows that we're a commercial radio station. . . . I don't try to be the non-profit organization. We're here to make a buck. I have a budget. . . . I have to get X number of dollars in, but I know what my annual cost of the operation is.
>
> But having said that, there's an overriding and everlasting understanding that part of our mission as a broadcast operation, that's owned and operated by an African American, is to not only serve in the public interest, which is mandated by licenses, but also to operate in a manner that reflects the promotion of Afrocentricity in the most significant manner.

Anderson concluded, "Because what 'DAS does as an African American owned and operated radio station brings pride to the rest of the African American community."

PROFIT AS POWER

For black radio, the struggle toward community activism was over-shadowed by the need for economic empowerment. The partnership between African American media and African American business prom-ised a cultural perspective and a social, political, and economic platform that could not be ignored in a capitalistic society. Mark Newman (1988) posits: "Race raised black entrepreneurship to a higher level because it added a powerful motivation to profits and innovation, namely pride of progress . . . [B]lack entrepreneurship in the media was a business venture first and a stride for racial progress second" (pp. 3-8).

Within the African American community, black/urban radio's role is seen as business leadership and community activism. KJLH-FM was the 1992 George Foster Peabody Award recipient for its coverage of the Los Angeles riots from its Compton, California, studio. The station's coverage of the riots was simulcast across the world. Karen Slade, KJLH station manager, stressed that there are two goals of black/urban radio:

> One [is] to put money back into the community so that [it] can thrive and prosper, and two, to support your clientele. So if the inner city buys

your product, or supports your store, you need to put money back into the community. . . . And that's an ongoing argument. . . . But this is the same kind of recognition that another broadcaster is going to have because let's face it, there's the audience, but then there's the advertising community, and we need both. (Slade, personal communication, March 2, 1993)

In the case of WDIA-AM/WHRK-FM, Memphis, one of their most successful promotions in terms of community outreach and corporate sponsorship is a trip to Africa during Black History Month[4] that is cosponsored by Budweiser. According to WDIA/WHRK Vice President/General Manager Rick Caffey:

We [are in] partnership with Budweiser to do something that is both educational and informational and hopefully will pay off in the end for the lucky winner. We're doing something similar with Coca-Cola, where we're giving away a thousand dollar scholarship for the best essay that deals with a topic on black history. What we are finding is that there are a lot of corporate sponsors very receptive to tying into what we already are tied into and that's the community . . . one of the ways we try to steer them is things dealing with education and cultural enlightenment. . . . That's what the challenge is for our format . . . [promoting that] it's not just radio and [demonstrating] the power and influence [black/urban radio] has [in] the African American community. (Caffey, personal communication, February 11, 1991)

African Americans spend over $250 billion dollars annually. They listen to radio for almost 3½ hours every day, which is about 30 minutes longer than white consumers. To reach African American buyers, the most effective format, in terms of time spent listening, is black/urban radio (F. Brown, 1990).

By the year 2000, the U.S. Census Bureau has projected that 40% of the nation's population will be African American and Hispanic. African Americans "continually" buy more name brand products than any other ethnic group (F. Brown, 1990, p. 22). Many major advertising agencies, however, still overlook the potential of the African American consumer. A November 1990 report released by Katz Radio stated: "The rise in black purchasing power is having an impact on the national economy [but the African American consumer] continues to represent a missed opportunity for the nation's businesses" (Schuyler, 1990, p. 15).

Black-owned radio, in its struggle to compete for national advertising dollars with nonblack radio stations, has developed political savvy in dealing with the corporate sector. Indeed, research has indicated that the political clout of African Americans, especially in local government, has been important in the amount awarded to minority businesses in government contracts (MacManus, 1990). Not surprising, black-owned radio—both commercial and noncommercial—has helped sponsor a number of civic organizations and has championed a number of political, social, and economic causes. One such noncommercial station is KCEP-FM, Las Vegas, which is licensed to and operated by the Economic Opportunity Board of Clark County. General Manager Al Johnson pointed out: "We're the only urban station in the state of Nevada. Without this station there would be no voice for the black community, nor for the other minorities here that are growing just as fast" (Love, 1991c, p. 53).

Many African American consumers have traditionally lacked financial resources and family capital, and have relied on income in low-paying jobs (MacManus, 1990). In 1990, however, one in ten African American households earned $50,000 or more (Schuyler, 1990). To succeed in business, African Americans are often forced to alienate themselves from their cultural heritage, especially in corporate white America (Anderson & Harris, 1990). Black/urban radio, through its community service activity, has addressed the need to educate African American youth on the importance of their cultural heritage and to prepare them for the future. WDAS (Philadelphia) and WDIA (Memphis) have sponsored trips to cultural museums and Africa (R. Caffey, personal communication, February 11, 1991; E. S. Collins, personal communication, June 24, 1992).

Education, although important, is only part of the solution, for those who have remained in urban areas have been faced with limited employment opportunities (Moore & Laramore, 1990). That is why black expositions have been viewed as an important part of the community service agenda at black/urban commercial stations. Black expositions showcase African American art, history, music, and black-owned businesses; provide opportunities through career conferences and job fairs; and sponsor scholarships to African American colleges. These expositions have been made possible through the financial commitment and leadership of black/urban radio stations throughout the country, such as KDIA in Oakland, California—which began broadcasting in 1922, making it one of the oldest stations in the country—and WTLC in Indianapolis ("Black Radio," 1970; Love, 1991a). These expositions are viewed as significant cultural and political events in the African American community. (A. Brown, personal communication, August 27, 1993; "WTLC," 1990). Cooperation from local businesses and state and national corporate sponsors has been instrumental to the success of these expositions.

African American-owned radio on a local and regional level has addressed employment issues and developed strong ties to the business community since the 1940s. According to WBEE-AM General Manager Carl David Farley, his station showcases area businesses during the annual Chicago Jazz Festival, which has "an estimated attendance over 250,000 people during its three day stay in Grant Park on Chicago's Lakefront" (*Chicago Jazz*, 1992). WBEE Chairman of the Board Charles Sherrell said he is proud of the station's heritage and community involvement as well as its rapport with local retailers. He added, "That is the signature of the NABOB [National Association of Black-Owned Broadcasters] Radio Stations. We know what's going on in our communities, and we do whatever we can to improve our communities" (Schuyler, 1990, p. 22).

THE CASE OF INDIANA BLACK EXPO

The Reverend Jesse Jackson started Operation Breadbasket in the late 1960s, when he was involved in the Southern Christian Leadership Conference (A. Brown, personal communication, August 27, 1993). Operation Breadbasket was a historic event in the civil rights movement. Radio station WVON held Operation Breadbasket in what is known today as the "old Chicago amphitheater" and aired a portion of the show live. Anthony J. Meyer (1971) recalled:

Several thousand participants gathered in a huge old-fashioned movie theater, its stage filled with the Operation Breadbasket choir, posters announcing black-owned produce. . . . By 9 a.m. it was packed. One four and a half hour meeting included the black national anthem, gospel music from the Breadbasket Choir, Jesse Jackson's hard prose-poetry drawing strategies for black liberation, boycott announcements, economic advice, political planning, the powerful response of thousands of hands clapping in rhythm, Scripture, poetry and interviews. (p. 16)

Meyer (1971) added, "One sign dominated the stage, posing a basic Operation Breadbasket question: 'HAVE YOU FED SOMEONE TODAY?' " (p. 16).

The idea for the Indiana Black Expo grew out of Operation Bread-basket. WTLC-FM listeners in Indianapolis (back from a visit to Chicago) proposed what turned out to be the first in a long line of black expositions for Indiana:

> They thought that an exposition that brought together minority busi-nesses as well as white businesses to reach out to the black community would have great appeal here in Indianapolis. They believed that with an entertainment component added, it would work. (A. Brown, cited in "WTLC," 1990, p. 50)

According to Indianapolis WTLC-FM Station Manager Amos Brown (personal communication, August 27, 1993), a bipartisan committee was formed that "cut across all cliques, and all groups within the African American community here." This committee invited WTLC to partici-pate in the event. WTLC, at that point, had been "on the air two years as the only 24-hour station serving the then Negro community" (A. Brown, personal communication, August 27, 1993). The station man-agement and ownership, at the time, made the decision to back the expo by donating airtime, in particular, public service time, and by setting up a booth to broadcast live from the event. "That is how that relationship began," Brown said.

In 1971, the first exposition was held in Indianapolis. Brown continued,

> It was designed to be an exposition of black-owned businesses showcas-ing their businesses to whites as well as the black community—[and] white businesses showcasing their stuff to the black community. Enter-tainment, athletic events, a variety of different things all under one umbrella. (A. Brown, personal communication, 1993)

It included an All-Star Game between the American and National Baseball Leagues as well as a golf tournament, exhibits, and a concert.

From its inception, the Indiana Black Expo, in partnership with city and state government agencies and radio station WTLC, has been committed to the following goals: (a) to create and maintain increased awareness and appreciation of African American culture and heritage; (b) to implement and support youth programs that foster educational, professional, and personal development; (c) to support economic development initiatives that benefit all sectors of the community; and (d) to promote activities that enhance the intellectual, physical, and spiritual development of individuals and society (Indiana Black Expo, 1993a).

Over the years, guests have included the Reverend Jesse Jackson, Lou Gossett Jr., elected officials from across the country, and chief executive officers from large companies. WTLC is the largest in-kind corporate sponsor for Indiana Black Expo, providing approximately $350,000 worth of airtime to promote the various events and activities surrounding the summer celebration each year (A. Brown, personal communication, August 27, 1993). In return, WTLC has exclusive (radio) broadcast rights from the exposition, airing approximately 30 hours live from the Convention Center at the Hoosier Dome for a four- to five-day period:

> We generate our dollars selling advertising in our live coverage of the event. And all of the proceeds go directly to Indiana Black Expo as an organization, which then allows them to do youth programs, allows them to do community education programs in education and social service, and a variety of others things in the community. (A. Brown, personal communication, August 27, 1993)

Unlike many other black business expositions, the Indiana Black Expo is a nonprofit organization with a volunteer board of directors. Up until about eight years ago, the entire organization was all volunteer. Now they have a paid staff of about 20 to 30 people with a volunteer board.

After Indianapolis was established as the site for the Indiana Black Expo, different cities with sizable African American populations within the state organized subchapters (i.e., in East Chicago, Gary, Evansville, and 12 other locations). At first, these subchapters served to encourage people from all over the state to attend the Indianapolis exposition each year. Now, however, several of those cities hold their own mini-black expos, and the dollars generated go back into the local chapters. A. Brown (1993, personal communication) explained that the Indiana Black

Expo helped alleviate the "severe inferiority complex" of the African American community:

> In other words, Indianapolis had no image . . . nobody really knew that there was a sizeable black population in this city. What expo did was give this black community something to say: "This is ours, we created it, we built it without anybody else's help, it is ours." The people feel a proprietary sense of ownership in the event. And people literally wait all year for it. And if they can attend any of the events connected to it, even if it is a concert event, they'll say I went to Black Expo.

IBE Summer Celebration 1993, which was held June 28 to July 4 at the Indiana Convention Center & Hoosier Dome, proclaimed a family theme—National African-American Family Summit—with many exhibits and events structured around the theme. IBE is organized very much like Unity Day in Philadelphia, yet with a stronger business component. For over 23 years, according to a 1993 program guide, Indiana Black Expo has provided

> the best in cultural entertainment, youth education and scholarship programs, economic trade shows, religious celebrations, and networking opportunities. . . . IBE, Inc. is a non-profit, nonpolitical organization devoted to improving the quality of life in Indiana and emphasizing programs which uplift the tradition and condition of African-American citizens. Through its programs, IBE supports a variety of initiatives to achieve broad cultural and socio-economic goals. (Indiana Black Expo, 1993b, pp. 32, 89)

Brown noted that both promotions were citywide unifying events. Unity Day was created by a radio station, and IBE "started from the community and the radio station chimed in. And both work hand-in-hand." The city of Indianapolis purchased approximately 20 booths for the 1993 Summer Celebration. Brown elaborated:

> So the city is spending several thousands of dollars in direct contributions to the organization. The city also provides some other services, and some other assistance to the expo. The city recognizes that this is an important part of what goes on in this city. It brings dollars into the coffers of the city. Your hotel rooms fill up.

Events included health fairs, children's programs and youth summits, sporting events, music heritage festivals, worship services, and

Operation Breadbasket. There were also many African American family workshops with topics such as elementary and secondary education, higher education, economic and community development, health care, civil and criminal justice, youth development, values, ethics and spiritual development, women's issues, African American male issues, governmental affairs and political structure, and African American history and genealogy (including a tour of the Turner Fair III Historical Institute). In addition, IBE featured "the first annual Indiana Black Expo Business Networking Forum" (*Hotter,* 1993).

Reverend Charles Williams, president of the Indiana Black Expo, said he, along with an executive volunteer board, decided to

> explore substantive issues which impact the everyday living of African-Americans including health, wellness, economics, spiritual awareness, education, and politics. In this decade, we have witnessed the deterioration of the family as well as an increase in violence in society, especially affecting the African-American male. (Indiana Black Expo, 1993b, p. 37)

Both Unity Weekend and the IBE Summer Celebration involve year-round planning, beginning in the fall of each year: "What's the theme, how can we help, why don't you look at this, this is what worked, what didn't work, what can we do, how can we [show] support?" (A. Brown, personal communication, August 27, 1993).

One of the things that has worked well for WTLC is a broadcast booth that looks more like a living room. Brown said the exposition's format changed around the time Bryant Gumbel started on the *Today Show*:

> We then did a booth in the round with chairs and a couch, kind of a living room setup. And that's how we started having our announcers learn to interview. So we went from a music dominated remote to a talk dominated remote. So I would say of that 29 to 30 hours, 70 percent of what we do is talk over those 4 to 5 days. And that is the antithesis. So it really isn't a remote.

WTLC announcers play the role of program hosts, similar to the hosts of *Good Morning America* and *The Today Show*. With wireless microphones, the announcers "literally roam in the exhibit hall . . . and talk to people so that [they]'re not just confined to a broadcast booth."

Brown continued, "When we started 23 years ago, it was a typical remote. I mean, we literally took two turntables and the cartridges, and we played records from the event." Then one year, the program director decided to uplift the image of black radio announcers "as more than just jocks who spin records."

Each year, the expo draws approximately 500,000 people from all over the nation (Indiana Black Expo, 1993b). As Reverend Williams (personal communication, August 20, 1993) pointed out, however, attendance is only one factor from which IBE has measured success:

> You measure success by how many jobs you are able to get for the unemployed through our job fair, by how many lives you've touched through our health fair (to help you provide some kind of medical services to those that don't have insurance). You measure success by the number of scholarships you give minority students going to college. You measure success by increase in attendance over the last five years, by how people feel when they leave the expo, the kind of positive spirit they walk away with, and the joy we bring to the African American community.

In August 1993, KMJM-FM, St. Louis, following the lead of WTLC, held its 2nd Annual Missouri Black Expo. JoAnne Destito, KMJM marketing/promotion director, explained:

> We're in infancy stages—in terms of expanding. We have a couple of on-air personalities who came from [WTLC] in Indianapolis. Because Indiana's expo is so big, recording artists just die to go there. . . . [WTLC] has a bigger role than we do at this point. (Destito, personal communication, August 27, 1993)

Missouri Black Expo workshops have included how to fund your child's education, how to get a job, and how to find child care as well as motivational speakers such as Les Brown (Vollard, 1993). In 1993, there were a total of 63 self-improvement seminars "mostly tied to the theme 'Children Are the Future' " (Vollard, 1993, p. E8). The 1992 Expo drew 35,000 attendees, and in 1993, over 80,000 people attended the three-day event "with more than 15,000 attendees arriving opening day" (p. E8).

Aside from KMJM's involvement in the Missouri Black Expo, the station "is very visible in the community," emceeing at banquets, fund-raising for children's homes and the United Negro College Fund, and participating (and involving others) in walk-a-thons:

A lot of things that we do are community oriented and because we're an urban station, it's a very very big deal to be out in the community. I think more so than a general market station because people are looking at you, and what are you doing for the black community. Yes, you're playing music but there has to be more than radio. (J. Destito, personal communication, August 27, 1993)

In fact, the audience is very responsive. In addition to the comments from listeners at the events, Destito explained, "We get a lot of letters about things that we do. I really liked this, or I didn't like that."

CONCLUSIONS AND IMPLICATIONS

WTLC's partnership with IBE and the city of Indianapolis is an example of black/urban radio's outreach in the African American community. Other partnerships between commercial radio stations, cities, and expositions, such as KMJM's involvement in the Missouri Black Expo and WDAS's Unity Weekend, are model cases of Newman's (1988, pp. 3-8) "pride of progress"—in other words, racial equality via black entrepreneurship.

Rick Caffey, vice president of WDIA/WHRK, said that successful radio is a combination of cultural awareness and practical business skills:

It's part of the heritage and legacy. People don't view [W]DIA as my station or the owner's station. They view WDIA as their radio station. And I tell you, business spends millions of dollars marketing their product to get their customers to claim their product as their own product, and [W]DIA has that type of relationship, rapport with its listeners. (Caffey, personal communication, February 11, 1991)

Caffey added that if the station is responsive to its community, then the rest will follow:

As far as our commitment to community, I don't look at it as something we consciously do to get ratings, we do it because it is the right thing to do. And as a result, we get ratings.

Events like Unity Day and Indiana Black Expo bring together the African American community and demonstrate the power of African

American entrepreneurship. These events also demonstrate the power of community service promotional radio and the potential of media-business partnerships. The incredible response from listeners also indicates that these expositions are tapping into many of their everyday concerns—how to get the most from their money, how to fund their children's education, and how to start their own business.

Unity Weekend is one example of community service promotional activity committed to social, economic, and spiritual empowerment. African American radio's promotional agenda has included many hours of working toward solutions for urban problems. Typical promotions have advocated attending church, keeping the family together, educating youth, getting parents involved in schools, stopping the violence on the streets and in the schools, combating the urban influence of drugs, and promoting citizenship through ongoing voter registration efforts and civic pride (e.g., Sheppard, 1983). These promotions have encouraged positive social and economic change in the African American community. Unity Day, like the Indiana Black Expo, is a symbol of black entrepreneurship.

Coretta Scott King has praised radio for its leadership role in the African American community. Now more than 25 years since the death of her husband Martin Luther King Jr., she has urged *Fortune* 500 companies to follow the lead of black/urban radio by establishing dialogue with communities across the country and providing more educational programs that address "social problems" (Love, 1992, p. 46). It would appear that business expositions and family unity days are the vehicle for economic and social change, and this message might be best communicated via black/urban radio.

NOTES

1. Using interviews and documentation, Newman (1988) compiled a "composite profile . . . of 34 black air personalities . . . representing 15 cities from Brooklyn to Seattle" (p. 139). He found that at least 21 of the 34 personalities had "some higher education" and over half had earned a college degree.

2. Wood is a former communications professor at Howard University and the first African American broadcaster to work for Mutual Broadcasting in 1950.

3. WDIA became the first black format radio station in the nation in 1949. See Cantor's (1990) *Wheelin' on Beale*.

REFERENCES

Anderson, T., & Harris, W. M. (1990). A socio-historical and contemporary study in African-Americans in U.S. corporations. *Western Journal of Black Studies, 14*(3), 174-181.

Black consumer: Myths shattered. (1991, June 21). *Radio & Records*, p. 20.

Black radio: On a high wire with no net. (1970, August 31). *Broadcasting*, p. 46.

The broadcasting yearbook. (1993). Washington, DC: Broadcasting Publications, Inc.

Brown, F., Jr. (1990). African-American broadcaster: The link to their communities. *Pulse of Radio, 5*(46), 22.

Cantor, L. (1992). *Wheelin' on Beale.* New York: Pharos.

Chapman, W. (1991, January). The Illinois experience: State grants to improve school's parent involvement. *Phi Delta Kappan*, pp. 355-357.

Chicago jazz festival proposal. (1992, July 29). WBEE-AM, Harvey, IL.

Cusic, D. (1990). *The sound of light.* Bowling Green, OH: Bowling Green State University Popular Press.

Day of music draws thousands to Cooper Creek. (1991). [Duplicate from promotional file of WOKS-AM/WFXE-FM]. Columbus, GA: *Columbus Ledger-Enquirer*.

George, N. (1988). *The death of rhythm & blues.* New York: Pantheon.

Ghee, K. L. (1990). Enhancing educational achievement through awareness in young black males. *Western Journal of Black Studies, 14*(2), 77-89.

Hale-Benson, J. E. (1986). *Black children: Their roots, culture, and learning styles.* Baltimore: John Hopkins University Press.

Hare, B. R. (1988-1989). African-American youth at risk. *Urban League Review, 12*(1-2), 25-38.

Hilliard, A. G., III. (1987-1988). Reintegration for education: Black community involvement with black students in schools. *Urban League Review, 11*(1-2), 200-208.

Hotter than the Fourth of July Celebration '93. (1993). [brochure]. Indianapolis: Indiana Black Expo, Inc.

Indiana Black Expo. (1993a). *Indiana Black Expo, Inc.* [Brochure]. Indianapolis, IN: Author.

Indiana Black Expo. (1993b). *Indiana Black Expo National African-American Family Summit Summer Celebration* [Program guide]. Indianapolis, IN: Author.

Jacob, J. E. (1987-1988). Taking the initiative in education: The National Urban League Agenda. *Urban League Review, 11*(1-2), 13-17.

Johnson, P. (1992). Black/urban is in touch with the inner city: What can educators learn from this popular medium? *Education and Urban Society, 24*(4), 508-518.

Johnson, P., & Birk, T. A. (1993). The role of African-American owned radio in health promotion: Community projects targeting young African-American males. *Urban League Review, 16*(2), 85-93.

Kozma, R. B., & Croninger, R. G. (1992). Technology and the fate of at-risk students. *Education and Urban Society, 24*(4), 440-453.

Lornell, K. (1988). *Happy in the service of the Lord: Afro-American gospel quartets in Memphis.* Urbana: University of Illinois Press.

Love, W. (1990a, October 5). Ganging up on gangs, radio fights crime. *Radio & Records*, p. 50.

Love, W. (1990b, September 14). 12-year tradition: WDAS celebrates unity. *Radio & Records*, p. 97.

Love, W. (1990c, November 9). WLOU turns 40 in classic style. *Radio & Records*, p. 48.

Love, W. (1991a, August 2). AM report card. *Radio & Records,* p. 46.

Love, W. (1991b, July 26). Celebrating tradition, WQUE, KJMS observe Juneteenth Day. *Radio & Records,* p. 42.

Love, W. (1991c, October 4). KCEP-FM: The Lone Ranger. *Radio & Records,* p. 53.

Love, W. (1991d, June 14). WXYV's winning ways. *Radio & Records,* p. 48.

Love, W. (1992, January 17). Keeping the dream alive. *Radio & Records,* p. 46.

MacManus, S. A. (1990). Minority business contracting with local government. *Urban Affairs Quarterly, 25*(3), 455-473.

Meyer, A. J. (1971). *Black voices and format regulations: A study in black-oriented radio.* Stanford, CA: Institute for Communication Research.

Moore, T. S., & Laramore, A. (1990). Industrial change and urban joblessness. *Urban Affairs Quarterly, 25*(4), 640-658.

Newman, M. (1988). *Entrepreneurs of profit and pride: From black-appeal to radio soul.* New York: Praeger.

Schuyler, J. (1990). Black-owned radio in the '90s. *Pulse of Radio, 5*(45), 15, 22.

Scott, J. W., & Black, A. (1989). Deep structures of African-American family life: Female and male kin networks. *Western Journal of Black Studies, 13*(1), 17-23.

Settel, I. (1967). *A pictorial history of radio.* New York: Grossett & Dunlap.

Sheppard, N., Jr. (1983, March 15). Black-oriented radio: A key in Chicago's election. *New York Times,* p. 24.

Slaughter, D. T., & Kuehne, V. S. (1987-1988). Improving black education: Perspectives on parent involvement. *Urban League Review, 11*(1-2), 59-74.

Smith, A. (1988-1989, Summer-Winter). Responsibility of the African-American church as a source of support for adolescent fathers. *Urban League Review,* pp. 83-90.

Spaulding, N. W. (1981). *History of black oriented radio in Chicago 1929-1963.* Unpublished doctoral dissertation, University of Illinois, Urbana-Champaign.

Thompson, T. L., & Cusella, L. P. (1974). Muddling through toward small wins: On the need for requisite variety. In L. Donohew, H. E. Sypher, & W. J. Bukoski (Eds.), *Persuasive communication and drug abuse prevention* (pp. 317-333). Hillsdale, NJ: Lawrence Erlbaum.

Unity promotional video. (1991). Philadelphia: WDAS-AM/FM.

Unity weekend overview. (1992). [Press release]. Philadelphia: WDAS-AM/FM.

Vendor list Unity '92. (1992). Philadelphia: WDAS-AM/FM.

Vollard, V. (1993, August 22). Black Expo here has doubled size since last year. *St. Louis Post-Dispatch,* p. E8.

WTLC and the Indiana Black Expo '90. (1990, August 24). *Radio & Records,* pp. 50-51.

15

Music in African American Culture

PORTIA K. MAULTSBY

Since the nineteenth century, African American music has been the subject of scholarly inquiry. Approaches to most of these studies employ traditional Western models, which emphasize the study of music as sound. This approach relies on the written score for interpretation, implying that music is a universal language and that culture is insignificant in determining meaning. An alternative and more comprehensive approach "treats music as a functioning part of human culture and as an integral part of the wider whole" (Merriam, 1964, p. 3). Pioneered by anthropologists and ethnomusicologists, this approach enables researchers to examine various social and cultural issues related to music-making: the role of music in culture; its functions and meanings in the organization of culture groups; musical origins; and music sound as a manifestation of cultural values, beliefs, worldviews, and behavior.

In African American culture, music is an integral part of daily life. As such, it reflects the social and cultural organization of African Americans, translating life into living sound and recording the experiences of African Americans as a marginalized group in society. Therefore, the use of research methodologies and analytical frameworks that consider social and cultural issues is crucial to investigations of African American music. Studies that disregard these issues result in inaccurate historical and analytical interpretations. This chapter will examine various approaches of scholars to the study of African American music and the use of music as a resource to examine African American culture with special attention given to post-World War II popular culture.

STUDIES IN AFRICAN AMERICAN MUSIC: EARLY APPROACHES AND PERSPECTIVES

Literature on African American history and culture abound with firsthand accounts of black musical performances, which provide detailed information about aesthetic issues, performance contexts, and the music-making process. Researchers such as Bruce Jackson (1967), Dena Epstein (1977), Eileen Southern (1983b), and Southern and Josephine Wright (1990) annotate a wealth of primary source materials—diaries, memoirs, journals, letters, novels, travel accounts, missionary reports, slave narratives, and so on—that describe performances of African and African American music in the Americas during the seventeenth, eighteenth, and nineteenth centuries. Many of these accounts, however, expose cultural bias and Eurocentric perspectives of observers who lacked previous exposure to and an understanding of African and African American cultures.

Accounts of black religious services, for example, describe the singing as "boisterous," "noise," "uncouth," and "barbaric" (Epstein 1977, pp. 201, 220, 228, 292; Jones, 1842/1969, p. 266; Southern, 1983b, p. 84). The use of these and other value-laden terms exposes the inability of observers to interpret music sound within the appropriate cultural framework—one that considers African-derived rather than European aesthetic principles.

The response of white observers to the slaves' reinterpretation of European songs further illustrates the cultural bias. When missionaries introduced the Protestant musical repertoire to slaves, the latter brought relevance to this tradition by reinterpreting European aesthetic ideals through an African prism. In the process, the song as originally conceived ceased to exist as slaves altered the structure, melody, rhythm, and tempo, and added hand clapping, foot stomping, and dance in accordance with African aesthetic principles (Epstein, 1977, pp. 217-358; Kilham, 1870, p. 306; Russell, 1895, pp. 84-85). Missionaries and other whites criticized this practice because the slaves' musical renditions did not conform to the European concept of reverence and refinement (Epstein, 1977, p. 201; Myers, 1972, pp. 482-483; Watson, 1819, pp. 62-63).

Whites also objected to the reinterpretation and creation of song texts, which they assessed to be "nonsensical" "disjointed affirmations," "absurd," and "incomprehensible" (Epstein, 1977, p. 223; Jones, 1842/ 1969, p. 266; Watson, 1819, pp. 62-63). Such descriptions reveal that whites assigned meaning using a Western cultural model. They failed to recognize that the song texts conformed to African linguistic structures and used coded words to convey both sacred and secular meanings. The latter feature, often referred to as double entendre, symbolized a unique religious expression, a black cultural identity, and a black worldview (Asante, 1990, pp. 19-33; Fisher, 1990; Turner, 1949).

Coded texts, which prevail in the body of original slave songs known as Negro spirituals, were used to communicate plans for clandestine meetings and to provide instructions for slaves to escape from bondage, as illustrated in the songs "Steal Away," "Go in the Wilderness," "I Am Bound for the Promised Land," and "Deep River" (Fisher, 1990). Despite cultural bias, inaccurate interpretations, and other flaws evident in the early accounts of slave singing, they provide data for examining the ways in which African Americans survived an oppressive existence and preserved their cultural identity. Therefore, they are invaluable to studies of African American history and culture.

During the twentieth century, scholars and music critics began constructing, deconstructing, and reconstructing histories of African American music. Although most of these works are on specific genres and performers, a few (Floyd, 1995; Locke, 1936/1968; Roach, 1992; Southern, 1983a) survey the entire tradition. The first scholarly studies on African American music focused on Negro spirituals. The introduction to the first collection of Negro spirituals, *Slave Songs of the United States* (1867), edited by William Allen, Charles Ware, and Lucy Garrison, as well as the research of African American intellectuals (Dett, 1918, 1923; Du Bois, 1903/1953; Hurston, 1935/1976; James, 1950/ 1973; Jessye, 1927; Johnson & Johnson 1925-1926; Locke, 1925/ 1970, 1936/1968; Work, 1915, 1923) represent early attempts to provide a sociocultural context for understanding the complexities of this tradition. These researchers (many of whom were university-trained musicians) uniformly identify Africa as the cultural source for Negro spirituals. Their writings also explore a number of issues related to evolution, aesthetics, meaning, function, and the preservation of Negro spirituals as concert music.

The perspectives of African American scholars were largely overshadowed by those of white researchers who, in ignoring cultural and social issues related to music-making, questioned the originality and presumed African origin of Negro spirituals. Richard Wallaschek (1893, pp. 60-62), a Viennese philosopher, formulated the theory that Negro spirituals were mere imitations of European compositions. Wallaschek had never visited Africa or America nor had he ever heard actual performances of African and African American music. He based his theory on the skeletal transcriptions of African American music found in *Slave Songs of the United States*.

The editors of this collection acknowledged the limitations of both their musical training and the Western notational system to accurately represent nuances of the African American musical aesthetic. Noting the uniqueness and complexity of this aesthetic, they confessed that their transcriptions "will convey but a faint shadow of the original" song (Allen et al., 1867, pp. iv-vi). Wallaschek's theory about origins disregarded this and similar comments found in other nineteenth-century publications that reveal the importance of the performance aesthetic in assessing originality and artistic merit. His conclusions, therefore, illustrate how the omission of cultural data that contextualize musical performances results in inaccurate interpretations.

Newman White, professor of English (1928), George P. Jackson, professor of German (1933, 1943), and sociologist Guy B. Johnson (1930), from Duke University, Vanderbilt University, and University of North Carolina, respectively, were among the first scholars to conduct comparative studies on white folk hymns and Negro spirituals. Advancing Wallaschek's theory, they argued that Negro spirituals were mere inept imitations of Euro-American hymnody. Like Wallaschek, their findings were skewed by their inappropriate research methodology and theoretical framework. Using data gathered primarily from white hymnals, performances by white singers, and transcriptions by white collectors, none of which included the nuances of African American musical performances, White, Johnson, and Jackson drew conclusions about Negro spirituals. Despite this profoundly flawed analytical model, the theory of a white origin for the Negro spiritual and other black folk forms, nevertheless, became central to the scholarship on African American music for many decades. The field research of anthropologists and folklorists provided new data that challenged the validity of the white origins theory. As outlined below, these data document the African roots of African American music.

Music critic Henry Krehbiel (1914), anthropologists Richard Waterman (1943, 1952) and Melville Herskovits (1958), and folklorist Alan Lomax (1968) conducted the most comprehensive, seminal, comparative studies on African and African American music. Applying a quantitative approach, they documented specific musical elements common to both traditions. Krehbiel based his research on descriptions of African American performances (folk and arranged traditions) found in primary and secondary sources. He also analyzed 527 songs from published and individual collections. Unlike many scholars, Krehbiel recognized the limitations of Western notation systems in conveying the nuances of African and African American musical performance. His analysis, which considers discrepancies between printed versions and live performances, reveals that African and African American music share common elements, structural features, and aesthetic qualities—many of which are foreign to European musical traditions. Although valuable to studies in African American music, Krehbiel's quantitative approach does not consider the function and meaning of music in African American life or changes that occur in musical traditions.

Richard Waterman, Melville Herskovits, and Alan Lomax also used a quantitative analytical model to study the African origins of African American music. Employing a different research methodology, they conducted fieldwork in Africa, where they observed and recorded musical performances and interviewed musicians. Their analysis considers not only aesthetic issues but cultural traditions and the sociocultural context for music performance as well. Their approach and conclusions have provided the most lasting model for subsequent qualitative and interdisciplinary studies on African American music.

After the 1930s, the focus of research on African American music shifted from Negro spirituals to jazz and blues. Most of these studies are either descriptive or biographical, and rarely consider cultural traditions, performance contexts, and the perspectives of African Americans. Yet, performance contexts provide the basis for interpreting and understanding the creative process, musical aesthetics, and role of music in community life, among other issues. Crucial to historical and analytical studies on jazz and blues are the criteria used to identify innovative performers. The selection criteria frequently expose the aesthetic preferences, musical backgrounds, and cultural viewpoints of white critics rather than those of the African American community from which the music emerges (Charters & Kunstadt, 1962; Hammond, 1977; Jones, 1970; Kofsky, 1970; Leonard, 1962).

For example, the designation of Benny Goodman, rather than Fletcher Henderson (Goodman's African American arranger) and/or Count Basie (the African American jazz musician who introduced the swing style to Goodman), as the "King of Swing" illustrates the existence of cultural bias in constructing African American musical histories. Goodman was better known by white critics and the general public because he performed in venues and had access to various forms of media promotion denied to African American musicians. Fletcher Henderson and Count Basie established their careers performing in venues frequented by African Americans. Within this context, jazz and blues performances mirrored the social norms and cultural aesthetics of African Americans. These issues are crucial to interpreting the significance of these and other genres in African American life.

The few studies published prior to the 1970s that examine jazz and blues within a sociocultural context include the writings of Nat Hentoff and Albert J. McCarthy (1959), Paul Oliver (1960), Hentoff (1961), Leroi Jones (1963, 1970), Neil Leonard (1962), A. B. Spellman (1966), and Charles Keil (1966). These works provide insight into various cultural and social forces that influenced musical creativity and shaped the lives and worldviews of performers.

CONTEMPORARY VIEWS
OF AFRICAN AMERICAN MUSIC

The emergence of the Black Power movement in the late 1960s inspired the reexamination of African American history and culture within the context of an African heritage. Building on the work of earlier scholars, more recently historians (Blassingame, 1972; Genovese, 1974; Harding, 1981; Holloway, 1990; Levine, 1977; Raboteau,

1978; Stuckey, 1987), folklorists (Abrahams, 1970; Davis, 1985; Dundes, 1973; Roberts, 1989; Wiggins, 1987), music scholars and critics (Maultsby, 1990; Nketia, 1973, 1981; Oliver, 1970; Small, 1987; Wilson, 1974, 1981), and sociologist Paul Gilroy (1993a, 1993b) have employed interdisciplinary and qualitative models that led to the exploration of topics that previously had been excluded or partially investigated by earlier researchers. These topics include (a) the sociocultural context for musical evolution and performance, (b) the embodiment of cultural values in the creative process, (c) continuity and change in music traditions, (d) the concept of a black music aesthetic, (e) the social role of performers, and (f) the meaning of music. Over the past three decades, scholars have made strides addressing these and other issues. Notable works on blues and jazz include those by researchers Tony Russell (1970), James Cone (1972), Albert Murray (1976), Michael Haralambos (1975), Mike Rowe (1975), Jeff Titon (1977), William Ferris (1978), Robert Palmer (1981), David Evans (1982), Daphne Harrison (1988), William Barlow (1989), Alan Lomax (1993), Frank Kofsky (1970), Valerie Wilmer (1970), Nathan Pearson (1987), David Baker (1990), Burton Peretti (1992), and William Kenny (1993).

Despite the efforts of scholars to provide broader perspectives on African American music, they barely have scratched the surface. Research interests have been narrowly focused, and post-World War II urban and contemporary musical expressions have been neglected. This omission, in part, results from priorities scholars have established and attitudes they have developed about contemporary traditions. Since the 1970s, many scholars of African American culture, and particularly African Americans, have deemed it urgent to rewrite past histories or to "set the record straight"—"a record," according to folklorist Adrienne Seward (1983), "that historically has not profited from a Black perspective" (p. 52).

The neglect of research topics in African American music also results from the attitude held by many scholars about the value of traditions that are less than 50 years old. An inability to look beyond finite historical periods in the examination of African American culture severely limits the development of a fuller and more holistic treatment of this culture. Resistance to cultural change interferes with the acceptance of new music and other cultural forms that, on the surface, appear to be radical departures from valued, well-established traditions. Musical traditions that scholars now routinely study (e.g., urban black popular music) were ignored by many in past decades who were unwilling to acknowledge the validity of cultural expressions produced within disadvantaged social environments.

Thirty to fifty years from now, current music traditions will become a part of the African American musical legacy. If researchers do not document contemporary traditions, future researchers will be confronted with the problems that so severely plague the study of African American music today. It is imperative that scholars develop different attitudes about the importance of contemporary music and other genres in formulating a holistic understanding of contemporary African American culture.

Biased perceptions of scholars about contemporary culture have limited current scholarly interpretation of post-World War II musical expressions. Over the last three decades, book-length studies on blues and jazz traditions have focused primarily on rural blues, big bands, and New Orleans and avant-garde jazz, thus omitting contemporary styles. Gospel and popular music are other genres that have been neglected by scholars. The pioneering research of gospel music scholars Pearl Williams-Jones (1970, 1975, 1977), Horace Boyer (1973a, 1973b, 1974, 1979), Mellonee Burnim (1980, 1983, 1988), Kip Lornell (1988), Ray Allen (1991), Bernice Johnson Reagon (1992), and Michael Harris (1992), however, exposes the cultural significance of this tradition and provides theoretical models for analysis.

Music critics Phil Garland (1969), Rochelle Larkin (1970), Arnold Shaw (1970, 1974, 1978), and sociologist Charlie Gillett (1970) were among the first to conduct research on African American popular traditions. A decade later, researchers including music critics Joe Radcliffe (1980), Gerri Hirshey (1984), Peter Guralnick (1986), Nelson George (1988, 1992), David Toop (1991), Robert Pruter (1991), Joseph Eure and James Spady (1991), S. H. Fernando (1994), Adam Sexton (1995), and musician Johnny Otis (1993) contributed to this effort.

As a music produced and marketed as a commodity for profit, scholars have historically questioned the artistic merit and significance of popular music in African American community life. My own research (Maultsby, 1979, 1983, 1986) reveals that this genre is invaluable to comprehensive studies on African American and American popular culture. Collectively, the various popular music styles chronicle post-

World War II African American history and document changes that have taken place in the culture at large. In essence, the music provides a window through which intellectuals can examine the attitudes, values, lifestyles, and worldviews held by African Americans during each decade following World War II.

The first postwar popular styles are known as *rhythm and blues*, a term used broadly by the music industry from 1949 to 1968 to identify music performed by black artists in an identifiably black style. Rhythm and blues records the experiences and survival strategies of blacks whose position in society was defined by either segregation in the South (Jim Crow laws) or discriminatory practices of northern cities. Songs such as "Drinkin' Wine Spo-Dee-O-Dee" (1949) by Stick McGhee and His Buddies, "Don't You Know I Love You?" (1951) by the Clovers, "Shouldn't I Know?" (1951) by the Cardinals, "Mamma, He Treats Your Daughter Mean" (1953) by Ruth Brown, "Shake, Rattle and Roll" (1954) by Joe Turner, "Annie Had a Baby" (1954) by the Midnighters, "Greenbacks" (1955) by Ray Charles, "Finger Poppin' Time" (1960) by Hank Ballard and the Midnighters, "I (Who Have Nothing)" (1963) by Ben E. King, "Walking the Dog" (1963) by Rufus Thomas, and "A Change Is Gonna Come" (1965) by Sam Cooke present a black perspective on life during the two decades immediately following the war.

Theory rather than practice has traditionally separated the sacred and secular worlds of black America. The boundary that separated these worlds during the twentieth century became illusive when the two merged in new and different ways during the civil rights and Black Power movements. These movements, which used music to communicate messages of equal rights, black unity, black pride, self-help, and an identification with African cultures, juxtaposed and fused spirituals, hymns, and gospel with rhythm and blues as well as newly created protest songs. In the process, folk spirituals became gospel songs; both spirituals and gospel songs became protest songs; and protest songs became spirituals or gospel and soul music (Reagon, 1980, 1987). Similar to trends of the nineteenth century, African American sacred and secular music traditions folded into a single musical form and communicated a single message—racial unity, racial equality, black pride, and cultural autonomy.

While the music of the "movement culture" sold millions of recordings under the rubric of *soul music,* its political message spread throughout

African American communities, who listened and responded to the words of wisdom and solutions for change. Recordings such as "Say It Loud I'm Black and Proud" (1968) and "I Don't Want Nobody to Give Me Nothing" (1969) by James Brown and "We're a Winner" (1967) and "This Is My Country" (1968) by the Impressions are among many songs that document the philosophy and strategies adopted by African Americans during their struggle to overcome imposed racial, social, political, and economic injustices. The gospel-derived performance style and the message of determination that characterize these songs document the interrelatedness of African American sacred and secular traditions.

Throughout the 1970s, African Americans took advantage of new opportunities to improve their social and economic status and to increase their political power. For the first time since Reconstruction, African Americans believed they were well on their way to achieving first-class citizenship while maintaining their cultural identity. Resistance to affirmative action programs, school desegregation, busing, and other federal policies designed to integrate African Americans fully on equal terms into the mainstream, however, hindered their efforts (Campbell, 1971; Gill, 1980; Jones, 1977; Schuman & Hatchett, 1974; Triandis, 1976). Varying feelings about progress toward social change resounds in the music. "Inner City Blues" (1971) by Marvin Gaye, "Down and Out in New York City" (1973) and "Funky President" (1974) by James Brown, "Survival" (1975) and "Give the People What They Want" (1974) by the O'Jays, "(I'm Just Thinking About) Cooling Out" (1978) by Jerry Butler, and "Ain't No Stopping Us Now" (1979) by McFadden and Whitehead illustrate the range of responses to progress toward social equality during the 1970s.

American culture experienced many changes following World War II; perhaps the most noticeable of these was the emergence of youth culture. In the 1950s and 1960s, many white youth rejected the values, standards, and lifestyles of mainstream America and turned to African American and other minority cultures as models. They especially were attracted to the urban culture that evolved when southern rural blacks migrated to urban centers during the World War II era. From this culture, white youth adopted their fashions, language, dances, and music, which added a new kind of excitement, flair, and color to postwar American culture. African American music became popular among this group.

In the 1950s, while broadcasting rhythm and blues to African American communities over 50,000-watt stations, white deejays John Richbourg (known as John R.) of Nashville and Alan Freed of Cleveland, and later New York, catapulted rhythm and blues into the white community. The overwhelming acceptance of black popular music by white teenagers generated negative responses from the white middle class (Jackson, 1991; Moffitt, 1985). Music critics and southerners, in particular, resented the youth's positive response to rhythm and blues music. They attributed the values, unruly behavior, and rebellious spirit of white youth to the influences of this form of black musical expression. Consequently, the Citizen's Council of Greater New Orleans, Inc., and other southern states organized coalitions and campaigned to rid public venues and the airwaves of rhythm and blues music. As part of this campaign, which included press conferences and public meetings, they distributed the following flyer:

STOP

Help Save the Youth of America

DON'T BUY NEGRO RECORDS

(If you don't want to serve negroes in *your* place of business, then do not have negro records on your juke box or listen to negro records on the radio.)

The screaming idiotic words, and savage music of these records are undermining the morals of our white youth *in America.*

Call the advertisers of the radio stations that play this type of music and complain to them!

Don't Let Your Children Buy, or Listen To These Negro Records

For additional copies of this circular, write

CITIZEN'S COUNCIL OF GREATER NEW ORLEANS, INC.
509 Delta Building,
New Orleans, Louisiana 70112

These and other forms of protest proved to be ineffective. White youth continued to listen to and buy African American music. By the mid-1970s and resulting from the mass dissemination of African American music, other cultural components had permeated every artery in mainstream culture. Black slang such as *jive turkey, hip, dude, bad* (for good), *what's happenin', give me five, cool,* and *sock it to me* gained widespread usage among white Americans as did various cultural customs including the soul handshake and the slapping of hands to greet one another. African-derived hairstyles (Afro, cornrow, and braids) also became popular among a sizable segment of white America (Robinson, 1980).

From the 1940s until the mid-1980s, most record companies produced music performed by African Americans primarily for consumption by black people. Within this context, musicians created out of their experiences as black people, drawing inspiration from everyday life. Their music captures the ethos, collective sensibilities, and cultural aesthetics of African Americans while the song lyrics tell the story of black life in America from a black worldview. The various lyric themes and musical styles that constitute the black popular tradition reveal the diverse and dynamic nature of African American culture. Song titles such as "Let's Party and Get Down," "Survival," "Bad Luck," "Black Pride," "Hard Times," "Coolin' Out," "Don't Let Go of Your Dreams," "Ghetto Life," "Respect," "Inner City Blues," "Cheatin' in the Next Room," "Down and Out in New York City," "Bustin' Loose," "Parents Just Don't Understand," and "Ain't No Stopping Us Now" represent the broad range of responses to social, political, and economic realities.

Since the mid-1980s, hip-hop culture and black musicians, in particular Michael Jackson and rap artists, have provided white America with new concepts regarding music, dance, language, and fashion. In the 1980s, white youth blasted rap music on portable radio-cassette players (known as "ghetto boxes" in black communities) as soundtracks for street corner break dance competitions (a style of dance that combines acrobatics and pantomime with fast, flashy footwork). They also adopted hip-hop jargon and wore hip-hop fashions including baggy pants, silklike shirts, T-shirts, tennis shoes, jogging outfits, and Michael Jackson's white-sequined glove worn on one hand ("An Old Look," 1989; "Where Black Is Gold," 1991; "Where the Homegirls Are," 1991).

The popularity of African American music outside the black community has resulted in its commercial exploitation and that of other cultural products as well. Adhering to society's discriminatory social policies while responding to the demand for black music by white youth in the 1950s, record companies produced adulterated versions of this music (known as cover records) using white artists. These performers, whose interpretations were influenced by Western musical conventions, diluted the vocal stylings and instrumental arrangements of recordings made by black artists.

Pat Boone, the McGuire Sisters, the Crew Cuts, and Georgia Gibbs are among the many artists who recorded cover versions that record companies marketed to mainstream society under the pop label. When white youth discovered the original black artists via radio, cover versions became less appealing. Their preference for authentic black music beginning in the mid- to late 1950s led to imitations of this sound by white artists including Elvis Presley, Jerry Lee Lewis, Joe Cocker, the Righteous Brothers, Boz Scaggs, the Rascals, Janis Joplin, the Bee Gees, and Linda Ronstadt (Garofalo, 1990, pp. 57-90).

The mass dissemination of adulterated and imitative black popular styles created new markets for consumption and new contexts for performance. This commodification altered the music's aesthetic, meaning, and function. Additionally, the music industry's discriminatory practices kept most African American performers out of mainstream markets. Both record companies and the mass media resisted promoting black artists in white markets until economically forced to do so (Connelly, 1982a, 1982b). Music Television Video's (MTV) inclusion of African American top-selling artists (other than those whose music could be classified as rock 'n' roll) did not begin until 1983 in response to the mounting protest from black artists, record companies, music critics, and various local communities. By the late 1980s, black music, especially rap music, had become integral to MTV's programming (Garofalo, 1990, pp. 106-110).

Popular music styles are in constant evolution. Frequent stylistic changes in this tradition have been interpreted as "faddish." This view, which results from the short life span of hit records, does not consider the social and cultural functions of music in African American communities. New popular music styles are created during each decade when established performers alter their style to reflect shifts in values, attitudes, and behavior, and when new performers of a different generation create their own song style. During the 1970s, for example, six different styles of popular music coexisted. Three of them—soul, ballads, and jazz fusion—evolved in the 1960s and remained popular in the 1970s. The 1970s generation of performers created three new styles—funk, disco, and rap. The coexistence of music styles from two eras in the 1970s reflects the diversity of social environments, value systems, attitudes, and worldviews prevalent during the decade of "equal opportunity."

Throughout the 1980s, musical expressions from the 1970s remained popular (the exception being disco) along with a new funk style labeled techno-funk—the creation of the 1980s computer-space-age generation of African American performers. Among the first songs recorded in this style were "Planet Rock" (1982) and "Looking for the Perfect Beat" (1983) by Afrika Bambaata & Soulsonic Force and "Space Is the Place" (1982) and "Pack Jam" (1983) by the Jonzun Crew. Techno-funk is distinguished from the traditional, or 1970s, funk style by the use of synthesizers, computers, and other technology. Both funk styles are characterized by lyric themes of "party," "have a good time," and "dance, dance, dance." Vocal arrangements favor group chanting over solo voices, and rhythm overshadows the melody in musical arrangements. A repetitive bass pattern provides the foundation for polyrhythmic structures resulting from repetitive, stratified melodic lines. In lieu of promoting social awareness or an intellectual agenda, funk music is dance music or "happy music" designed to provide relief from stressful situations and daily routines. Therefore, funk musicians encourage people to have fun and be happy by freely expressing themselves in any manner (Clinton, 1977; Maultsby, 1979; personal interviews with Frank Alstin, songwriter-bass guitarist, Philadelphia, 1982, and James Alexander, songwriter-bass guitarist and leader of the funk group the BarKays, Los Angeles, 1983).

The evolution of techno-funk and its use in the rap tradition (beginning with "The Message" in 1982 by Grandmaster Flash and the Furious Five) illustrate continuity and change in African American culture. While maintaining the essence of the original funk style, the 1980s and 1990s generation of musicians used different resources to express contemporary ideas. Computers, space movie soundtracks, and video games provided new sound resources for African American musicians, which they employed in ways that continued to reflect black musical and aesthetic norms. These musicians also incorporated the vocabulary from contemporary language styles in their lyrics.

CONTEMPORARY AFRICAN AMERICAN POPULAR MUSIC AND THE ACADEMY

Popular music provides an invaluable resource for documenting the complex and diverse nature of contemporary African American culture.

As a teaching and research tool, it can be used to enhance the learning environment and to provide the perspective of African Americans on contemporary issues. Prior to the 1990s, only a few universities offered courses specifically on African American popular music. Subsequently, and largely due to the efforts of ethnomusicologists, sociologists, and mass media and cultural studies scholars (Baker, 1993; Berry, 1993; Dyson, 1991, 1996; Gilroy, 1993a; hooks, 1990; Rose, 1994; Ross & Rose, 1994; Wallace, 1992; West, 1988), this music slowly is finding a place in the academic curriculum.

Among intellectuals, rap music has received the most attention. It has been the subject of conference papers, journal articles, and books and has become part of the academic curriculum in African American, American, and cultural studies, folklore, ethnomusicology, mass communication, sociology, and English. This attention given to rap music, in part, results from student interest, the controversy surrounding its lyrics, and the emergence of cultural studies as a viable field of study within and among disciplines.

The inclusion of courses devoted specifically to African American popular and other urban musics in the undergraduate and graduate curricula will contribute to broadly trained scholars in twentieth-century popular culture. Curricula at both levels should include both historical and performance courses. Within the context of the latter, students can gain a better understanding of issues related to cultural aesthetics while developing their creative talents and providing entertainment. Performing ensembles also serve to preserve a musical legacy, which in future decades will include current popular music styles. Educators must begin now to create an academic structure to preserve this legacy and to prepare future scholars for research, teaching, and curricula development in urban, ethnic, cultural, American, and African American studies.

Investigations of contemporary African American culture should emphasize interdisciplinary and intragenre studies. The former approach will enable scholars to better understand the complexities of environmental forces that influence both continuity and change within culture and the ways in which cultures adapt to change. For example, the shift from a blues-derived rhythm and blues music to a gospel-based sound (known as soul music) in the 1960s coincides with the emergence of the civil rights and Black Power movements. The cultural,

social, and political significance of soul music, therefore, can be understood only if examined within this context.

Intragenre studies will allow for a more comprehensive examination of
interactions that take place among cultural genres and the features that
unify them as a conceptual whole. Contemporary game songs, for example, combine popular music forms with contemporary dance styles and
street talk. Rap music derives its structure, content, language, and performance from a folk-based communication style that employs rhythm
and rhyme. The concept of rappin' as a black style of communication
prevails in black preachers' sermons, politicians' speeches, children's
games, and "the dozens" (a form of verbal competition that involves the
exchange of insults). Rap music, which embodies these and other black
traditions, can be used to illustrate the cross-fertilization of genres as well
as cultural traditions that undergird African American creativity.

Rap music also provides a source for examining the multidimen-
sional use of music in African American communities. Similar to other
African American musical forms, rap serves historical-political, cultural, and social functions. It records the responses of inner-city residents to their environment, their perspectives on social ills that ad-
versely affect their lives, and the forces that determine their position in
society. Serving cultural and social purposes, rap music provides a
vehicle for group interaction, an outlet for creative expression, and a
forum for competitive play (personal interview with Grandmaster
Flash, leader and DJ for the rap group Grandmaster Flash and the
Furious Five, Los Angeles, 1983).

Establishing new courses in nontraditional areas requires scholarly
resources and funding. Unlike established fields of study, primary
documents on African American popular music are virtually nonexistent. This situation, coupled with the scarcity of substantive secondary
sources, often prevents course development. Scholars whose research
agenda includes popular music must take the lead in establishing
academic validity by providing the necessary research and teaching
resources. Collecting these data requires us to humble ourselves to the
knowledge of those who may or may not possess earned academic
degrees but possess a wealth of knowledge that they are willing to share.
Our knowledge of contemporary culture can be greatly enhanced by
the experiences of those who create, perform, market, and sell African
American popular music and culture.

While on leave from Indiana University to conduct research on black popular music from 1982 to 1983, 1984 to 1985, and 1991 to 1992, I interviewed performers, songwriters, producers, and music industry personnel who provided me with a wealth of primary data. Despite several hundred hours of taped interviews, additional research is needed to fill in missing data.

Conducting research on contemporary African American culture requires a substantial amount of funding. Herein lies the problem: Who will provide long-term funding for this type of research? The current political climate, mainstream attacks on popular culture, and the threat from the current Republican Congress to eliminate funding for the arts and humanities pose a dilemma for possible funding agencies. Proposal reviewers may view popular music as less than meritorious because it does not represent a traditional area of study and because of limited funding resources. Funding agencies currently have no designated category for popular music studies, as exist for folk and classical music. Our nation could be well served by agencies and foundations reviewing this omission.

Popular and other forms of music are invaluable resources for examining African American history and culture. They provide a window through which scholars can examine African American perspectives on their cultural and social life, including ritualized celebrations and other cultural traditions; worldviews, beliefs, and attitudes; strategies to overcome racial injustices; and experiences as a marginalized group in society. African American music also can be used to document the widespread influence of African American culture on mainstream society and world cultures. Even though some investigations of this music reflect cultural bias and inaccurate interpretations, recordings, live performances, descriptions of performances, and interviews with performers, among other data, provide additional sources for analysis. When examined within the appropriate cultural and social framework, these sources can aid in objectively assessing the artistic merit of African American music and its significance in black community life.

REFERENCES

Abrahams, R. D. (1970). *Positively black*. Englewood Cliffs, NJ: Prentice Hall.

Allen, R. (1991). *Singing in the spirit: African-American sacred quartets in New York City.* Philadelphia: University of Pennsylvania Press.

Allen, W. F., Ware, C., & Garrison, L. (Eds.). (1867). *Slave songs of the United States.* New York: A. Simpson.

Asante, M. K. (1990). African elements in African-American English. In J. Holloway (Ed.), *Africanisms in American culture* (pp. 19-33). Bloomington: Indiana University Press.

Baker, D. N. (Ed.). (1990). *New perspectives on jazz.* Washington, DC: Smithsonian Institution Press.

Baker, H. (1993). *Black studies, rap, and the academy.* Chicago: University of Chicago Press.

Barlow, W. (1989). *Looking up at down: The emergence of blues culture.* Philadelphia: Temple University Press.

Berry, V. (1993). Crossing over: Musical perceptions of black adolescent culture. *Journal of Popular Music Studies, 5,* 26-39.

Blassingame, J. W. (1972). *The slave community.* New York: Oxford University Press.

Boyer, H. (1973a). *An analysis of black church music with examples drawn from services in Rochester, New York.* Unpublished doctoral dissertation, University of Rochester.

Boyer, H. (1973b). Gospel music comes of age. *Black World, 33,* 42-48, 79-86.

Boyer, H. (1974). An analysis of his contributions: Thomas A. Dorsey, father of gospel music. *Black World, 23,* 20-28.

Boyer, H. (1979). Contemporary gospel. *Black Perspective in Music, 7,* 5-8.

Burnim, M. (1980). *The black gospel music tradition: Symbol of ethnicity.* Unpublished doctoral dissertation, Indiana University.

Burnim, M. (1983). Gospel music: Review of the literature. *Music Educators Journal, 69,* 58-61.

Burnim, M. (1988). Functional dimensions of gospel music performance. *Western Journal of Black Studies, 12*(2), 52-61.

Campbell, A. (1971). *White attitudes toward black people.* Ann Arbor: University of Michigan, Institute for Social Research.

Charters, S. B., & Kunstadt, L. (1962). *Jazz: A history of the New York scene.* Garden City, NY: Doubleday.

Clinton, G. (1977). In living funk. *Soul, 11,* 16.

Cone, J. (1972). *The spirituals and the blues: An interpretation.* New York: Seabury.

Connelly, C. (1982a). Rock radio: A case of racism? *Rolling Stone, 384,* 53-55.

Connelly, C. (1982b). Rock radio puts out a "whites only" sign. *Miami News,* p. 3C.

Davis, G. L. (1985). *I got the word in me and I can sing it, you know: A study of the performed African-American sermon.* Philadelphia: University of Pennsylvania Press.

Dett, N. R. (1918). The emancipation of Negro music. *Southern Workman, 47,* 172-176.

Dett, N. R. (1923). A flashlight on music students. *Southern Workman, 52,* 336.

Du Bois, W. E. B. (1953). *The souls of black folk.* Greenwich, CT: Fawcett. (Original work published 1903)

Dundes, A. (Ed.). (1973). *Mother wit from the laughing barrel.* Englewood Cliffs, NJ: Prentice Hall.

Dyson, M. E. (1991). Performance, protest, and prophecy in the culture of hip-hop. *Black Sacred Music, 1,* 13-23.

Dyson, M. E. (1996). *Between god and gangsta rap.* New York: Oxford University Press.

Epstein, D. J. (1977). *Sinful tunes and spirituals: Black folk music to the civil war.* Chicago: University of Illinois Press.

Eure, J. D., & Spady, J. G. (1991). *Nation conscious rap.* Los Angeles: PC International Press.

Evans, D. (1982). *Big road blues: Tradition and creativity in the folk blues*. Berkeley: University of California Press.

Fernando, S. H., Jr. (1994). *The new beats: Exploring the music, culture and attitudes of hip-hop*. New York: Anchor/Doubleday.

Ferris, W. (1978). *Blues from the delta*. New York: Anchor.

Fisher, M. M. (1990). *Negro slave songs in the United States*. New York: Carol. (Original work published 1953)

Floyd, S. A. (1995). *The power of black music: Interpreting its history from Africa to the United States*. New York: Oxford University Press.

Garland, P. (1969). *The sound of soul*. Chicago: Regnery.

Garofalo, R. (1990). Crossing over: 1939-1989. In J. L. Dates & W. Barlow (Eds.), *Split image: African Americans in the mass media* (pp. 57-121). Washington, DC: Howard University Press.

Genovese, E. D. (1974). *Roll Jordan roll: The world the slaves made*. New York: Pantheon.

George, N. (1988). *The death of rhythm & blues*. New York: Pantheon.

George, N. (1992). *Buppies, b-boys, baps and bohos: Notes on post-soul black culture*. New York: HarperCollins.

Gill, G. R. (1980). *Meanness mania: The changed mood*. Washington, DC: Howard University Press.

Gillett, C. (1970). *The sound of the city*. New York: Outerbridge & Dienstfrey.

Gilroy, P. (1993a). *Small acts*. New York: Serpent's Tail.

Gilroy, P. (1993b). *The black Atlantic: Modernity and double consciousness*. Cambridge, MA: Harvard University Press.

Guralnick, P. (1986). *Sweet soul music*. New York: Harper & Row.

Hammond, J. (1977). *An autobiography: John Hammond on record*. New York: Ridge.

Haralambos, M. (1975). *Right on from blues to soul in black America*. New York: Drake.

Harding, V. (1981). *There is a river: The black struggle for freedom in America*. New York: Vintage.

Harris, M. W. (1992). *The rise of gospel blues: The music of Thomas Andrew Dorsey*. New York: Oxford University Press.

Harrison, D. D. (1988). *Black pearls: Blues queens of the 1920s*. New Brunswick, NJ: Rutgers University Press.

Hentoff, N. (1961). *The jazz life*. New York: Dial.

Hentoff, N., & McCarthy, A. J. (Eds.). (1959). *Jazz*. New York: Holt, Rinehart & Winston.

Herskovits, M. J. (1958). *The myth of the Negro past*. Boston: Beacon.

Hirshey, G. (1984). *Nowhere to run: The story of soul music*. New York: Times Books.

Holloway, J. (Ed.). (1990). *Africanisms in American culture*. Bloomington: Indiana University Press.

hooks, b. (1990). *Yearning: Race, gender and cultural politics*. Boston: South End.

Hurston, Z. N. (1976). Spirituals and neo-spirituals. In N. Huggins (Ed.), *Voices from the Harlem Renaissance* (pp. 344-347). New York: Oxford University Press. (Original work published 1935).

Jackson, B. (Ed.). (1967). *The Negro and his folklore*. Austin: University of Texas Press.

Jackson, G. P. (1933). *White spirituals in the southern uplands*. Chapel Hill: University of North Carolina Press.

Jackson, G. P. (1943). *White and Negro spirituals*. New York: J. J. Augustin.

Jackson, J. A. (1991). *Big beat heat: Alan Freed and the early years of rock & roll*. New York: Schirmer.

James, W. L. (1973). The romance of the Negro cry in America. In A. Dundes (Ed.), *Mother wit from the laughing barrel* (pp. 430-444). Englewood Cliffs: NJ: Prentice Hall. (Original work published 1950)

Jessye, E. (1927). *My spirituals.* New York: Robbins Engel.

Johnson, G. B. (1930). *Folk culture on St. Helena Island.* Chapel Hill: University of North Carolina Press.

Johnson, J. W., & Johnson, J. R. (1925-1926). *American Negro spirituals* (Vols. 1, 2). New York: Viking.

Jones, C. C. (1969). *Religious instruction of the Negroes in the United States.* New York: Negro University Press. (Original work published 1842)

Jones, F. C. (1977). *The changing mood in America: Eroding commitment?* Washington, DC: Howard University Press.

Jones, L. (1963). *Blues people.* New York: William Morrow.

Jones, L. (1970). *Black music.* New York: William Morrow.

Keil, C. (1966). *Urban blues.* Chicago: University of Chicago Press.

Kenny, W. H. (1993). *Chicago jazz: A cultural history 1904-1930.* New York: Oxford University Press.

Kilham, E. (1870). Sketches in color. *Putnam's Monthly, 15,* 304-311.

Kofsky, F. (1970). *Black nationalism in music.* New York: Pathfinder.

Krehbiel, H. (1914). *Afro-American folk songs.* New York: Frederick Ungar.

Larkin, R. (1970). *Soul music!* New York: Lancer.

Leonard, N. (1962). *Jazz and the white Americans.* Chicago: University of Chicago Press.

Levine, L. W. (1977). *Black culture and black consciousness.* New York: Oxford University Press.

Locke, A. (1968). *The Negro and his music.* Port Washington, NY: Kennikat. (Original work published 1936)

Locke, A. (1970). The Negro spiritual. In A. Locke (Ed.), *The new Negro* (pp. 199-213). New York: Athaneum. (Original work published 1925)

Lomax, A. (1968). *Folk song style and culture.* New Brunswick, NJ: Transaction.

Lomax, A. (1993). *Land where the blues began.* New York: Pantheon.

Lornell, K. (1988). *Happy in the service of the Lord: Afro-American gospel quartets in Memphis.* Urbana: University of Illinois Press.

Maultsby, P. K. (1979, June 9). Contemporary pop: A healthy diversity evolves from creative freedom. *Billboard,* pp. BM-10, BM-22, BM-28.

Maultsby, P. K. (1983). Soul music: Its sociological and political significance in American popular culture. *Journal of Popular Culture, 17*(2), 51-59.

Maultsby, P. K. (1986). Rhythm & blues (1945-1955): A survey of styles (monograph). In N. Kilkenny & R. Selim (Eds.), *Black American popular music* (Program guide, pp. 6-19, 22-23). Washington, DC: Smithsonian Institution/Museum of American History, Program in Black American Culture.

Maultsby, P. K. (1990). Africanisms in African-American music. In J. Holloway (Ed.), *Africanisms in American culture* (pp. 185-210). Bloomington: Indiana University Press.

Merriam, A. P. (1964). *The anthropology of music.* Evanston, IL: Northwestern University Press.

Miller, J. (1862, August 9). Negro songs. *Dwights Journal of Music,* pp. 148-149.

Moffitt, P. (1985). The sound of soul. *Esquire, 103,* 21-22.

Murray, A. (1976). *Stomping the blues.* New York: McGraw-Hill.

Myers, R. M. (Ed.). (1972). *The children of pride; A true story of Georgia and the Civil War.* New Haven, CT: Yale University Press.

Nketia, J. H. K. (1973). The study of African and Afro-American music. *Black Perspective in Music, 1*, 7-15.

Nketia, J. H. K. (1981). African roots of music in the Americas: An African view. In *Report of the 12th Congress* (pp. 82-88). London: American Musicological Society.

An old look is new again. (1989, October 16). *Newsweek*, pp. 77-79.

Oliver, P. (1960). *The meaning of the blues.* New York: Collier.

Oliver, P. (1970). *Savannah syncopators: African retentions in the blues.* New York: Stein and Day.

Otis, J. (1993). *Upside your head! Rhythm and blues on Central Avenue.* Hanover, NH: University Press of New England.

Palmer, R. (1981). *Deep blues.* New York: Viking.

Pearson, N. W. (1987). *Goin' to Kansas City.* Urbana: University of Illinois Press.

Peretti, B. W. (1992). *The creation of jazz: Music, race and culture in urban America.* Urbana: University of Illinois Press.

Pruter, R. (1991). *Chicago soul.* Urbana: University of Illinois Press.

Raboteau, A. J. (1978). *Slave religion: The invisible institution in the antebellum South.* New York: Oxford University Press.

Radcliffe, J. A. (1980). *This business of disco.* New York: Billboard/Watson-Guptill.

Reagon, B. J. (1980). Descriptive notes. In *Voices of the civil rights movement: Black American freedom songs 1960-1966* (recording, RO23). Washington, DC: Smithsonian Institution, Program in Black American Culture.

Reagon, B. J. (1987). Let the church sing "freedom." *Black Music Research Journal, 7,* 105-118.

Reagon, B. J. (Ed.). (1992). *We'll understand it better by and by: African American pioneering gospel composers.* Washington, DC: Smithsonian Press.

Roach, H. (1992). *Black American music past and present* (2nd ed.). Melbourne, FL: Krieger.

Roberts, J. W. (1989). *From trickster to badman: The black folk hero in slavery and freedom.* Philadelphia: University of Pennsylvania Press.

Robinson, L. (1980). The blackening of white America. *Ebony, 35,* 158-162.

Rose, T. (1994). *Black noise: Rap music and black culture in contemporary America.* Hanover, NH: University Press of New England.

Ross, A., & Rose, T. (Eds.). (1994). *Microphone fiends: Youth music and youth culture.* New York: Routledge.

Rowe, M. (1975). *Chicago breakdown.* New York: Drake.

Russell, H. (1895). *Cheer! boys, cheer! Memories of men and music.* London: John Macqueen, Hastings House.

Russell, T. (1970). *Black, whites and blues.* New York: Pathfinder.

Schuman, H., & Hatchett, S. (1974). *Black racial attitudes: Trends and complexities.* Ann Arbor: University of Michigan, Institute for Social Research.

Seward, A. L. (1983). The legacy of early Afro-American folklore scholarship. In R. M. Dorson (Ed.), *Handbook of American folklore* (pp. 48-56). Bloomington: Indiana University Press.

Sexton, A. (Ed.). (1995). *Rap on rap: Straight-up talk on hip hop culture.* New York: Delta.

Shaw, A. (1970). *The world of soul.* New York: Cowles.

Shaw, A. (1974). *The rockin' '50's.* New York: Hawthorn.

Shaw, A. (1978). *Honkers and shouters.* New York: Collier.

Small, C. (1987). *Music of the common tongue.* New York: Riverrun.

Southern, E. (1983a). *The music of black Americans: A history.* New York: Norton.

Southern, E. (Ed.). (1983b). *Readings in the music of black Americans*. New York: Norton.

Southern, E., & Wright, J. (Compilers). (1990). *African-American traditions in song, sermon, tale, and dance, 1600s-1920: An annotated bibliography of literature*. New York: Greenwood.

Spellman, A. B. (1966). *Four lives in the bebop business*. New York: Pantheon.

Stuckey, S. (1987). *Slave culture: Nationalist theory and the foundations of black America*. New York: Oxford University Press.

Titon, J. (1977). *Early downhome blues: A musical and cultural analysis*. Urbana: University of Illinois Press.

Toop, D. (1991). *Rap attack 2: African rap to global hip hop* (rev. ed.). New York: Serpent's Tail.

Triandis, H. C. (Ed.). (1976). *Variations in black and white perceptions of the social environment*. Urbana: University of Illinois Press.

Turner, L. (1949). *Africanisms in the Gullah dialect*. Chicago: University of Chicago Press.

Wallace, M. (1992). *Black popular culture* (G. Dent, Ed.). Seattle, WA: Bay.

Wallaschek, R. (1893). *Primitive music: An inquiry into the origin and development of music, songs, instruments, dances and pantomimes of savage races*. London: Longmans, Green.

Waterman, R. (1943). *African patterns in Trinidad Negro music*. Unpublished doctoral dissertation, Northwestern University.

Waterman, R. (1952). African influence on the music of the Americas. Selected papers of the XXIX International Congress of Americanists, *Acculturation in the Americas* (pp. 207-218). (Sol Tax. Ed.). University of Chicago Press.

Watson, J. (1819). Methodist error in readings in black American music. In E. Southern (Ed.), *Readings in the music of black Americans* (pp. 60-64). New York: Norton.

West, C. (1988). *Prophetic fragments*. Trenton, NJ: Africa World Press.

Where black is gold: From music to magazines, media firms get hip to African-American culture. (1991, December 2). *Newsweek*, pp. 42-43.

Where the homegirls are: From Paris to New York, rap rises to the runways. (1991, June 17). *Newsweek*, p. 60.

White, N. (1928). *American Negro folk songs*. Cambridge, MA: Harvard University Press.

Wiggins, W. H. (1987). *O freedom! Afro-American emancipation celebrations*. Knoxville: University of Tennessee Press.

Williams-Jones, P. (1970). Afro-American gospel music. In V. Butcher (Ed.), *Development of materials for a one year course in African music for the general undergraduate student* (pp. 201-219). Washington, DC: U.S. Department of Health, Education and Welfare.

Williams-Jones, P. (1975). Afro-American gospel music: A crystallization of the black aesthetic. *Ethnomusicology, 19*, 373-385.

Williams-Jones, P. (1977). The musical quality of black religious folk ritual. *Spirit, 1*, 21-30.

Wilmer, V. (1970). *Jazz people*. New York: Bobbs-Merrill.

Wilson, O. (1974). The significance of the relationship between Afro-American music and West Africa. *Black Perspective in Music, 2*, 3-22.

Wilson, O. (1981). *The association of movement and music as a manifestation of a black conceptual approach to music*. London: American Musicological Society.

Work, J. W. (1915). *Folk song of the American Negro*. Nashville: Fiske University Press.

Work, J. W. (1923). Negro folk song. *Opportunity, 1*, 282-294.

16

Rap Music, Black Men, and the Police

VENISE T. BERRY
HAROLD LOONEY JR.

Cultural theory research as developed by scholars such as Raymond Williams, Stuart Hall, James Carey, John Fiske, and others has been crucial in the recognition of people as active participants in their own media experiences. Today, cultural theory is used to better understand all forms of media and cultural practice. According to Hanno Hardt (1992):

> The media constitute a major terrain for critical analysis and political or social action, since they dominate the cultural sphere of modern societies. They are important, because they help produce the understanding of a social totality by bringing together and, if necessary, reconciling conflicting and confusing fragments of reality. The study of media raises questions of power and ideology as necessary and significant issues of cultural practice. (p. 190)

In his work with cultural studies, Henry Giroux (1983, p. 37) has also identified questions of power and ideology in the media. He argues that there is a need to give the traditionally voiceless a voice, to allow them to affirm their own histories through the use of language, a set of social relations, and a body of knowledge that critically constructs and dignifies the cultural experiences that make up the tissue, texture, and history of their daily lives.

As these scholars suggest, cultural existence is a crucial component of the mediated experience. The emphasis on power and ideology is important, particularly where the construction of knowledge, meaning, and values is involved. This chapter seeks to document that construction through historical forces, media practices, and lived experience as it exists within the contemporary relationship between rap music, black men, and the police. More, this analysis is a culturalist's exploration that ultimately demonstrates how rap music encompasses the power and ideology of urban black male populations specifically in relation to their experiences with the police.

Within this struggle to locate power and ideology, rap music is a valuable genre. It provides a voice for the voiceless—young black men. It reflects and affirms an important lived experience in black culture— the urban experience. And it is an essential form of black cultural communication. Unlike many artists who simply sing songs that are written for them by others, rap artists write their own lyrics based on personal experience and cultural existence.

This analysis first builds the foundation with a contextual overview of black music's use as a prominent form of cultural communication. Next, it explores the cultural functional reality between black men and the police. Then, it examines cultural musical messages about the police found in selected songs. Finally, it discusses the importance of this cultural legacy for the African American community and contemporary society.

BLACK MUSIC AS COMMUNICATION

Music among African people has always served as an important form of communication. There was music for every custom, festival, ceremony, or dance. Southern (1971) writes: "Ceremonial music composed the largest part of the musical repertory of a village people. Music accompanied religious ceremonies and rites associated with birth, initiation, marriage, healing, war and death" (pp. 5-6).

In the United States during slavery, that communicative tradition continued as slave songs and spirituals took on meaning and depth that enabled cultural survival. Black musical style became interwoven with black consciousness. Cone (1972) explains: "It shapes and defines black being and creates cultural structures for black expression. Black music is unifying because it confronts the individual with the truth of black existence and affirms that black being is possible even in a commercial context" (p. 5).

Cone says one of the prime functions of African music is to recite the history of black people: "When Africans came to America that art of storytelling and reflection came too" (p. 15). Black music contains meaning on both emotional and literal levels. For example, the well-known song "Steal Away" carried a spiritual message that served as an emotional release as well as a metaphoric message about secret meetings that were held by slaves during the early nineteenth century (Cone, 1972, p. 16).

According to Keil (1970), black music continued to reflect messages about historical conditions and lived experience. In his work with blues music, Keil found that themes of manhood as well as related issues concerning sex, aggression, control, and identity were basic to any examination of the blues. As early as 1970, he called for a more detailed analysis of blues lyrics to "describe with greater insight the changes in male roles within the Negro community as defined by Negroes at various levels of socio-economic status and mobility within the lower class" (p. 74). Keil also believes that the lyrical content of city blues, urban blues, and soul blues presented examples of varying sorts of adjustments made to urban living conditions.

Soul music was a composite of several earlier black musical forms— blues, jazz, and spirituals—and it brought forth a more potent style of black cultural consciousness. As Maultsby (1983) explains:

> Performers of soul music, in communicating the philosophy of the Black Power Movement, promoted black pride and self-awareness. The African derived fashions and hair styles encouraged an identification with the mother country, while the song lyrics advocated national black unity. Through these texts, soul singers not only discussed the depressing social and economic conditions of black communities, but they also offered solutions for improvement and change. (p. 51)

Today, rap music continues this tradition of creating meaning and expression through black music and style. After a number of years of being lulled into complacency by popular music and disco, rap music has reintroduced black identity and consciousness. It has evoked an empowering voice for urban black communities. As Toop (1984) suggests, "Rap is a spoken newspaper, a fax from the wax; on the other side, rap fits into the storytelling tradition of oral history and symbolic teaching" (p. 188).

Knowledge is a key component of much of rap music, and many rap artists speak about their efforts to inform America. For example, rap artist KRS-One says he is a teacher—a street corner scholar who spent his days as a high school drop out reading in the New York public library (Light, 1991). As a strong advocate for self-education, his name, KRS-One, stands for "knowledge reigns supreme over nearly every-one." The Poor Righteous Teachers (PRT) define themselves as "Black men who gain knowledge of themselves and then take it as their duty or obligation to teach and resurrect the poor" (Poor Righteous Teach-ers, 1991, p. 60). One member of PRT, Wise Intelligent, explains, "I see rap as being a gardening tool due to the fact that we are planting seeds. We are trying to plant seeds in the minds of black youth. . . We're teaching black youth that their history goes beyond slavery" (Poor Righteous Teachers, 1991, p. 68).

Maultsby (1985) says such new styles do not evolve independently of existing traditions but evolve out of them. She explains:

> New forms of black musical expression are, in essence, new impulses drawn from the environment, blended with the old forms and given a new shape, a new style, and a new meaning. . . . Black music is a manifestation of black culture and it serves a communication function within the tradition. Because rap music exists as a functional entity within black America, the creation of this new style discloses shifts in values, attitudes and social needs. (p. 11)

BLACK MEN AND THE POLICE: THE REALITY

> Can we help you? They asked as I stepped to the cherry top
> What's going on I replied to the two cops
> Just get back in the car and sit down!
> back in the car and sit down!
> in the car and sit!
> sit!

The triple K rednecks broke illegally
treat a simple question like a major felony
Well, I'm not the one to fade on a punk rush
Front me hard, be prepared for my rough touch
Get back in the car and sit down! . . . F— You!
Sit—F— You!
Sit—F— You!

Bad boys, tables turned unaccustomed to my northern flavor
Never seen a brother demonstrate such proud behavior
Double take—must have thought a nigga would be faded
What did you say?
They asked, so I restated. F— You!
This time they heard the words clear with diction
So the gaffle was on and they rushed in with conviction. (Looney,
1993)

This is not the song of a popular "gansta rapper" but the true 1982 experience of a black male college graduate, Harold Looney. The cultural functional reality concerning black men and the police has always been one of distrust and disrespect. It is a situation that existed long before NWA's controversial 1988 rap song "F— tha Police" was released and triggered a warning letter from the FBI.

According to Looney, the event described in his rap introduction occurred in Pensacola, Florida. He was 21 years old and trying to define himself as a black man in a society that seemed resolved to keeping him in, what he called, "modern slavery": flipping burgers and mopping floors. Looney described the officer's forceful tone and general disrespect when he and his friend were stopped for no apparent reason (at least no reason that Looney was told). That disrespect created frustration and his pride kicked in:

I stood motionless as the officer repeated his demand, get back in the car and sit down. F— you was my automatic response. The police officers looked at each other then looked at me in disbelief and asked me to repeat what I said, so I did. The officers grabbed me. They tried to throw me to the ground. I did not fight back, but I stood straight and still. My body was so stiff that the officer had to wrap his leg around mine to sweep me to the ground. They cuffed my hands behind my back and stood me up against the police car. When one officer attempted to spread my legs apart he kicked my foot so hard my tennis shoe flew off. The other officer frisked me and pushed me into the back of the police car. When they saw my Illinois driver's license they told me in a cocky and insulting way that they were going to show me that I was not dealing with the Illinois police.

According to Looney, his friend was from Alabama, so he chose to play by the rules of southern police politics. He suppressed his voice and remained very submissive. Many black males recognize the situation and try to survive in this same way, even when falsely accused. Elijah Anderson (1990) says:

> In the elaborate script of the streets, the black male is an ambiguous figure who arouses the utmost caution and is generally considered dangerous until he proves he is not. Therefore, black men make a conscious effort to reassure the officers that they are not dangerous, fearing any action will provoke them. (pp. 193-194)

Looney's friend played the game correctly and he was released on bail the next day. Looney's verbal defiance earned him several charges: two counts of aggravated assault and battery on a police officer, resisting arrest with violence, and obstructing justice. Looney described his treatment inside the legal system as enlightening. He said he continued to be treated as if he were nonhuman:

> During the court preceding, the judge and the public defender made decisions that affected my life as if I were not even there. I could only respond to questions that were asked directly to me. And I was removed from the courtroom at one time for responding to a question from the judge with the word, "yeah." There was an obvious double standard. It was okay for the officers or judge to disrespect me and address me in any manner they chose, but I was to be submissive and respectful at all times.

Looney's bail was set at $250,000. Because he could not raise the money to post a bond, he remained in jail. He said he knew it didn't matter to the system that he lost his job while he was there. By the time his trial took place, the charges included hitting one of the officers. In court, he finally got the chance to explain to the judge the officer's disrespect. Looney admitted that he had cursed at the officers but denied hitting either of them. The prosecuting attorney asked Looney if the officer's statement made him angry enough to curse automatically, how could he be so sure that he didn't also strike as a reflex action. Looney responded with confidence that he was sure because he had spent a month in jail thinking about the incident. When the trial finally ended, Looney was acquitted of all charges.

These kinds of stories are prominent among black men in black neighborhoods, where this problematic historical legacy continues. It is a well-known fact that Huey Newton and Bobby Seale formed the Black Panthers in 1966 in Oakland, California, specifically to stop the rampant police abuse in that community toward black men (Fletcher, Jones, & Lotringer, 1993). Chicago writer Ahmad Rahamn discusses similar experiences in the 1960s and 1970s in a documentary called *The Promise Land* (1995):

> We saw the police as an occupying army that did not live in our community. They came in our community just to touch [our] life as often as they could with white power and let [us] know that white power runs the city of Chicago.

In some cases, the brutality has been so excessive that black men have died. For example, in 1993, two white police officers in Detroit were convicted of the beating death of Malice Green. Green was a 35-year-old, unemployed black male. He was arrested outside of a suspected crackhouse because he refused to open his hand for the two police officers. It was reported that Green was unarmed when his skull was torn off by 14 blows to the head ("Detroit Cops," 1993). These officers will serve jail time, but many don't. Gannette News Service reporter Rochelle Sharpe found in her research on the 100 worst brutality lawsuits that the officers found guilty for abuse usually went undisciplined and were rarely fired. She reported that some officers actually received promotions and others were given early retirement with full disability after a conviction (cited in Weathers, 1992).

A 1993 study released by sociologist Joe Feagin at the University of Florida examined national and regional newspapers between January 1990 and May 1992 and found 130 brutality incidents. The study reported that in 97% of the brutality cases documented across the country, African Americans or Latinos were the victims and in 93% of those cases the assaults were by Caucasian officers ("National Study," 1993).

Even prominent black male figures in this country have had these kinds of experiences with police. Politician Jesse Jackson told a *USA Today* reporter that all three of his sons had looked into the barrel of an officer's gun. Washington University Professor Gerald Early once described being harassed by police while window shopping in a predominantly white Missouri suburb ("National Study," 1993). Even a black undercover police officer has experienced his fellow officers' use of excessive force. In 1988, Sergeant Don Jackson in a hidden camera news exposé had his head shoved through a glass window during a routine traffic stop by a white police officer. The charges were dismissed after a Long Beach jury dead-locked ("Milestones," 1991).

This is not to suggest that police officers don't have a difficult and dangerous job or that all police are excessive, but the ongoing legacy of abuse of black men by police has been well documented. When the Senate Law Enforcement Hearings were held in 1991, the Justice Department had 15,000 brutality cases on file; some had been there as long as six years and had never been acted upon (Gest et al., 1991). Actor Blair Underwood told the Senate subcommittee that "a silent fear has been generated within black men across the nation. For now, there is a fear that the enemy is dressed in blue" ("National Study," 1993, p. 17).

BLACK MEN AND THE POLICE: THE MUSIC

These same experiences between black men and the police are described in many types of black music over a long period of time. One example comes from two 1960s blues tunes by Lil' Son Jackson in which a policeman named Charlie Cherry who abused black men was the focus.

> Well, he'll cut you if you stand, shoot you if you run.
> You better stay right here 'til Charlie Cherry come.
> Now he arrested my brother, tied him to a tree.
> You could hear him crying please don't murder me. (in Sackheim, 1993, p. 138)

The Last Poets created musical poetry in the 1960s and 1970s that dealt with racial tension and injustice. In a story about Ho Chi Minh, they described an American soldier who offered to build an army base for Ho Chi Minh. When he refused the assistance, was told by the soldier that he must be insane because the soldier is the world's policeman—"Uncle Sam" (Last Poets, 1992, p. 69). Ho Chi Minh continues to be defiant, so the soldier threatens to send jets, tanks, and helicopters to destroy him.

Gil Scott-Heron also includes police brutality in a number of his songs. In "The New Deal" he says he's been "harassed by police," and in "The Revolution Will Not Be Televised," he explains:

> The Revolution will not be televised. There will be no pictures of pigs shooting down brothers on the instant replay. (Scott-Heron, 1990, p. 47)

Stevie Wonder in 1973 included in his popular tune "Living for the City" an incident surrounding the police and what's seen as an unfair legal system. In the middle of the song, between musical verses, a dramatized scene describes a black man arriving in New York City by bus. He is approached by another man who asks him about a package. It is obvious that the newcomer does not know what is going on in this situation. Suddenly, we hear police sirens in the background and the police forcefully arrest the naive newcomer while the real criminal gets away. The scenario jumps to the courtroom, where the newcomer is convicted by a jury and sentenced to 10 years in prison, despite his innocence.

Although incidents of police brutality can be found in earlier black music examples, nowhere is it more prominent than in rap music. There has been a steady stream of rap songs involving the tenuous relationship between police and black men. One of the early rap groups, Grandmaster Flash and the Furious Five, in a 1982 song called "The Message," raps about an incident in which they are harassed by police while they stand talking on the street in front of their house. "The Fugitive" in 1986 on Whodini's *Back in Black* album paints a scenario about a criminal on the run from police, but his crime is his music—rap music. In "Illegal Business" (1988) by KRS-One, another side of the black male-police connection is presented. The song is about the link between local drug dealers and crooked police who take payoffs.

By 1988, rap music had not only survived what critics said would be a short-lived trend but invaded the popular music charts. NWA was one of the first groups to radically address the problematic relationship between black men and police. Their video for "F— tha Police" (on *Straight Outta Compton,* 1988) dramatized a trial where a police officer was accused of racial discrimination and police brutality. Members of NWA—MC Ren, Ice Cube, and Easy E—served as the prosecutor's witnesses, and Dr. Dre was the judge. Each witness took the stand to explain their experience with police brutality. Ice Cube described how police seemed to believe that they had the right to kill him because of his skin color. His testimony involved verbal defiance against the unfair battery and aggression toward black men:

> F— tha police coming straight from the underground.
> A young nigga got it bad cause he's brown and not the
> other color, so police think they have the authority to
> kill a minority. F— that shit cause I ain't the one
> For a punk mother f—— with a badge and a gun to
> be beating on and thrown in jail. (NWA, 1988, cited in Stanley, 1992,
> p. 235)

The average American had been reluctant to admit that there was abusive or excessive force used by police when black men were involved, and subsequently black men were denied a forum to address this injustice. But the 1991 videotape of Rodney King's beating brought police brutality into the light, and the issue finally began to receive the attention it deserved. The Rodney King beating also heightened the issue of police brutality for many rappers. Ice Cube continued to include police issues in his raps after his split from NWA. His 1991 album *Death Certificate* was filled with defiant and contemptuous messages concerning police brutality.

On the cover of his cassette/CD *2PACALYPSE NOW*, Tupac Shakur included the police along with other enemies: "F— all Police, Skinheads, Nazi whatever!!" (Philips, 1992, p. 17). The lyrics from one song off that album, "Soulja's Story," discussed how black men fear the police and how the Rodney King incident had confirmed Tupac that he needed to protect himself even if it meant shooting the cop first.

Ice T's controversial "Cop Killer" was written and performed prior to the King incident. The inspiration for the song came from Ice T's and the band members' personal experiences along with incidents among family and friends of police abuse. The abuse specifically took place at the hands of the LAPD, during the many years they lived in

South Central Los Angeles. The police saga of 1991 was actually produced as a thrash heavy metal song rather than rap, but because Ice T is a well-known rapper, the song was added to the controversy that surrounded rap music and violence. One of the major problems with the coverage of this song was that most critics ignored the initial verse that set up the scenario. This song was not about going out and killing all cops but was directly aimed at bad police, and especially the LAPD:

> This next record is dedicated to some personal friends of mine the LAPD. For every cop that has ever taken advantage of somebody, beat 'em down or hurt them because they had long hair; listened to the wrong kind of music; were the wrong color . . . whatever the reason to do it. (Ice T, 1991)

In his book *The Ice Opinion,* Ice T (1994) discusses the lack of balance in critical analysis when it comes to his music:

> During the exact same time my song was being condemned, the film *Unforgiven* was winning critical praise across the country. What's *Unforgiven* about? A cop killer. Eastwood takes justice into his own hands after his buddy is unjustly murdered by a corrupt cop. What's Cop Killer about? A black youth takes justice into his own hands after his buddies are murdered by corrupt cops. (p. 180)

At 14 years old, KRS-One was a homeless runaway sleeping on steaming New York City sidewalk grates. About ten years later, he has become a popular rap star. In his 1993 CD, *Return of the Boom Bap,* KRS-One raps that his grandfather, great-grandfather, and great-great-grandfather all had to deal with abuse from cops. He asks: When will it stop? The CD contains two songs specifically dealing with police issues, "Black Cop" and "Sound of da Police."

> The black slave turn black cop is not logical . . . but
> very psychological. Haven't you heard it's black cops
> killing black kids in Johannasburg [sic]. What's up black cop,
> yo what's up. Your authorization says shoot your nation
> You want to uphold the law . . . what would you do to me?
> To say no is to diss the whole black community
> You can't play both sides of the fence . . . 1993 mad kids
> get intense. (Black Cop, 1993)

. . . overseer, overseer—officer, officer, you need a little clarity check.
The overseer rode around the plantation, the officer patrols all the
nation. The overseer he took stock in what ya doing, the officer will
pull you over for just what he's pursuing.
The overseer had the right to get ill, and if you fought him, the
overseer had the right to kill.
The officer has the right to arrest, and if you fight back put a hole in
your chest. (Sound of Da Gouce, 1993)

All rap songs that deal with black men and the police are not
negative. Many show the officer as simply doing his or her job. For
example, The Fat Boys's "Jailhouse Rap" (1984) is a satirical look at an
illegal food binge. The Fat Boys get up in the middle of the night and
have no food in the house. They end up in a restaurant and can't pay
for the food they eat, so they go to jail. The Fresh Prince's hit "Parents
Just Don't Understand" (1989) included his driving without a driver's
license and getting stopped by a police officer.

Finally, Heavy D and the Boys included a black police officer in their
video *Mr. Big Stuff* (1987). The video narrative is about how Heavy D
talks his uncle into letting his group perform in his nightclub even
though they are underage. At the end of the performance, a black police
officer enters the club and questions the uncle about the underaged
kids. The police officer warns he had busted him earlier and says that
he can bust him again. The uncle explains that he doesn't know how
all the kids got in his club. Then, the police officer sees the camera,
looks directly into it, and tells the operator: "Stop!" The officer puts
his hand over the lens and the video goes black.

CONCLUSION

Rappers, particularly these black male rappers, often reflect their
cultural reality with police within their music's lyrics. Through rap
music, they are able to bring that experience to the public and, in their
own way, challenge what they see as unfair authoritative practices. This
analysis documents the struggle over ideology as it takes place through
this musical communication process. The representation of self and the
creation of cultural identity are crucial to the production and consumption of rap music despite its commodification. Yet, the message from

much of mainstream ideology is that all rap music is limited, repressive, and condescending.

From an oppositional viewpoint, these cultural participants are located outside of the mainstream, yet they are impacting the mainstream society through their music. Rather than labeling such rappers as violent, racist, sexist, or nihilistic—as many critics have—this analysis demonstrates through cultural interpretation how important their music is and why it is crucial to examine this music from within the experience, as well as from without.

It is the cultural ideology of bell hooks (1990) that informs this analysis. In her discussion of the need for black people to construct self and identity as oppositional and liberatory, hooks identifies cultural criticism as an important function in black life. And despite the fact that the opposition and liberation take place within a system of hegemonic values and practices, she maintains that this is still an important stage in developing an alternative cultural paradigm. hooks (1990) explains:

> It is no accident that "rap" has usurped the primary position of rhythm and blues music among young black folks as the most desired sound or that it began as a form of "testimony" for the underclass. It has enabled underclass youth to develop a critical voice, as a group of young black men told me, a common literacy. Rap projects a critical voice, explaining, demanding, urging. (p. 27)

Much of hooks's writing involves documenting and validating the black cultural experience as well as moving the agency of that experience away from the margins. As this examination suggests, cultural experience is a prominent focus of black male rappers and their music often represents their reality as black men in America. This analysis indicates that cultural consciousness is, therefore, a powerful and active mode of musical communication outside of the margins, particularly if the rapper's own cultural experience is taken into account.

At this time in American history when Reaganomics has made poverty, hate, and greed synonymous with democracy, the level of anger in the music of black male rappers is proportional to the level of anguish in their lived experiences. And it is the anger in rap music that has forced Americans, black and white, to receive, relate, and react. The images and ideology in rap music concerning black men and the police are all tied together within the issues of community, culture, and experience.

These rappers and their music posit a self-conscious effort to find voice and challenge "the system" through that voice. Oppositional and liberational themes for many black male rappers are protected by a refusal to articulate anything but the truth: their truth.

The issue of slavery was forced onto the public agenda for debate on July 5, 1852, by Frederick Douglass when he delivered a moving speech affirming the need for a more powerful voice against slavery in America:

> At a time like this scorchy irony, not convincing argument, is needed. Oh! Had I the ability and could reach the nation's ear, I would today pour out a fiery stream of biting ridicule, blasting reproach, withering sarcasm, and stern rebuke. For it is not light that is needed, but fire. It is not the gentle shower, but thunder. (as quoted in Foner, 1950, p. 192)

The issue of police brutality is being forced onto the public agenda today through rap music's thunder. Rap music is a contemporary example of Douglass's scorchy irony, biting ridicule, blasting reproach, withering sarcasm, and stern rebuke. It exposes the problematic relationship between black men and the police in direct response to the musical experience of the urban black male today. The relationship between rap music, black men, and the police reflects a viable connection between historical forces, media practices, and lived experience, particularly when explored from a cultural perspective.

REFERENCES

Anderson, E. (1990). *Streetwise: Race, class and change in an urban community.* Chicago: University of Chicago Press.

Cone, J. (1972). *The spirituals and the blues: An interpretation.* New York: Seabury.

Detroit cops get 12-25 years in Malice Green death. (1993, November 1). *Jet, 85,* 25.

Fletcher, J., Jones, T., & Lotringer, S. (1993). Chronology of the Black Panther Party. In D. B. Wahad, M. Abu-jamal, & A. Shakur (Eds.), *Still black, still strong: Survivors of the U.S. war against black revolutionaries* (pp. 221-242). New York: Semiotext (E).

Foner, P. S. (1950). *The life and writings of Frederick Douglass pre-Civil War decade 1850-1860.* New York: International.

Gest, T., et al. (1991, April 1). Why brutality persists. *U.S. News and World Report,* p. 24.

Giroux, H. (1983). *Theory and resistance in education: A pedagogy for the opposition.* Boston: Bergin.

Hardt, H. (1992). *Critical communication studies: Communication, history and theory in America.* London: Routledge.

hooks, b. (1990). *Yearning: Race, gender and cultural politics.* Boston: South End.

Ice Cube. (1991). *Death certificate* [CD]. Los Angeles, CA: Priority Records.

Ice T. (1991). *Body count* [CD]. Los Angeles: Sire/Time Warner.

Ice T. (1994). *The ice opinion.* New York: St. Martin's.

Jackson, Lil' S. (1987). Charlie Cherry I and II, Dallas. On M. Leadbitter & N. Slaven (Compilers), *Blues records 1943-1970: A selective discography* [recording]. Ris: London. (Original songs recorded July 10, 1960).

Keil, C. (1970). *Urban blues.* Chicago: University of Chicago Press.

KRS-One. (1993). *Return of the boom bap* [CD]. New York: Zomba Recording/Jive.

Last Poets. (1992). *Vibes from the scribes* [Compilation of song lyrics]. Trenton, NJ: Africa World Press.

Light, A. (1991, May 30). Wisdom from the street. *Rolling Stone, 605,* 41-42.

Looney, H. (1993). [Rap written at University of Iowa Summer Research Program].

Maultsby, P. (1983). Soul music: Its sociological and political significance in American popular culture. *Journal of Popular Culture, 17*(2), 51-59.

Maultsby, P. (1985). The role of scholars in creating space and validity for ongoing changes in black American culture. In B. J. Reagon (Ed.), *Black American culture and scholarship: Contemporary issues* (pp. 11-26). Washington, DC: Smithsonian Institute.

Milestones. (1991, May 27). *Time, 137*(21): 72.

National study reports white cops' beatings of blacks reveal "dirty secrets of racism." (1993, May 3). *Jet, 84,* 14-18.

NWA. (1988). *F— tha police* [video]; *Straight Outta Compton* [CD]. Hollywood, CA: Priority Records.

Philips, C. (1992, October 13). Testing the limits. *Los Angeles Times*, Tuesday Home ed., Pt. F, p. 1.

Poor Righteous Teachers. (1991). Poor Righteous Teachers [Interview]. In *Nation consciousness rap* (pp. 59-76). New York: PC International Press.

Rahamn, A. (1995). *The promise land* [film] (N. Libran, Executive producer). BBC: Discovery Productions.

Sackheim, E. (Compiler). (1993). *Blues lines.* Hopewell, NJ: Ecco.

Scott-Heron, G. (1990). *So far, so good* [Compilation of song lyrics]. Chicago: Third World Press.

Shakur, T. (1991). *2PACALYPSE NOW* [CD]. New York: Interscope/Atlantic.

Southern, E. (1971). *The music of black Americans: A history.* New York: Norton.

Stanley, L. (Ed.). (1992). *Rap the lyrics.* New York: Penguin.

Toop, D. (1984). *Rap attack 2: African rap to global hip hop.* London: Pluto.

Weathers, D. (1992, November). If you are a victim of police brutality. *Essence,* pp. 23, 137.

Index

About the Contributors

Sharon Albert-Honore is Assistant Professor in Communications Media at Alabama State University in Montgomery. Her dissertation (1995) is titled *Freedom of Expression and African-American Community Radio*, and her research also involves critical race theory and minority voice within mainstream culture. She has worked as a freelance journalist for more than 15 years. She received her doctorate in journalism and mass communication from the University of Iowa in 1995.

John T. Barber is Assistant Professor and the Acting Chairman in Telecommunications at Morgan State University in Maryland. His research interests involve the press portrayal of African American and white U.S. representatives and the creation of a multicultural news paradigm. He has published in the *Howard Journal of Communication* (Spring 1990). He received the Alan Bussell Award for Student Research in Mass Communication at AEJMC (1986) and the top three papers award for research in political communication from the Eastern Communication Association in 1990.

Venise T. Berry is Assistant Professor in the School of Journalism and Mass Communication at the University of Iowa. Her research interests involve the cultural examination of African American images in the media. Her publications include book chapters in *Adolescents and Their*

Music (1994) and *Cecilia Reclaimed: Feminist Perspectives on Gender and Music* (1994) along with journal articles in the *Journal of Popular Music Studies* (Summer 1993) and *Popular Music and Society* (Fall 1990). She is cultivating her creative writing talent through her first novel, *So Good* (1996).

Thomas A. Birk is Assistant Professor in the Department of Radio-Television at Southern Illinois University at Carbondale. His research interests include media sales, management, and promotions. He has coauthored several articles and paper presentations. His journal articles have appeared in the *Urban League Review* (1993) and *Excellence and Equity* (1993), among others.

Sharon Bramlett-Solomon is Associate Professor in the Walter Cronkite School of Journalism and Telecommunication at Arizona State University in Phoenix. Her research interests involve media images and portrayals of Americans of color and the media's projection of racial issues, race relations, and racial change. Her journal articles have appeared in *Mass Communication Review* (1994), *Newspaper Research Journal* (Fall 1991; Summer/Fall 1993), and *Journalism Quarterly* (Fall 1991, 1992; Spring 1989), among others.

Ruth Elizabeth Burks is Assistant Professor in English at Macalester College in St. Paul, Minnesota. Her research interests are equally divided between film and literature. She has contributed to *Black Women Scholars/Work and Struggle: Selected Papers from the 1994 Black Women in the Academy Conference* (1995), *Black Women Writers (1950-1980): A Critical Introduction* (1984), and the *San Francisco Review of Books* (1975). She receive her doctorated in English from the University of California, Los Angeles, in 1993 and is also a graduate of the American Film Institute.

Eddith A. Dashiell is Assistant Professor in the E. W. Scripps School of Journalism at Ohio University in Athens. She completed her dissertation in 1992, titled *Getting to the Supreme Court of the United States: The Social Characteristics of Supreme Court Media-Related Libel Cases Since Times v. Sullivan.* Her research interests are law and policy. She has a chapter in Michael Bugeja's *Living Ethics: Developing Values in Mass Communication* (1995).

Tricia M. Farwell is a graduate student in the Walter Cronkite School of Journalism and Telecommunication at Arizona State University in Phoenix. Her research interests involve mass media cultivation and socialization.

Oscar H. Gandy Jr. is Professor of Communication in the Annenberg School for Communication at the University of Pennsylvania. His research interests involve the political economy of information. He is the author of *The Panoptic Sort* (1993) and *Beyond Agenda Setting* (1982). His research on racially comparative risk is supported in part by a Freedom Forum Media Studies Center Fellowship (1993-1994).

Herman Gray is Associate Professor in Sociology at the University of California at Santa Cruz. He is the author of *Watching Race: Television and the Sign of Blackness* (1995). His expertise concerning African Americans and the media is evident in his participation in a number of video documentaries including *Color Adjustment* and *Signal to Noise*.

William A. Harris is Assistant Professor in Sociology at Boston College. He is currently researching upward mobility among African Americans, with the goal of explaining and enhancing the process. He is completing a manuscript titled *Up From Poverty: Stratification and Mobility Among African-Americans* (1996). His past research has focused on social problems, legitimation, and the sociophysiology of status organizing processes and was published in *Social and Economic Studies* (1992, 1993) and *Sociological Theory* (1992).

Phylis Johnson is Assistant Professor in the Department of Radio-Television at Southern Illinois University at Carbondale. Her research interests include radio programming, promotions, and content regulation. She has published articles in the *Journal of Radio Studies* (1993/1994, 1995), *Urban League Review* (1993), *Excellence and Equity* (1993), and *Education and Urban Society* (1992), among others. She has worked in radio in Houston, Philadelphia, and St. Louis.

Jacquie Jones is filmmaker and critic who writes frequently about the black image in popular culture and has contributed to important anthologies such as *Black Popular Culture, Black American Cinema,* and *Picturing Us: African American Images in Photography* as well as numerous magazines and journals. She was formerly the editor of *Black Film Review,* the leading journal on African diaspora film. In addition, she has done film programming for various festivals and institutions, including the Smithsonian Institution, the Festival of New Latin American Cinema, and the Washington, DC, International Film Festival.

Harold Looney Jr. is a Consultant in the Media and Technology Department at Anderson Consultants in Chicago. He participated in the 1993 Summer Research Opportunity Program at the University of Iowa and received his bachelor's degree from the University of Illinois in 1994. His interests include computer technology, interactive television, the Internet, multimedia, and broadband communication.

Carmen L. Manning-Miller is Associate Professor in the Department of Journalism at the University of Mississippi. Her research interests involve cognitive processing models for political persuasion via the mass media, structural biases of mass communication content, and longitudinal design methodology. She has published articles in *Journalism Quarterly* (1993), *Journalism Educator* (Winter 1993), *Journal of Mediated Communication* (December 1993), and the *Howard Journal of Communications* (in press). She is completing a book project on women, politics, and the mass media.

Portia K. Maultsby is Professor in Afro-American Studies at Indiana University in Bloomington. Her research includes gospel and popular music. She has published chapters in *We'll Understand It Better By and By: African-American Pioneering Gospel Composers* (1992), *Africanisms in African American Culture* (1990), and *More Than Dancing* (1985), and her journal articles have appeared in *Black Music Research Bulletin* (Spring 1989) and *Journal of Popular Culture* (Fall 1983), among others. She is completing a book manuscript titled *From Backwoods to City Streets: Post War II Black Popular Music.*

Reginald Owens is Assistant Professor and the Publication Director for the Department of Communication at Grambling State University in Louisiana. His research interests involve the African American communication environment and the African American press in social change. He has extensive print media experience, including the *Austin American Statesman, Nokoa the Observer,* the *Houston Informer,* the *Houston Post,* and the *Philadelphia Tribune.* He has completed several summer sabbaticals in the newsrooms of the *Nashville Tennessean,* the *Philadelphia Tribune,* and the *New Orleans Times Picayune.*

Jyotika Ramaprasad is Associate Professor in the School of Journalism at Southern Illinois University at Carbondale. Her research interests are international news, advertising, and consumer behavior. She has published articles in the *Journal of Advertising* (Fall 1995), *Journalism Quarterly* (Fall 1992; Winter 1990), the *Asian Journal of Communication* (1993), the *Journal of Advertising Research* (January/February 1992), *Gazette* (1983), and the *Newspaper Research Journal* (Summer 1991; Fall 1987).

Karen M. Smith is a graduate student in American Studies at the University of Iowa in Iowa City. Her research centers on African American cinema and independent women's cinema. Her dissertation will focus on the work of black women filmmakers. Her essay on feminist pedagogy will be published in the book *In Struggle: Selected Essays From Defending Our Names.*

Alice A. Tait is Associate Professor of Journalism at Central Michigan University. Her research taps into a number of areas such as the civil rights movement, disabilities and the mass media, and the portrayals of African Americans on television. Her publications include the *Western Journal of Black Studies* (in press), the *News Computer Journal* (1992), the *Handbook on Mass Media in the United States* (1994), the *Michigan Academician* (1989/1990), and the *Negro Educational Review* (1987). She is chairperson of the communication division of the Michigan Academy of Arts and Sciences.